The World's Greatest
Leg-Spin Bowlers

THE WORLD'S GREATEST
Leg-Spin Bowlers

JACK POLLARD

Foreword by
Shane Warne

Leg-Breaks, Googlies, Chinamen and Devious Plots

ROBERT HALE • LONDON

Acknowledgments

The photographs in this book came from All Sports through their agents, the Australian Picture Library, from *Inside Edge* magazine, from the *Sydney Morning Herald*, the Melbourne *Sun-Herald*, the Melbourne *Age*, the personal albums of bowlers discussed, the author's collection, or are the work of the outstanding English cricket photographer Patrick Eagar. The statistics are the work of Ross Dundas, official statistician to the Australian Cricket Board and operator of the Sydney Cricket Ground's electronic scoreboard. Some of the vintage photographs in the book are from Stephen Green, curator of the museum and library at Lord's. The author and publisher would like to personally thank all of these people, and offer their special thanks to Shane Warne for his Foreword.

Front cover: Shane Warne, the brilliant Australian leg-spin bowler, at the 5th Cornhill Test in 1993. Photo courtesy of Patrick Eagar.
Back cover: Bernard Bosanquet, inventor of the googly.

© Jack Pollard 1994

First published in Great Britain 1995

ISBN 0-7090-5645-X

Robert Hale Limited
Clerkenwell House
Clerkenwell Green
London ECIR 0HT

Printed in Australia

Contents

Foreword

Shane Warne

Leg-spin bowling in which the ball turns across the batsman's legs towards the off stump was a proven way of getting players out even in the days of the under-armers. The variations that can be achieved bowling over-arm by rolling the wrist, such as the flipper, topspinner, or googly, are comparatively recent additions to the spinner's bag of tricks.

I discovered this reading Jack Pollard's great new book on leg-spinners, and found myself intrigued by his account of how Bernard Bosanquet won an Ashes series for England against Australia in 1903–04 when he introduced the googlie or bosey. He did it in Sydney when he had a spell of 5 for 12 to finish with 6 for 51 by bowling what our papers called 'off-breaks with a leg-break action'.

This is just one of the triumphs by a wrist-spinner set down in Pollard's book. He takes a close look at all the outstanding leg-spinners from the cricket nations. There are chapters on Australians like Ranji Hordern, Arthur Mailey, Clarrie Grimmett, Bill O'Reilly and Richie Benaud. But he has not forgotten Tich Freeman, who took 200 wickets seven times in an English season, South Africans like Reggie Schwartz and Aubrey Faulkner, the Pakistani Abdul Qadir, India's Anil Kumble, nor the New Zealander Billy Merritt.

I had not heard of most of them but they certainly show that leg-spin is an international art which cricketers struggle to master wherever they are born. I have been credited with reviving the method when it was close to dying out, but there were a lot of guys before me who kept rolling their wrists successfully.

It's not an easy job. When I started off in Test cricket in January 1992, I took only one wicket for 228 runs in two Tests. But I had a taste of test cricket and I wanted to give myself the best chance. So I got super fit and things have improved since then.

It all started to fall into place at Columbo against Sri Lanka, when Allan Border gave me a chance to win a Test.

I took 3 for 12 and we won. I had 7 for 52 against the West Indies at the end of that year (1992) and by the time I got to New Zealand and grabbed 17 wickets in three Tests I felt the ball was coming out of my hand the way I had always wanted.

Then came the 1993 English tour when all my dreams came true and I beat Clarrie Grimmett's 63-year-old record of 29 wickets in five Tests by taking 34 wickets in six Tests. I was tickled to read in the book that Grimmett always declined to comment in his media interviews on whether he bowled googlies, flippers or topspinners. The old fox just refused to say if he bowled anything special, though a lot of great batsmen said he did.

Keeping batsmen guessing about your variations is all part of the leg-spinner's approach. We did it in England in 1993 when Border surprised the Poms by throwing me into the first match of the tour at Worcester. At Worcester it was a case of don't show them too much, use your variations sparingly.

After that exciting first ball in a Test in England, which nipped right across the pitch and hit Mike Gatting's off bail, Border let me bowl what I wanted and I tried my full range. The googly was a bit disappointing but made me realise I had to work on it. At Edgebaston, I thought I could bowl Gooch around his legs. Allan liked the idea, and it worked, which was amazing.

Most of the leggies discussed in Jack Pollard's book have enjoyed similar highlights because they were all top men in their craft. Before television they may not have received the media coverage my wickets got, but they all knew some bad days, too. You have to expect it.

South Africa was the first time I had done the wrong thing. And I've learnt from it. The thing that annoyed me the most was that because I've had a little bit of success, and then they see the South African incident, they think it has all gone to my head, which is not true. I'm still the same bloke I was two years ago. Keep spinning and just do it.

1

The First Tweaker

Allan Gibson Steel was a nimble, pugnacious all-rounder who played for Lancashire from 1877 to 1893, for Cambridge University from 1878 to 1881, and captained England in four of his 13 Tests. He was a cricketer of immense influence from his schooldays at Marlborough, rated second only to the great Dr W.G. Grace amongst players of his time, who served as president of the Marylebone Cricket Club during a golden era of big cricket.

Steel hit eight centuries in compiling 6,767 first-class runs at 29.29, repeatedly flaying bowlers with fierce drives on both sides of the pitch. He made 135 not out for England against Australia at Sydney in 1882–83, and 148 against Australia at Lord's in 1884, a match-winning innings. He was a clever, accurate right-arm slow bowler, who spun the ball widely, took 164 wickets in his first full season of first-class cricket (1878), the year he took 13 for 73 for Cambridge against Oxford at Lord's. He snared a hat-trick against Oxford the following year, had a best analysis of 9 for 63 for Lancashire against Yorkshire at Manchester in 1878, and in a career frequently interrupted by his work at the bar took 789 wickets at 14.78. As a captain he had a wonderful winning sequence: Marlborough over Rugby, Cambridge over Oxford, Gentlemen over Players, Lancashire over Yorkshire and England over Australia.

Photographs of Steel disclose an alert, pop-eyed, slightly built man with a luxuriant dark moustache every bit as thick as Merv Hughes' and a liking for pillarbox hats and sashes about the waist. It comes as no surprise to find that he was one of England's finest barristers. The respected English googly bowler Ian Peebles said A.G. Steel pioneered overarm wrist-spin bowling in international cricket and that he was the first tweaker.

'There is something so tempting to an inexperienced player in seeing a ball chucked up in the air slowly and simply, it looks so very easy to hit, so peculiarly guileless, that a wild slog is frequently the result, too often followed by disastrous consequences,' A.G. Steel wrote in the Badminton Library edition on cricket in 1904.

Steel discovered the leg-spin that reduced famous batsmen to harassed impotence in matches with his brothers, Ernest Eden Steel, Douglas Quintin Steel, both accomplished slow bowlers, and Harold Banner Steel, a fine middle-order batsman whose career was upset by a football injury. The Steels came from West Derby, Liverpool, where A.G. was born on 24 September 1858, and in the north of England they matched the fame of the Grace family in the south.

A.G. Steel was the man who befriended Australian ophthalmic surgeon Dr Rowley Pope while Pope was involved in advanced studies at Edinburgh University. He was impressed by the batting that had won Pope a place in one Test against England at Melbourne in 1884–85 following an innings of 170 for Melbourne Cricket Club against I Zingari at Richmond. Steel suggested Pope apply for membership of the MCC and personally proposed his application. Pope played a lot of cricket thereafter with the Steels in MCC teams charged with the job of promoting cricket in small villages and schools.

When A.G. Steel made his first-class debut in 1878, bowling had only just evolved from underarmers who favoured grubbers to round-armers who resorted to lobs, and then to overarmers who found that their actions, although unpopular with players who regarded it as cheating, allowed them subtle variations in pace. Steel and his brothers took overarm a step further by producing spin with wrist and fingers.

The underarmers had spun the ball from the leg from the middle of the eighteenth century, when members of the Hambledon club popularised cricket on Broadhalfpenny Down in Hampshire. There clever bowlers like 'Lumpy' Stevens and characters known as 'Hogsflesh' and the 'Little Farmer' developed the art of bowling 'jerkers'. Their work was carried on by Richard Francis and the Rev. John Mitford, who acclaimed Lumpy as the 'finest bowler this world ever rejoiced in when living and lamented over when dead'.

From Hambledon the game moved to the first Lord's ground in Dorset Square, where John Willes attempted to introduce round-arm bowling for Kent against MCC in 1822. He was no-balled and stormed off the field in protest. Willes had learnt round-arm from his sister who adopted the style to get round her crinoline petticoat. Soon Edward Budd, William Lambert, William Hillyer and Fred

The first overarm leg-break bowler, Allan Gibson Steel, whose cricket was restricted by his work as a barrister. He took 164 wickets in his first full season of first-class cricket.

Lillywhite were experimenting with deliveries that lifted and spun from a round-arm delivery.

Hillyer was known as 'Topper' because he always bowled in a top hat. Like Lillywhite, he was on the Lord's ground staff, 'shuffling to the crease as if carrying hot plates he wanted to set down', but releasing round-armers easily and economically that curled in the air and turned with what was called venomous speed from leg to off.

Australia in its formative years produced similar bowling tricksters. The *Sydney Gazette* said in 1832 that no gentleman could expect to dangle on a lady's apron-strings unless he could boast of his cricket skill. One of those whose boasting was justified was James McKone, best known exponent of the dreaded Sydney grubber whose spinning underarms were said to have had a 'subterranean touch'. McKone was the hero of many matches in Sydney Domain, and near the end of his career took 5 for 25 and 5 for 11 to give New South Wales a surprise win in her first inter-colonial match against Victoria in Melbourne in 1856. Another colonial bowling giant was William Henty, who sent down the first delivery in Australian first-class cricket. Henty took nine wickets to give Tasmania victory over Victoria at Launceston in 1851.

Even in those early days the quest for bias led bowlers to try a variety of grips and wrist movement, but at each stage of the development from underarm to round-arm and eventually to overarm, exponents of the new technique were accused of cheating. In 1858–59, Tasmanian umpires refused to allow round-arm bowling by Victorians, insisting it was foul play.

Victoria won both the inter-colonial matches that summer against Tasmania, with round-arm specialists Gideon Elliott and Tom Wills peppering Tasmania's batsmen with deliveries like cannon shot which spectators in Launceston and Hobart regarded as a form of treachery. Elliott's 9 wickets for 2 runs to dismiss Tasmania for 33 runs in the match in Launceston remains the most economical bowling analysis in Australian first-class cricket. Elliott learned his skills in Surrey, where he was born in 1828, before being lured to Australia in his twenties by the gold rushes.

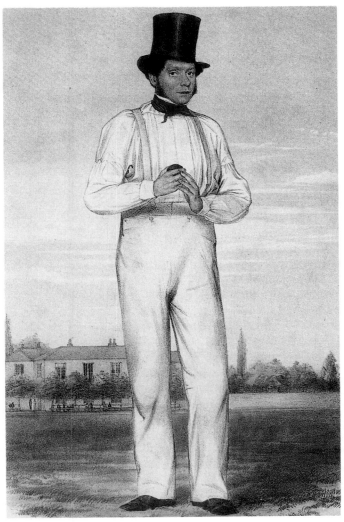 

William Hillyer, left, who turned leg-breaks with 'venomous speed' bowling in a top hat, with Fred Lillywhite, whose experiments with round-arm wrist spinners were influenced by his ample stomach.

At the time Elliott was proving such a destructive force in the Australian colonies a former bricklayer named William Clarke enjoyed remarkable success with his All England XI. Clarke, a slow underarm bowler, was captain, secretary, promoter, and business manager for the All England XI which he founded in 1846. The team played in almost 40 country centres in its first three years and was so successful between 1850 and 1860 that a second travelling team, known as the United England XI, was formed.

Clarke married the widow Chapman, who kept the Trent Bridge Inn, at the rear of which Clarke developed a ground that became world famous. Before his team's matches Clarke habitually made a careful study of each of their opponents at practice, puffing on a cigar as he decided on methods to dismiss them cheaply, declining to practise himself. Clarke took 2,385 wickets in seven years of touring with his XI, rich pickings for a bowler who had lost an eye in a childhood accident and only discovered cricket late in life. He was one of the first bowlers to realise that all batsmen have a blind spot just outside the leg stump and slightly in front of the batting crease and on rough, lumpy pitches he achieved leg-breaks with his fingers that yielded an average of 340 wickets a season.

There were, of course, many other bowlers who exploited this weakness outside the batsmen's legs. John Bickley, a thickset round-armer who also operated in a top hat, preferred to walk rather than run to the wicket and had notable success with Nottinghamshire and the All England XI, swinging his right arm with speed which confounded many a complacent adversary. Bickley repeatedly produced an unplayable delivery by pitching just outside the leg stump and breaking with destructive pace towards the off stump. His opportunities for advancement were few and he often had to return to his trade as a silk-glove weaver simply to earn a living. His great coup came on 9 July 1856, when he took 8 wickets for 7 runs for England against a combined team of Kent and Sussex on a rain-affected Lord's pitch.

The most famous bowler of the period, however, was Frederick William Lillywhite, hailed as the 'Nonpareil Bowler' through his feats for the All England XI and his 10 years on the Lord's ground staff. Lillywhite regarded himself as an unmatched bowling machine, superior to all other exponents of the art. He rated his skill so highly he was given to smoking a pipe while he bowled. His conception of ideal cricket: 'Me bowling, Pilch batting and Box keeping wicket—now that's real cricket'. When he was reprimanded by his captain for refusing to take a simple return catch, he said: 'When I've bowled the ball, I've done with her, and leaves her to my field'.

Lillywhite's sustained accuracy in bowling his slows for hours at a time enabled him to play a major role in the change from underarm to round-arm bowling, which was legalised in 1835. Round-arm bowling of Lillywhite's type, with the arm raised above the level of the elbow, has in fact been used for variety by leg-spinners like Clarrie Grimmett, Colin McCool, and even Shane Warne.

Lillywhite was an earthy, truculent figure mentally tough enough to resist all criticism of his technique by experts like Thomas Lord and John Nyren. 'I bowl the best ball in England and if I thought about every ball they'd never get a run,' said Lillywhite, who David Frith, the Anglo-Australian writer, credited with taking 685 wickets with his 'peculiars' in one rich three-year spell. Frith said Lillywhite bowled fewer than a dozen wides in 27 years of cricket. Asked if he could land the ball on a small piece of paper at the other end of the pitch, Lillywhite said: 'Yes, and I could shift the paper and still hit it'.

Lillywhite, bowling in a top hat and cotton braces stretched over his beer-drinker's paunch, revolutionised the whole art of bowling and caused young cricketers previously dedicated to express bowling to take a long look at the tricks and subtleties of slow bowling. It seemed incredible that such an ungainly figure could hoodwink fine batsmen so consistently. Lillywhite's arrogance hid the reasons for his success right up until the time he died of cholera in 1854 at the age of 62, but a handbook he published in 1844 provided one clue: 'By holding the ball slightly askew, with the thumb well across the seam, you will find by working the wrist as the ball leaves the hand, that it will assist you to cut and rick at the wicket, such balls that are very troublesome to get rid of'. Like Bill O'Reilly a century later, Lillywhite considered fast bowling by schoolboys nothing short of 'cruelty to animals'.

The most accomplished of the sons Fred Lillywhite left was John, born in 1826 when his father was 34, a short, stocky, strongly built man who in his mature years sported a magnificent set of whiskers. He reduced his pace as he passed through his teens and became renowned as a 'mud bowler' because of his success with slows on wet pitches. John refused to tolerate the dictatorial control of William Clarke and left the All England XI to join the rival United All England. Weak eyesight restricted John with the bat, but he was good enough as a bowler to gain employment at Lord's in 1856 and play for MCC until 1860. With his brothers, James and Frederick, he built up a prosperous family business and became the founder of a *Cricketers' Companion*, a pocket-sized annual which from 1849 until 1866 was cricket's best read reference.

John Lillywhite's major contribution to cricket, however, came at The Oval in 1862 in a match he umpired. Surrey was chasing an England total of 503 when Edgar Willsher, commonly known as Ned, came on to bowl his high-action left-arm slows. Lillywhite had had many chances to study Willsher's bowling as a player and after one delivery he warned Willsher that by raising his bowling arm above the shoulder he was breaking the law. Most professionals believed Willsher infringed the ethics of the game and some even considered he threw the ball, but despite the warning he continued with his high overarm style.

One-eyed William Clarke, the former bricklayer who developed a famous ground and a more famous team, bowling spinners that fooled 2,385 batsmen.

Lillywhite no-balled Willsher six times in succession and in a fit of pique Willsher threw down the ball and stalked off the field. The eight professionals in the England team went with him, leaving the umpires, the batsmen and two amateurs on the field. Lillywhite was admired for his courage, but Willsher had the spectators' sympathy. Officials tried to persuade Lillywhite to resume without calling Willsher but he refused, and rather than lose the gate money from the match, play continued with a replacement umpire. No more no-balls were called and the match ended in a draw.

Willsher's so-called humiliation aroused widespread discussion, much of it overheated nonsense in which north of England cricketers accused southerners of prejudice against them. Lillywhite was alleged to have been ordered in advance to no-ball Willsher to save Surrey from a humiliating defeat.

The upshot was that in June 1864 the laws of cricket were amended to abolish restrictions on the height of the bowler's arm at delivery, and overarm bowling became legal. Overarm bowling ushered in a whole new breed of artful, scheming bowlers, many of them erratic romantics who believed they could now produce unplayable deliveries of prodigious turn without hours of hard net practice.

One of these, James Cobbett, born at Frimley in Surrey in 1804, was described in Pycroft's *The Cricket Field* as a bowler capable of deliveries that had new life in them. Cobbett wrapped his fingers around the ball, which he delivered with his wrist in a horizontal position. 'At delivery,' said Pycroft, 'he threw his bowling hand back, his fingers seemingly unglued joint by joint till the ball quitted the tips of them last. No bowling so fair, and with so little rough play or violence, ever proved more effective than Cobbett's.' Unhappily, Cobbett died at 38 in his London bat shop.

But the English bowlers who initially mesmerised Australians were the exponents of the lob, a method with a success record that defies belief. Australia was denied the spectacle of Teddy Walker, one of the great exponents of the art, wheeling down his lobs, but Robert Crispin Tinley, who gave up pace bowling to bowl corkscrews for the All England XI, came to Australasia with the second England touring team captained by George Parr in 1863–64. Advance publicity suggested that Tinley could virtually make the ball talk and he did not disappoint. In a team that included only 12 players, Tinley bowled in 37 innings and collected 250 wickets at five runs apiece.

On ill-prepared pitches outside the major centres, Tinley hoodwinked batsmen with ridiculous ease, and when Parr's team went to New Zealand for a match against Twenty-Two of Otago, Tinley bowled unchanged in both innings, giving his colleagues more leisure time than they expected by routing opposing batsmen. Unfortunately, Tinley retired before Test cricket began in 1877, although his methods lingered on.

At The Oval in 1884 when Australia's batsmen mastered nine English bowlers, the Rt Hon. Alfred Lyttelton

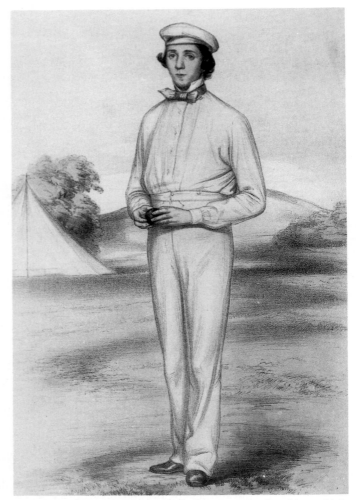

Edgar Willsher, no-balled for bowling over the shoulder, which led to rule changes and the introduction of overarm as a legal bowling style.

discarded his wicket-keeping gloves and pads and took 4 for 19 with lobs. His technique was aired in the first of all Tests when England's attack became frustrated by the batting of Charles Bannerman, and Tom Armitage resorted to lobs which commentators said could not have been reached with a clothes prop. The last prominent user of the lob, George Simpson-Hayward, returned his best analysis, 6 for 43, in the first of his five Tests in South Africa in 1909–10, and finished that series with 23 wickets. Thereafter he depended more on slow underarm leg-breaks than lobs until his retirement in 1914, with 503 wickets at 21.39 to his credit.

Deviation from the leg to the off, comparatively easy in underhand days, demanded greater skill from overarm bowlers. The leg-break, well bowled, became the most dangerous of all balls but the hardest to master. The spin or rotary motion from right to left that had been achieved with the fingers now had to be imparted by turning the wrist over at the moment the ball left the hand, with the fingers imparting a powerful twist to the ball.

Ian Peebles, who once confounded Bradman with a

wrist-spinner in an Old Trafford Test, made a close study of its origins and had no doubt A.G. Steel pioneered the technique in international cricket. Steel wrote what remains the definitive work on bowling for the Badminton Library edition on cricket in 1888. 'The skill, science, and practice which are necessary before a man can throw a good salmon fly, or before he can bring down a good average of high rocketing pheasants, are equally necessary for one who wishes to become adept at bowling,' said Steel. 'Bowling may not require the same good eye as batting but it demands more practice and experience, and a far greater exercise of mental qualities. The object is to out manoeuvre the batsman.'

Steel dealt with the leg-break before all the other types of bowling. 'The trap laid for the batsmen in this style of bowling,' he said, 'is the danger he incurs unless he is actually to the pitch of the ball; if he falls into the snare, the ball is certain to go up in the air owing to the twist of the ball causing it to hit the side rather than the centre of the bat.'

Steel's record was that of a man who knew what he was talking about. He spun Cambridge to a dramatic win as a freshman, taking 8 for 62 in Oxford University's first innings and later, on a worn pitch, 5 for 11, sending Oxford back for only 32 in their second innings. This 1878 haul of 13 for 73 remains the varsity record. Steel played a major role in Cambridge University's defeat of Australia that summer in two days, and finished his first season on top of England's bowling averages with 164 wickets at 9.43 each.

At The Oval from 6 to 8 September 1880, Steel introduced overarm leg-spin to international cricket in the first Test on English soil. He took 3 for 58 in Australia's first innings from 29 four-ball overs, and 2 for 73 in the second innings from 31 four-ball overs. Jovial, sunny-natured, he was economical but never concerned if he was hit, and remained an automatic selection for the Gentlemen against the Players from 1880 to 1888 and for England when work permitted.

Steel not only fulfilled the promise of his remarkable school career—his masters believed he should have played for England while still at Marlborough—but by establishing himself as the most consistent wicket-taking spinner of his time helped lift cricket's strength in the north of England. As the dominance of the wandering elevens waned, Lancashire through the Steel brothers, 'Monkey' Hornby, and Richard Barlow, Nottinghamshire through Alfred Shaw, William Gunn, Arthur Shrewsbury and Dick Attewell, and Yorkshire through Bobby Peel, Edmund Peate, George Ulyett and Lord Hawke provided powerful opposition for even the strongest southern counties. Gloucestershire may have had the Graces, Middlesex a seemingly endless array of talented amateurs like the Walkers, the Lytteltons and the Fords, and Surrey Walter Read, George Lohmann and Bobby Abel, but they could never be sure of beating these northern counties.

The result was county cricket of such a high standard

Englishmen believed it was supreme in the world. Hence their profound shock when overseas teams began arriving and, at The Oval in May 1878, Australia beat an MCC team led by W.G. Grace—but excluding Steel who was grouse shooting—in a single afternoon. From their victory in the first Test a year earlier in Melbourne, Australians had shown they could give even the smartest England bowlers big problems.

Steel quickly showed he was not overawed by the Australian challenge. His brilliance in taking 164 wickets at nine runs each and his hand in the defeat of Australia by an innings at the age of 20 has never been matched by a freshman. At The Oval in 1880 he took the first Test wicket attributed to a leg-spinner when he had Australia's Billy Murdoch caught at short leg by Billy Barnes off his fourth ball. Almost before Murdoch disappeared into the pavillion, another Steel leg-break scattered Tom Groube's stumps, leaving Australia in a slump from which she never recovered. Steel's 42 runs in his only innings and his five wickets in the match helped England to a five wickets win.

William Lillywhite, son of the great 'Non-Pareil' Fred Lillywhite, like most wrist-spinners of his time, always bowled in a top hat.

Two years later Steel bowled less because he was being saved for his batting but he still managed 152 wickets at 6.57 in all matches on his only tour of Australia. The next best English bowler, C.T. Studd, managed 60 wickets. Steel also headed the batting averages with 561 runs at 30.61. At Sydney when Australia won the extra Test added to England's itinerary, Steel produced his marvellous 135, England's sole consolation in a four-wicket defeat. All this in a player carrying a leg injury for most of the tour.

After this trip Steel's work at the bar curtailed his first-class cricket but he still made 18 appearances for the Gentlemen. Given his natural gifts, county captains soon realised he was a bowler who could dispense with practice. He played his last Test at The Oval in 1888, showing glimpses of his rare bowling cunning and his wonderful eye with the bat. He took 9 for 63 for Lancashire against Yorkshire at Manchester in 1878 and the following year bowled unchanged throughout both innings with his old Oxford University rival A.H. Evans for the Gentlemen against the Players.

A clubmate of Steel's at the MCC was Billy Williams, who played 27 matches for Middlesex between 1885 and 1902, toured the West Indies with Arthur Priestley's team in 1896–97, and was reputed to have taken more than 100 wickets every summer for 50 years for MCC teams, all of them with leg-spin. Williams was certainly one of the most successful early devotees of the art and revelled in bowling his wide breaks to Australian touring teams in the Lord's nets. He was also a noted Rugby footballer with Harlequins and a top-class Rugby referee, credited with laying out the ground on which Twickenham now stands.

Steel argued that leg-spin was of comparatively little avail on soft or sticky pitches, probably because his pace was too slow. Later exponents of the delivery like Sydney Barnes and Bill O'Reilly took advantage of these pitches by bowling at medium pace, although this did not enthuse true lovers of wrist-spin.

Ian Peebles, a lifelong student of the turning ball, preferred Steel's approach. 'I am not concerned with the impeccable Barnes or O'Reilly who spun the ball from the leg largely by using their fingers, but with the devotee who curls his wrist up in the region of his flask pocket, and with bared teeth and distorted countenance, gives it all he's got,' Peebles told readers of *Punch* magazine. 'What matter if it doesn't land in quite the right place, so long as it bursts like a bomb on a beehive; this is art for art's sake even if some captains do not appreciate the point. This is the true tweaker, the optimist, the sanguine gambler, the serpent among bowlers, venomous but vulnerable.'

Australia acknowledged the value of the leg-spinner by including balding, 32-year-old William Henry Cooper in

William Henry Cooper, the first notable Australian wrist-spinner. His wide turn mystified English batsmen at Melbourne in 1881–82.

the team for only the fifth of all Tests at Melbourne in the 1881–82 season. Cooper always bowled round the wicket and until they turned most of his deliveries looked like leg-side wides. He screwed the ball out of the side of his hand in the way a billiards marker screws a ball along the table and then brings it back to him. His deliveries were extraordinarily slow in the air, but spun quickly from the turf on pitching, twisting up to a metre into the batsman. He positioned all bar two of his fieldsmen on the leg side, all waiting for mishits.

Cooper had little experience but enjoyed dramatic success with his often wayward spin in giving Australians their first glimpse of wrist-spin at that Melbourne Test, taking 3 for 80 and 6 for 120. His victims included Arthur Shrewsbury, the Notts master who was said to be unbowlable. Cooper knocked back Shrewsbury's stumps in England's second innings with a ball that had the batsman shaking his head in disbelief at the width of the turn.

2

The Search for Twist

William Henry Cooper, Paul Sheahan's grandfather, was born at Maidstone in Kent on 11 September 1849, and was eight years old when his family settled in Australia. At the age of 27, his doctor advised him to get more exercise, and when Cooper suggested lawn bowls the medico said a more strenuous sport was required. Cooper joined South Melbourne Cricket Club as a rank beginner, became victim of the leg-spinning bug, and within three years played his way through the grades into first grade and the Victorian team. His striking display in his first-class debut against Lord Harris' touring English team in February 1879 stamped him as a match-winner. This was the first match between England and Victoria on level terms.

Cooper's wide turn enabled wicket-keeper Jack Blackham to make five stumpings in England's first innings, a feat since equalled but never surpassed. Cooper began by bowling English batting star A.P. Lucas with an enormous leg-break. He then had Lord Harris, Vernon Royle, Charlie Absolom and Sandford Schultz all stumped by Blackham, who got his fifth victim when he stumped Leland Hone off Harry Boyle. Cooper finished the match with 7 for 125 (5 for 79 and 2 for 46) off 56 overs, which was virtually responsible for Victoria's shock two-wicket win after four tense days.

Spinning the ball from a full extension of his 5 foot 9 inch frame, Cooper gave wicket-keepers big problems because of the sharpness and width of his turn. His club scorecards recorded a lot of byes but at the state level his combination with Blackham presented a major worry for the most talented batsmen, and together they accounted for many prize dismissals. Nine months after his debut Cooper took 7 for 37 off 16 overs for Victoria against New South Wales in Sydney and a year later had 5 for 44 against South Australia in Melbourne. Fifteen of his 28 overs were maidens, with batsmen too puzzled by his spin to score runs.

From 31 December 1881 to 4 January 1882 in Melbourne, Cooper secured the first five-wicket haul by a tweaker in Test cricket by taking 6 for 120 in England's second innings. He bowled 61 overs for these figures, 19 of them maidens, and despite the width of his spin that surprised even visiting umpire James Lillywhite had no wides called against him in a drawn match. This performance of skill and stamina made him a hero overnight in Melbourne, but the following month he was among 11 Victorian bowlers who took a hiding as New South Wales ran up 775 in Sydney, Murdoch scoring 321, Sam Jones 109 and Tom Garrett 163. This was the highest total in all first-class cricket to that time and the hammering Cooper received (1 for 120) cost him selection in the second Test. He recovered with 4 for 84 from 36 overs for Victoria v. A. Shaw's XI in Melbourne and although this did not earn him a place in the third and fourth Tests of that series, his confidence returned.

Victorian officials showed they disagreed with Australia's Test selectors by appointing Cooper captain and sole-selector for their 1882–83 team, and electing him a vice-president of the VCA. He justified this promotion by taking 5 for 89 for Victoria against Ivo Bligh's 1882–83 England XI but a hand injury kept him out of the Tests.

Cooper was chosen in the 1884 Australian team that toured England after several stars dropped out. His selection was hailed as a gamble in some newspapers and there was widespread speculation about how English batsmen would handle the spin which sorely troubled tour candidates in the selection trials. But would he land them in the right spot often enough?

With Victorians arguing that inside Cooper's thinly thached head lay a masterly tactical brain, Cooper inspired hopes that he would prove Australia's major hope in England by taking 15 wickets for 194 runs for the Australian tourists against South Australia en route to London. Later on the voyage, however, he became involved in a hectic game of shinty, which saw him collide with Alick Bannerman, who pushed him into an engine-room fan, severely damaging the spinning finger on Cooper's right hand.

The ship's doctor failed to mend the injury and in London the Queen's surgeon, Sir James Paget, advised that only a long rest could cure the injured ligaments. Sir James said it would have been easier to fix the injury had

Cooper broken a bone. Cooper played in only six of Australia's 32 matches, and his 136 overs on the tour, often painful, brought only seven wickets at 46.42 each.

Cooper retired from first-class cricket on his return home, leaving unanswered the argument that Englishmen would find him unplayable on turning wickets. At his best he was a remarkable bowler, capable of bowling for long periods with only two fieldsmen on the off side. He fielded brilliantly at point but was a moderate batsman, compiling only 247 runs in 39 first-class innings at 10.29. His 71 wickets at 24.49 was hardly convincing evidence of the need for more leg-spinners, but at least it was a start.

Cooper disappeared from the Victorian and Australian teams just as George Henry Stevens Trott was making his bid for a permanent spot in both teams. Trott, eldest of three talented Trott brothers, was a sad, lugubrious figure who, like Cooper, played for the South Melbourne club. The great South Australian all-rounder George Giffen described him as the finest all-round man Victoria ever sent to England. Trott hit nine centuries in compiling 8,804 first-class runs with skilful right-hand batting. He was never as murderous a hitter as his brother Albert, but he was just as fine a fieldsman and his tactical acumen earned him the Australian captaincy in eight Tests. Australia won five of those matches and in most of them Harry Trott bowled his leg-breaks with telling effect.

Trott, born in Collingwood on 5 August 1866, toured England four times with Australian teams, in 1888, 1890, 1893 and 1896—the last tour as captain—scored 1,000 runs on each of those tours and dismissed 175 batsmen on his four trips. Perhaps his finest bowling coup came on his last tour when he noticed how much Dr W.G. Grace's footwork had slowed as he aged. At the start of England's first innings Trott bowled slow leg-breaks to exploit Grace's weakness and had both Grace and Andrew Stoddart stumped, throwing the ball to his regular opening bowlers with England 2 for 23.

Harry Trott's idea of properly exploiting his leg-spinners was to bowl them in short spells, usually to solve a problem or test a batsman's faults. He was one of the first Australian bowlers to become known as a partnership-breaker because of his habit of ending worrying stands. He seldom bowled long spells, probably because he never enjoyed robust health, and he quickly took himself off when a batsman became accustomed to his turn.

A characteristic of leg-break bowlers down the years has been their sunny nature, their refusal to allow a few big hits from their bowling to upset them. Most of the great tweakers laughed a lot, shrugged off punishment, and directed all their concentration on the next delivery.

Harry Trott was an exception, a cricketer whose perpetual air of impending misfortune belied his skills and hid his enjoyment in playing. A lot of spectators encountering his gloomy facade wondered why he bothered going out on to the field at all, and even the most humourous events seldom drew a smile from him. No cricket academy would recommend his attitude.

His melancholia manifested itself after 12 summers in the Victorian eleven in 1897–98 when his health broke down and he went into a psychiatric institution. By then he had made such an immense contribution to Victorian cricket a testimonial was started on his behalf and the Melbourne Cricket Club began with a donation of 100 guineas.

He defied medical forecasts by playing again for Victoria in 1903–04, when he made nine runs in Victoria's infamous total of 15 against England, watching six of his team dismissed for ducks. Victoria's 15 remains the lowest score in Australian first-class cricket. In his 59 matches for Victoria, he hit 2,881 runs at 26.92 and took 181 wickets at 24.97 apiece. In all first-class cricket he hit nine centuries and dismissed 386 batsmen, taking five wickets or more in an innings with his leg-spinners 17 times. Clem Hill, a veteran of 49 Tests, and the famous Indian batsman Prince Ranjitsinhji, rated him the best Australian captain in their experience.

All the Trott brothers found an early grave. Albert shot himself in his London boarding house at the age of 41, leaving £5 in cash. Fred died in 1921 without achieving first-class status in a round of jobs as a professional ground bowler. Harry died in a Melbourne asylum in 1917 at 51, remembered as a man whose leg-breaks could revive despondent team-mates. A postman who delivered mail in South Melbourne, Harry Trott was the only bowler who could give Turner and Ferris, a notable bowling twosome, a spell without weakening the Australian attack.

There appeared in England in Harry Trott's time, a stubborn, pig-headed slow bowler who puzzled all Australian tourists, Walter Mead. He was born at Clapton, Middlesex, in 1868 but declined all invitations to play for the county of his birth and instead remained inactive until he qualified by residence to play for Essex, for whom he appeared in 332 matches over 19 seasons. He bowled right-arm with an easy, rhythmical action and could turn the ball either way even on good pitches. Opponents feared his leg-break and, in his mature years, his googly, but he preferred to bowl off-breaks.

Mead took 100 wickets in an English season 10 times, with 179 victims at 14.55 in 1895 his best. He dismissed nine batsmen in an innings three times for Essex, with 9 for 40 against Hampshire at Southampton in 1900 his best figures. Despite these splendid credentials and the obvious menace of his leg-break, he appeared in only one Test.

In May 1899, at Leyton, he hit the stumps eight times in capturing 14 wickets for 127 runs against Yorkshire. This performance won him a place in the England team against Australia the following month at Lord's. Mead was given 53 overs in Australia's first innings, but steadfastly refused to follow the instructions of his captain, W.G. Grace, to bowl leg-spinners. Instead he stuck with off-breaks, watched Australia score 421 and win the match by 10 wickets because of centuries (135 each) from Trumper and Hill. He was never again invited to play for

Perpetually morose Harry Trott, who opened the bowling in a Test with leg-spin and exploited Grace's slow footwork.

England, and when he died in 1954 *Wisden* aptly described him as 'an occasional' leg-break bowler.

One theory was Mead became so engrossed with his experiments to master the googly that this overshadowed his Test ambitions. He was certainly among the first to bowl off-breaks with a leg-break action. There was a lot of exploring going on as bowlers mastered the high, overhanging action overarm bowling allowed. However, the fear of punishment when they were wayward in a period of quick-footed batsmanship often stopped experimental balls getting a trial in matches.

One bowler who stuck with what he knew was W.G. Grace, who reached the stumps in a few shuffling strides and innocently rotated his arm in a pronounced round-arm swing that invariably produced good-length deliveries. Grace saw no reason to change to lofty overarm, and concentrated instead on imparting topspin to his round-armer. The famous lob bowler Digby Loder Armroid Jephson, of Cambridge (Blues in all his three years from 1890 to 1892) and Surrey (165 matches), wrote that when W.G. bowled 'the hand is large and the ball well concealed until the ball leaves by the back door over the knuckle of the little finger'.

The great Dr W.G. Grace preferred this round-arm style to overarm, but got a lot of topspin and turn from the leg on the ball.

Jephson, who wrote both songs and poems about cricket, unashamedly defended lob bowling in a curious piece for *Wisden*: 'We, the solitary few who still strive to hold upright the tottering pillars in the ruined temple of lob bowling, are today of small account. There is scarcely a ground in England where derision is not our lot, or where laughter and taunting jeers are not hurled at us'.

Jephson called leg spin bowling 'tosh', but conceded that it was a more effective method of getting rid of great batsmen on firm wickets than faster, guileless bowling. Among England's outstanding lob bowlers he rated Simpson Hayward and Edward Wynyard supreme. Leaders among the 'tosh' bowlers were the Rev. George Raikes, who once took 71 wickets in nine matches for Hampshire, and Frederic Geeson of Leicestershire. Geeson reverted to leg-breaks after objections to the legality of his medium-pacers, delivering balls so slow spectators wondered if they would arrive at the other end. The switch worked and at the age of 38 Geeson took 125 wickets at 26.64, many of them from stumpings when batsmen went down the pitch after his 'tosh'.

There was no belittling the leg-breaks of Sussex's Joe Vine, a leg-spinner who was seldom punished, and a good batsman to boot. David Frith in his book *The Slow Men*, said that Vine differed from those who were expert in imparting leg-spin to genuinely fast balls, such as Sydney Barnes, only in his trajectory, which was slower, and in his field-placing, which was heavily accented to the leg side. 'On his day, Vine could aspire to that magical, mystical but truly only theoretical delivery, the "unplayable",' wrote Frith. Vine's career stretched from 1896 to 1922, his forty-seventh year. He appeared in 421 consecutive matches for Sussex. In his first-class career he took 685 wickets at 28.52. His Test career was limited to only two matches for the 1911–12 England team in Australia, in neither of which he bowled.

Often preferred to Vine was Len Braund, who was considered a superior batsman and a match-winning slips fieldsman. Braund was slower through the air than Vine and was one of the few leg-spinners who could exploit a damp pitch as well as left-arm slow bowlers. He took 100 wickets in a season four times, with 172 at 19.80 in 1902 his best, and six times scored more than 1,000 runs in a season. His 17,801 runs included 25 centuries and a top score of 257 not out for Somerset against Worcestershire in 1913. Thirty-nine of his career total of 545 catches came in his 23 Tests.

Braund toured Australia three times and had to contend with fleet-footed top-order batsmen like Victor Trumper, Clem Hill and Joe Darling, whose determination to get to the pitch of the ball dispirited many a leg-spinner. It was a technique that had prevailed since the days of Australia's original slow bowler Tom Kendall, whose 8 for 109 helped win the first of all Tests in Melbourne. Like Kendall, Braund learnt that against cocky Australians, well-versed in facing leg-spin, variety and a command of flight and turn were essential.

On his first Australian tour in 1901–02, Braund took 21 Test wickets and averaged 36 with the bat. In 1903–04 he made a classic 102 at Sydney and took 8 for 81 at Melbourne. Facing the South African googly attack at Lord's in 1907, he scored 104. But he is probably best remembered for the catches he held in between discussing race form with his wicket-keeper. At Edgbaston in 1902 against Australia, he darted from slip to the leg side to get rid of Clem Hill. Even when he was hammered by batsmen like Gilbert Jessop, who once struck six boundaries from a Braund over at Bristol, he remained calm, and this same fortitude carried him through the loss of both legs as the result of World War II air-raids. He went to Lord's in a wheelchair, happily recalling old matches with friends. His spirit was indomitable.

One of Braund's contemporaries was the Nottinghamshire captain Arthur Owen Jones, who preferred to bowl his wide leg-spinners in short spells to try and break long stands or allow his stock bowlers to change ends. Jones was a wily captain, a brilliant fieldsman and a skilful opening batsman, but many thought he undervalued his wrist-spinners. From a low arm action, he released curling, dipping deliveries that hummed in the air and sometimes hit the pitch like firecrackers. They brought Jones 333 first-class wickets at 32.81 but he was only sparsely used in Tests though he could be an extremely hostile bowler in county cricket.

Jones toured Australia with Archie MacLaren's team in 1901–02 and captained the 1907–08 English team in Australia. Illness prevented him playing in the first three Tests but he left hospital to appear in the fourth and fifth Tests in a series Australia won 4–1. He never fully recovered from that illness and he died in 1914, aged 44, from tuberculosis, captaining Notts until a few months before his death.

Among Jones' team-mates in Australia in 1901–02 were leg-break bowlers of highly contrasting appearance and technique, Sydney Francis Barnes, Willie Quaife and Charlie McGahey. Quaife was one of the smallest cricketers to play for England at 5 feet 3 inches, and of such slight stature his pads always looked too big for him. He produced his leg-breaks from a low action which created official doubts about its legality, but escaped a life ban by raising his arm slightly to go on and take 931 first-class wickets at 27.32 runs each. He did not bowl in any of his seven Tests, scoring 228 runs at 19.00 in the

Spry's cartoon of the noted lob bowler Digby Loder Armroid Jephson, who had to overcome spectators' derision whenever he bowled. He believed leg-breaks 'tosh', fast bowling guileless.

Towering Charlie McGahey, as tall but not as bulky as Armstrong, delivered leg-breaks from a high, whippy action, taking 330 first-class wickets, none of them in Tests.

Warwick Armstrong, who perfected his leg-spinners as a ground bowler for the Melbourne Cricket Club, often bowled to packed legside fields.

middle order. McGahey was 6 feet 2 inches and released his leg breaks with a high, whippy action in which his right arm was fully extended. His career bag of 330 wickets, none of them in Tests, cost 31.21 runs apiece. Compared to Quaife, McGahey was a giant and each English winter he played top-class soccer for Tottenham Hotspur, Clapton Orient, Arsenal and Sheffield United.

As a bowler McGahey was noted for his success on rain-damaged or worn pitches. In 1906 at Leyton he cleverly exploited a crumbling pitch to take 7 for 27 for Essex against Notts, and in 1919 at Weston-Super-Mare he took 6 for 21 on a turning pitch for Essex against Somerset. He also had match analysis of 12 for 158 for Essex v. Gloucestershire in 1901 at Clifton and 10 for 64 for Essex against Notts at Leyton in 1906. He was the idol of spectators at Leyton, where he scored 18 of his 31 first-class centuries and took 152 of his wickets, and when he retired in 1921 after 400 matches for Essex the Leyton spectators jumped the fence and carried him shoulder-high from the ground.

McGahey's high, loose action was often compared to that of the giant Australian Warwick Windridge

Armstrong, who through a combination of leg-spin bowling, aggressive batting and arrogant demeanour made himself one of the most formidable cricketers of all time. Armstrong always liked to get his own way, but when he was first brought to Melbourne from his birthplace at Kyneton, to try out as a ground bowler with the Melbourne club, his bowling failed to impress and he was sent home.

Armstrong learnt to play cricket when he was educated at Cumloden School, Alma Road, and University College, Armadale, on the southern side of the Yarra. He bowled leg-breaks, from an uncommonly long approach, out of the back of his hand and topspinners over the top of his big right fist. Despite his bulky physique he could sustain a tight length for hours on end. He took more than 100 wickets on three English tours—1905, 1909 and 1921—but he probably made the biggest impact on his first tour in 1902 with his negative leg theory, operating to a packed leg-side field and drilling the ball unerringly down a path wide of the leg stump. Typical of his disdain for spectators was his effort in 1905 when he bowled 52 overs wide of the leg stump, 24 of them maidens, in the Trent Bridge Test won by England.

Armstrong found work as a pavilion clerk for the Melbourne club after that early snub and developed great accuracy bowling daily on the MCG practice wickets. He made his debut for Victoria in 1898–99 and was plucked from the Victorian XI to tour England with Joe Darling's Australian team in 1902 at the age of 23. He was then 10 stone in weight and 6 foot 2 inches tall, a gangling youth who had to stoop to get the bat onto the turf. When he retired from first-class cricket after 83 matches for his state in 1921–22 at the age of 42 he was 22 stone and widely known as 'The Big Ship', a weight increase attributed to his fondness for Scotch whisky, which he sold in such quantities after his departure from big cricket that the sales made him rich. On the way through his 24 years of big cricket he had seen many controversial events, not the least of them the introduction of the googly, the ball that revolutionised his beloved art of leg-spin bowling.

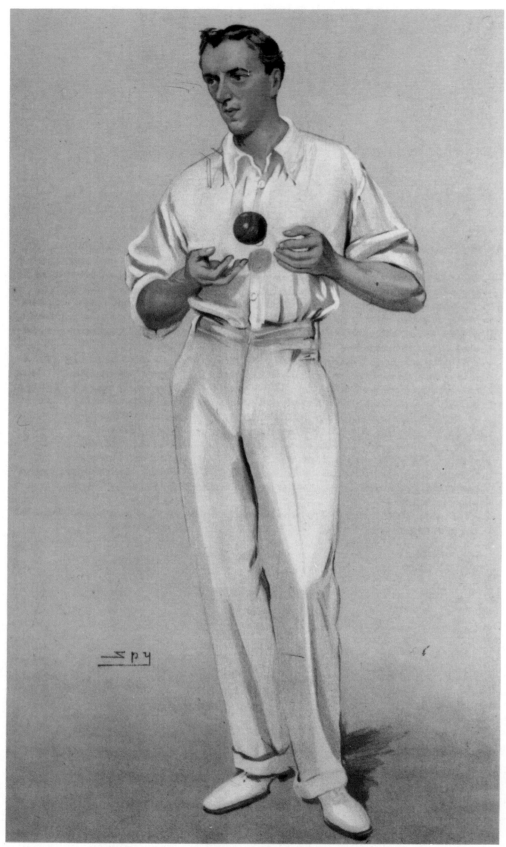

Spry's cartoon of Bernard Bosanquet, whose Test match coup in Sydney silenced sceptics who doubted that he had invented a new delivery, off-breaks with a leg-break action known as googlies in Australia and bosies in England.

3

The Bosanquet Revolution

Bernard James Tindal Bosanquet, born at Bulls Cross, Enfield, in Middlesex in 1877, began his cricket at Sunnymede School at Slough and at Eton as a fast bowler. His father, Lieutenant-Colonel B.T. Bosanquet (1843–1910), bowled off-breaks with a leg-break action to him from the time Bernard was six years old but the boy never queried his father about his methods. At Eton Bernard played a game called twisti-twosti, the object of which was to pitch a ball onto a table and make it turn or break in a manner that deceived the receiver at the far end. It occurred to him that if he could do the same thing on a cricket pitch, he could cause batsmen to make false strokes. Practising with a soft ball at 'stump-cricket', he gained enough control to try the same trick on a cricket pitch with a hard ball.

By 1899 Bosanquet had become the star turn during the luncheon interval in matches at Oxford University. The most famous batsmen on the opposing side were invited into a net and Bosanquet bowled them two or three leg-breaks. He then bowled his 'off-break' with the same action.

'If this pitched in the right place it probably hit him on the knee and everyone shrieked with laughter,' Bosanquet told *Wisden* in 1925. 'I was then led away and locked up for the day.' In the next two seasons he devoted considerable time to practising the googly at the nets and occasionally bowled it in unimportant matches. He said the first public exhibition of the googly was in July 1900, when he produced it at a critical moment for Middlesex against Leicestershire at Lord's.

Left-hander Sam Coe was on 98 for Leicestershire when he was clean bowled by a googly which Bosanquet said bounced four times. This brought ribald comment from all who watched but from an incident treated as a joke came what was hailed as a revolution in bowling. Only six weeks earlier he had taken his career-best 15 for 63 (6 for 48 and 9 for 15) opening the bowling for Oxford University bowling medium-pace against Sussex at Oxford, a match-winning display. But his knowledgable and influential Middlesex team-mates 'Plum' Warner and wicket-keeper Gregor MacGregor knew of the googly's potential. 'At that time I always tried to convey the impression that it was accidental and unintentional,' Bosanquet said. 'I did not want batsmen to be on their guard. I even persuaded "Plum" not to write about it and he refrained from doing so for almost a year.'

He continued to practise until he could bowl the googly at will, but his length and direction were often astray. But by the time Warner and others began to write about the ball in 1901 Bosanquet's control over the delivery had improved. 'I have always maintained that there was nothing new in the googly,' he said. 'For years leg-break bowlers had been occasionally turning the ball from the off. The difference was that I could produce it whenever I wanted to. Off-breaks were not new but my method of producing it with a leg-break action was the secret.'

Bosanquet's invention attracted plenty of scepticism but Australian batsmen needed no convincing on his effectiveness after their match at Lord's in 1902. 'The first time I bowled the googly against the Australians I had Joe Kelly out for a duck and he returned to the pavilion very puzzled,' Bosanquet said. 'Not one of the Australians initially tumbled to the fact that it was no accident.' Kelly, in fact, only attracted laughter when he told team-mates: 'There's a bloke out there bowling leg-breaks that turn in from the off.'

From the moment it became recognised that a ball could be bowled that left batsmen in doubt over which way it would break, Bosanquet came under close scrutiny. Commentators found him to be a gifted all-round sportsman who had represented Oxford at hockey and billiards and won Blues for cricket three years in a row as a fast-medium bowler and punishing right-hand middle-order batsman. He played fullback in soccer matches for the Old Etonians and threw the hammer for Oxford against Cambridge before making his debut for Middlesex in 1898. He did not know how much his father's use of the googly method in their backyard matches influenced him but agreed that it probably had an instinctive effect when he began turning the wrist over at the moment of delivery far enough to alter the axis of spin.

'I persevered with the googly chiefly because I found the lot of an average fast-medium bowler in a county side was not a happy one,' Bosanquet told *Wisden* readers.

B.J.T. Bosanquet, inventor of the googly, had long, sinewy fingers that took a firm grip on the ball, as shown here.

'It generally meant being put on under a sweltering sun on a plumb wicket when the other bowlers had failed and the batsmen were well set. If one was lucky enough to get a wicket, the original bowlers resumed, and unless the same conditions recurred one was not wanted again. If the wicket was difficult, one was never thought of. As a result, partly from a natural disinclination to work hard on hot days (how much more pleasant to walk up slowly and gently propel the ball in the air), and partly from a sneaking ambition to achieve bigger things I persevered with the googly.

'It took a lot of hard work but for a year or two the results were worth it, for in addition to adding to the merriment of the cricket world, I found that batsmen who smiled at the sight of me now showed a marked preference for the other end.'

Despite his wayward length Bosanquet created mayhem among leading English batsmen for several seasons. Arthur Shrewsbury, the great Nottinghamshire professional and sponsor of tours to Australia, claimed the googly was unfair. His Notts team-mate William Gunn was stumped off a googly when he was closer to Bosanquet than the batting crease.

When England's Test wicket-keeper Dick Lilley boasted that he could detect every googly Bosanquet bowled, Bosanquet's team-mates urged him to teach the Warwickshire hero a lesson. Bosanquet bowled Lilley two overs of leg-breaks and then changed to the googly action. Lilley attempted to play the delivery gracefully to leg and had his off stump removed, a fate which returned him, shamefaced, to a noisy dressing-room.

The value of surprise in successful googly bowling was persistently demonstrated on Bosanquet's North American tours, first with Plum Warner's team in 1898, then on a visit to the West Indies under Prince Ranjitsinhji, and finally in 1901 with a side Bosanquet himself led to the U.S. Warner baited the trap on arrival for the 1903–04 Australian tour when he described Bosanquet as a prolific bowler of bad balls. Australians were accustomed to furphies about mystery balls and scoffed at the idea of a new delivery, variously described as a googly, wrong-un, or bosey.

Warner had a choice of classy bowlers in Hirst, Arnold, Braund and Rhodes, which allowed him to keep Bosanquet under wraps until the vital days of the tour. Bosanquet impressed with 79 against Victoria in Melbourne, 99 against Northern Districts at Maitland, 124 not out against Tasmania in Hobart, deflecting attention from his bowling. In his Test debut at Melbourne in December 1903 his 2 for 52 and 1 for 100 did not look threatening because he bowled only leg-breaks. He was dropped from the second Test, and in the third Test had 3 for 95 and 4 for 73, again bowling mostly leg-breaks and topspinners.

Warner now decided to produce the googly. Bosanquet won the match against New South Wales in Sydney, scoring 114 and following with 6 for 45 against batsmen still unaware that his leg-breaks turned the wrong way. In New South Wales' second innings, with Warner chuckling as he watched, Bosanquet gave Australians the first look at the googly's menace. He was thrown the ball with Bert Hopkins in full flow after scoring 40 in 20 minutes. Hopkins hit two leg-breaks imperiously to the cover boundary. The next one, which Bosanquet confessed he delivered with a silent prayer, pitched on the same spot and drew the same stroke but dipped in flight and spun back from the off and hit Hopkins' middle stump. Bosanquet's 6 for 45 gave England victory by 278 runs, completing a richly satisfying all-round coup in which Bosanquet also made 168 runs and took 8 for 96.

This convinced Warner that the time was right to gamble on the googly in the Test. On the same Sydney Cricket Ground pitch where he had duped New South

Wales a fortnight earlier, Bosanquet had a spell of 5 for 12, polishing off Australia's second innings with 6 for 51 in a display that gave England an Ashes-winning 3–1 lead. Lilley stumped Clem Hill, Bert Hopkins and Hugh Trumble as they struggled to get to the pitch of the ball, and also caught Charlie McLeod, Foster taking a neat catch to complete the rout. It was an eventful Test with the crowd, impatient over delays in resuming after rain, bombarding the field with watermelons. But England's triumph on a tour funded by the Melbourne Cricket Club foiled the sceptics and won international acceptance for the googly.

Watching Bosanquet fool famous batsmen with his googly, a young Sydney dental student vowed to master the ball himself. Herbert Vivian Hordern, born at North Sydney on 10 February 1884, and nicknamed 'Ranji' because of his swarthy complexion, learnt to play cricket with the North Sydney district club and made his debut for New South Wales in December 1905. His 11 for 164 on debut was rated a fine effort, and included figures of 8 for 81 in Queensland's second innings.

He went to America to continue his dental studies before he got another chance to appear for his state and in 1907 as a university student toured England with the Pennsylvania cricket team, which completed a program against leading English schools. The following year he returned to England with the Philadelphian team for 10 first-class matches. Bowling off a longer run than other googly bowlers, Hordern developed deceptive flight and exceptional accuracy with the spinning ball. Despite his limited practice, he rejoined the New South Wales team in November 1910, immediately he returned from America. He took 4 for 60 and 5 for 70 and 3 for 59 and 1 for 25 in two matches against Queensland, 7 for 31 and 5 for 67 against Tasmania, 7 for 55 and 6 for 32 against Victoria, and on that form forced his way into the fourth Test in Melbourne against South Africa in February 1911.

Teams for this match showed the startling impact Bosanquet's ball had produced on selectors. Apart from Hordern and fellow googly bowler Syd Emery in the New South Wales side, South Africa included googly addicts George Aubrey Faulkner, Reginald Oscar Schwartz, Alfred Edward Ernest Vogler and Gordon Charles White as well as leg-spinner Sidney James Pegler. They had badly shaken English cricket in 1904 and 1907 following Bosanquet's technique.

Schwartz, born at Lee, Kent in May 1875, of Silesian parents, was the catalyst. He became obsessed with bowling off-breaks out of the back of his hand at St Paul's School and later at Cambridge. He played cricket with Bosanquet for Oxfordshire and Middlesex, and Rugby as a five-eighth for Richmond, Cambridge and England.

Australians impressed by Bosanquet's new delivery who decided to learn how to bowl it. Left, dentist Dr Herbert ('Ranji') Hordern; right, Victorian Syd Emery, affectionately known as 'Mad Mick'.

When he took a job in South Africa with Sir Abe Bailey, he taught the other Springboks the googly.

The Australians all found Hordern harder to read in the nets than any of the South Africans in the match. Hordern took Louis Stricker's wicket with the first ball of his second over in Tests, but had to go off with a dislocated finger. He returned to take 3 for 39 and 5 for 66, setting up Australia's victory by 530 runs. Sadly, Billy Murdoch, ex-Test captain, missed their triumph as he had died in the stands of a heart attack during the second day.

At Sydney in the fifth Test Hordern was sent in to bat while the pitch dried after Australia had lost her first wicket with only two runs on the board. He stayed to score a highly competent 50, lifting the total to 126 in a 124-run stand with Macartney (137) which set Australia on the way to a total of 364. He then did the bulk of Australia's bowling, taking 4 for 73 and 2 for 117 off 51 overs to finish the series with 14 wickets from his two Tests.

This impressive debut in Tests made Hordern an automatic selection in 1911–12, when he proved Australia's only hostile bowler against the touring English team. He had another splendid season, taking 35 wickets at an average cost of 24.05. He won the first Test for Australia in Sydney by taking 5 for 85 and 7 for 90, took 4 for 66 in the first innings of the second Test, 3 for 175 in the third Test, 3 for 137 in the fourth Test and, in what turned out to be his final Test, captured 5 for 95 and 5 for 66 in the fifth Test.

Hordern's dental practice forced him to retire after only seven Tests because of the risk of injury to his hands. His two summers had yielded 46 Test wickets at 23.36 and in only 33 first-class matches he finished with 217 wickets at 16.79. His unavailability for Australia's 1912 tour of England was a sad blow to all tweaker fans as he had already taken 110 wickets there at only 9.68 apiece on his 1907 tour with Pennsylvania University.

Hordern's figures in a relatively short career—he played in more Tests than Shield matches—entitle him to ranking with the great Australian wrist spinners. The outstanding critic A.G. ('Johnnie') Moyes said: 'The comparison between Hordern, Mailey and Grimmett is of more than academic interest. Two (Mailey and Grimmett) became world famous, but the third (Hordern) rarely comes into discussion because he played so little, but I'm inclined to rank him ahead of the others. He was as good as Mailey on hard wickets and better than Grimmett; in England he would have been as outstanding as Grimmett. With his command of length, his disguised deliveries, his ability to flight the ball, and his clever fingers, I do not see how he could have failed.'

Hordern did not bowl loose balls like Mailey and he turned both leg-break and googly as far as Grimmett. He gave no advance signals of the googly such as Grimmett's dropped shoulder. Moyes described how in Victor Trumper's testimonial match in Sydney in 1912–13 Trumper advised him to watch for Hordern's little finger lifting from the ball as he let go his googly. Moyes lost sight of the little finger, the ball broke the opposite way to expectations, and Sammy Carter stumped him. 'Fooled you, son,' said Carter and out Moyes went. No wonder C.B. Fry and Pelham Warner ranked Hordern the best googly bowler they ever encountered.

Hordern's ascendancy over the South African googly experts unfortunately gave Australians the impression that the South Africans lacked menace. This was a foolish view, considering the havoc the South Africans created among English batsmen on their 1907 English tour, when the Springboks won eight of their 11 matches before the first Test. The rubber was dominated by wrist-spin bowlers, with Colin Blythe, the Kent left-armer, taking 26 wickets for England and the googly quartet of Faulkner (12), Schwartz (9), Vogler (15) and Gordon White (4) taking 40 of the England wickets that fell in the three Tests.

On wet pitches South Africa's batsmen struggled against English bowlers experienced on these surfaces, but their googly bowlers troubled all England's leading batsmen. The first Test was drawn after Vogler took 7 for 128, scattering the stumps three times. England won the second Test, despite Faulkner's 6 for 17 which enabled South Africa to bundle England out for only 76. At The Oval, Tom Hayward became the first English Test batsman dismissed by the first ball of the match in England when he misread Vogler's sharp-turning googly. At the end of a tour on which their googly bowlers regularly hoodwinked county batsmen, Schwartz was invited to join an English team in Philadelphia.

Schwartz deserved this compliment as he had taken 137 wickets on South Africa's English tour for only 11.79 runs apiece. He took five wickets in an innings 12 times and fooled batsmen so palpably with his googly the delivery brought laughter from spectators. Vogler took 119 wickets, including 8 for 67 against a powerful MCC XI at Lord's, and dismissed five batsmen in an innings nine times.

Even these performances were not as highly ranked, however, as the all-round display by Aubrey Faulkner, whose spinners frequently looked unplayable. His 5 for 8 against Hampshire at Southampton was matched by a remarkable effort against England at Headingley when he worried all the English batsmen, taking 6 for 17, with all 10 England wickets falling to googlies.

Faulkner bowled his googlies at medium-pace and throughout his career proved a threat to great batsmen. He achieved unusual flight for a bowler of his pace and varied spin in both directions with a well-concealed yorker. All four South African googly bowlers shocked English cricket fans, but because of his good looks and his aggressive batting Faulkner won most headlines, finishing with 64 wickets at 15.82 and heading the South African batting with 1,163 runs at 29.82, with two centuries and a top score of 106 not out.

He completely mastered England in South Africa in 1909, taking 29 wickets with his googlies at 21.89 and scoring 545 runs at 60.55 in the five Tests. At Johannesburg in the first Test of that series Faulkner made

G.H. Simpson-Hayward, one of the last of the successful underarm bowlers, who kept going in this style for 156 matches for Worcestershire and appeared in five Tests for England.

78 and 123 and took 8 for 160 to ensure South Africa of victory by 19 runs. Googly exponents dominated this famous triumph, with Vogler taking 12 for 181 and accounting for Jack Hobbs, Wilfred Rhodes and Frank Woolley in both innings. This was the match in which lob bowler G.H. Simpson-Hayward took eight wickets in his only Test for England.

There was a touch of brilliance in all Faulkner did. After his marvellous batting in Australia in 1910–11, he settled in England and became one of cricket's finest coaches, tutoring hundreds of youngsters in the art of batting and wrist spin at the indoor school he owned. Freddie Brown, R.W.V. Robins, Stan Squires, Peter Smith and Doug Wright were among the successful tweakers who passed through his doors. He employed Ian Peebles as one of his assistants, a job in which Peebles had time to develop his spinners.

Handsome, popular Faulkner added to his fame in the army in World War I, winning the DSO and rising to the rank of major. He was recalled to the South African Test team in 1924 at the age of 43 but the old magic had gone and England's batsmen took 87 runs from his 17 overs without loss. He departed from Test cricket after lack of speed saw him run out for 12, attempting a run he would have easily made in his prime.

In his first-class career Faulkner took 449 wickets at 17.42, 82 of them in 25 Tests at 26.58, and scored 13 centuries in scoring 6,366 runs. His 1,754 runs in Tests included four centuries. As he aged he became increasingly prone to melancholia and he told Jack Hobbs in a radio interview in 1930 that he lamented not being able to stay young. 'These young fellows today don't know how marvellous it is to be young and to be able to get on with things.' A few weeks later he died by his own hand, suffocating on carbon monoxide from a gas fire.

Faulkner remained a fine bowler for most of his 49 years, spinning the ball abundantly, disguising his googlies from all but the eagle-eyed. He always insisted that Vogler was the best of the four South Africans who shook the cricket world in the decade before World War I because Vogler bowled his sharp-spinning googly at a brisk medium-pace. He liked to tell the pupils at his cricket school how Schwartz, one of that wonderful quartet, ended up only able to bowl the googly and completely unable to produce a leg-break however he twisted his wrist.

Faulkner's widow retrieved the blazer Faulkner had given to a friend just before he died. The blazer had solid gold buttons, and his estate was valued at only £273. He had a further £2 in his pockets as they carried his body away.

Bert Vogler approached the crease in a jerky manner and had an arm action that was anything but fluent. He was very difficult to read and although the googly was his stock delivery he mixed them up with a topspinner and a deceptively slow yorker. He began with Natal but switched to Eastern Province after making his first-class debut at 27 in 1903 against Transvaal. When he was

Albert Ernest Vogler, known as 'Bert', described as the world's best bowler after he went round England with a South African team specialised in the Bosanquet ball. He taught it to other Springboks.

enslaved by the joy of tweaking, he turned professional and joined the MCC ground staff at Lord's, appearing with brilliant success in several matches for MCC. Unfortunately for him his employers already had colonial players Frank Tarrant and Albert Trott on the staff and this frustrated his plans to qualify for Middlesex. Sir Abe Bailey, the great benefactor of South African cricket,

Arthur Mailey's classical side-on action allowed him to conceal the ball until the last moment of his delivery stride.

found a job for him back in South Africa and Vogler returned home to enjoy further success in domestic cricket. He took 10 for 26 in 12 overs for Eastern Province in a glorious day against Griqualand West and finished with 16 for 38 in the match.

Vogler played in all five Tests at home against England in 1905–06 when South Africa shocked the cricket world by winning the series 4–1, but found it difficult to get a bowl in such a successful attack, taking only nine wickets, and contributing splendidly with the bat by averaging 34.25.

At 31, he was a vital part of the four-pronged South African googly attack in England in 1907, and England's captain Reggie Foster called him the 'best bowler in the world'. Vogler took 119 wickets on that tour at 15.62, including 15 wickets in the three Tests at 19.66. In 1909–10 he took a record 36 wickets at 21.75 in the five Tests, South Africa winning a tense rubber 3–2. His last great showing came against England in 1909–10, when he took 12 for 181 in the first Test and 8 for 207 in the third Test, both at Johannesburg. He came to Australia in 1910–11 but lacked his old penetration. He kept playing with Scottish, Irish and English clubs and in 1912 appeared for an Irish XI against the touring South Africans, finishing with 393 first-class wickets at 18.27, 64 of them in Tests at 22.73, having with his team-mates brought the googly to its highest pitch of perfection.

Vogler's departure for South Africa deprived English first-class cricket of its leading exponent of googly bowling, leaving the field to a frustrated Kent medium-pace bowler named Douglas Ward Carr. He played for Oxford University in the Freshmen's match in 1891, but a football injury prevented him from appearing in major matches. Inspired by the mayhem Bosanquet had created, he switched to googlies and in 1909, at the age of 37, forced his way into county cricket, strengthening Kent's reputation for producing exceptional spinners.

Carr was so successful in his first full season that he forced his way into the Gentlemen's XI against the Players and at the end of that season played for England against Australia at The Oval, where he took 7 for 282 from 414 deliveries. His first innings analysis of 5 for 146 included a spell of 3 for 19 in his first seven overs in which he clean bowled Syd Gregory and had Noble and Armstrong leg before to balls that turned the opposite to their expectations.

This success caused Carr's captain Archie MacLaren to over-bowl him and the 69 overs he was given in the match proved too much for him, allowing the Australians to become accustomed to his break-backs. Carr kept going until 1914 and, although he finished with 334 first-class wickets, the element of surprise which made him triumphant in his initial season was gone.

Bosanquet suffered similar disappointment after his triumphs in Sydney and his memorable duels with the leading Australians in 1902–03. The mystery of his googlies disappeared. At Trent Bridge in the first Test of the 1905

One of an array of Australians who experimented with wrist-spin before World War I, George Garnsey. He took 80 first-class wickets with it, five times taking five wickets in an innings, but did not win a Test spot.

season his second innings figures of 8 for 107 paved the way to England's victory, but that was the end of him as a Test wicket-taker. He was not used in the rain-affected second Test at Lord's, and in the third Test at Headingley secured only one wicket from 19 overs. He was such a grievous disappointment selectors did not again favour him in an England XI.

He had enjoyed a marvellous match for Middlesex against Sussex that summer, when he took 5 for 75 and 8 for 53 and scored 100 not out in 75 minutes, but that was his last summer of glory. He attributed part of his decline to ribald newspaper comments about his googly and there is no doubt that noisy spectators' jokes about his bowling broke his confidence. He kept playing for Middlesex until 1919 and in 1908 hit a century in 25 minutes for Uxbridge against MCC.

Bosanquet seldom bowled in the last few seasons of a career that changed the entire conception of slow bowling, and endured much ridicule for deliveries that bounced three or four times. Australian tourists dubbed him the 'worst length bowler in England' and even his mentor Plum Warner said he bowled more bad balls than any Test bowler of his experience. Yet on his day he was a beguiling match-winner, capable of deluding the most astute batsmen. The big surprise in his statistics is not that he took 629 first-class wickets but that he also scored 21 first-class centuries. He died in Surrey in 1936 at 58, the father of a noted British television compere.

In Australia the development of Bosanquet's googly was interrupted by the premature retirement of Hordern, but a dedicated group of googly bowlers appeared, including Ray McNamee, George Garnsey, Charlie Barnes, Warwick Armstrong, 'Mad Mick' Emery, Jackie Matthews and Arthur Mailey. Not all of them mastered Bosanquet's delivery, but all of them rolled their wrists successfully enough for the Australian school to play a big part in furthering the style.

'The whole art of bowling is to make the batsman think that the ball he is about to receive is going to be one kind when it really is of quite a different nature,' Bosanquet said in a 1930 interview for *Cricket* with Neville Cardus. It was a concept Mailey, Emery and the others eagerly followed.

4

The Trailblazers

Wrist-spin bowling makes heavy demands on the temperament of its exponents. All those who followed A.G. Steel and B.J.T. Bosanquet quickly became aware their future depended a lot on how they reacted when their best-intentioned deliveries disappeared into the crowd. The batsmen's confidence soared, but success often came with the very next ball for bowlers who remained calm. A ball pitched in the right spot carrying the spin imparted by wrist and fingers could very quickly erase the batsman's smile, and was always more satisfying than anything pace or seam bowling provided.

Tweaking produced a breed of cricketers who had a philosophy all their own. Arthur Mailey, a master practitioner, said: 'Sometimes I am attacked by waves of accuracy, and I don't trust them'. Syd Emery, advised that he could become a great bowler, if he could control his googly, nodded and said: 'I could also become a great man if I could learn to control myself'. Both had great days when they floated balls up the pitch and the spin they contrived cut the ball down to deceive batsmen in flight or turn contrary to the batsmen's expectations. But they had to accept that when the ball pitched a fraction short or failed to take the bias planned, they could be mercilessly hammered.

New South Wales introduced two promising wrist-spinners into their team in 1904–05—Charlie Barnes, from the Redfern club, and George Garnsey, from the Burwood club. Garnsey was the sixth bowler used on his debut in a team that included Noble, Cotter, Hopkins, Howell and the North Sydney leg-spinner Fred Johnson. He had to be content with seven overs in the first Victorian innings (2 for 20) and 16.2 in the second innings (3 for 67). Barnes did not get a bowl at all in his match against Queensland because captains preferred not to introduce young bowlers until they became attuned to the atmosphere of first-class cricket. Garnsey had his chance the following summer against Queensland in Sydney when he took 6 for 71 and 6 for 45.

The struggle for the leg-spinner's job in the New South Wales XI intensified when Syd Emery started to produce outstanding figures in district cricket. But Garnsey was preferred to Emery and Barnes until Emery forced his way into the state team in December 1908, against South Australia in Adelaide. He had only a moderate debut although his rich potential was obvious. For the 1909 match in Sydney against Victoria, New South Wales went back to Barnes and he won the match for them with a stunning display of wrist-spin, taking 6 for 59 and 5 for 147 against a powerful Victorian batting line-up.

This earned Barnes a place in The Rest XI for two matches against the Australian XI just before the 1909 Australian team departed for England. In both matches he failed to impress. Meanwhile, Garnsey, Emery and Arthur Mailey were regularly turning in fine figures in club cricket. Emery grabbed his opportunity when he was picked for New South Wales against Victoria in December 1909, hitting the stumps six times in taking 7 for 28 (his career best) and 5 for 85. He followed this memorable effort on a firm Melbourne pitch against some of the best batsmen Australia had produced (Ransford, Armstrong, Smith, McAlister) with 5 for 55 and 1 for 39, all of them bowled, against South Australia in Sydney. In the return match against Victoria in Sydney, he was again on target, hitting the stumps three times in the first innings and once in the second.

The wrist-spin of Charlie Macartney and Ranji Hordern was preferred against South Africa in Australia in 1910–11 and in 1911–12 against England in Australia, but when Hordern retired and six top players declared themselves unavailable, Emery went into the Australian team for the triangular series in England in 1912. He made his Test debut in the first Test of that series against South Africa at Old Trafford, but it was his colleague, Jimmy Matthews, whose wrist-spin won all the headlines.

Matthews was a tough, persistent right-arm bowler with the build of a jockey, his skin darkened by a lifetime in the sun, who overcame his lack of height with a copybook technique. He kept the ball well up to the batsmen and on well-prepared pitches did not get much turn but a lot of topspin which rushed the ball on to the batsman. He was born at Williamstown, Victoria, in 1884, and learned the basics at Williamstown club. Later, with Essendon, St Kilda and the East Melbourne clubs, he developed his technique in breaks from his job as a groundsman.

Jimmy Matthews, the tough little Victorian wrist-spinner who took two Test hat-tricks in one day against South Africa in 1912.

He made his debut for Victoria against Tasmania in 1906–07, in his twenty-second year, with 5 for 93, dislodging the stumps of Test batsmen Ken Burn and Charles Eady. Then he pressed claims for a permanent spot in the Victorian team with an innings of 200 for Williamstown against South Melbourne. It soon became clear, however, that his promise lay in his bowling. His task looked formidable because the state's spinners, Warwick Armstrong, Gervys Hazlitt and Jack Saunders were successful Test bowlers, but in his second appearance against Tasmania Matthews took 7 for 49 and 5 for 42.

Steady improvement with the bat won him selection as an all-rounder in the Victorian XI that met South Africa in Melbourne in November 1910, and he responded with important contributions in an upset victory, scoring 51 with the bat and finishing with match figures of 6 for 46. This display earned him a regular place in the Victorian team and consistent wicket-taking and run-scoring took him into the Australian team against England at Adelaide as an all-rounder in January 1912. He took only one wicket for 96 runs but produced a valuable innings of 53 in Australia's second innings, enough to retain his place in the fourth Test at Melbourne where his 22 overs failed to produce a wicket.

Likeable, plucky, he was established as a good team man but far from a front-line bowler when he was chosen to visit England in Australia's triangular Test team after six leading players dropped out. The South Africans practised so often against their own squad of wrist spinners they were not expected to have the slightest difficulty with Matthews' bowling but he gave a performance unique in cricket history by taking a hat-trick in each innings on a firm, dry Old Trafford pitch that favoured batsmen. The six wickets in the hat-tricks were the only ones he took in the match and all fell on the second day.

Matthews made 49 not out in Australia's first innings of 448 after a cheeky 114 by Macartney and 121 littered with regal drives from Warren Bardsley, who added 202 for the third wicket. Faulkner played a masterly hand of 122 not out against the bowling of Bill Whitty, Syd Emery and Gervys Hazlitt, but with little support. At 7 for 265 Matthews took the ball, bowling Beaumont with the first delivery of his twelfth over, trapping Pegler lbw with his second, and Ward lbw with his third.

Following on, South Africa floundered against the pacy, swinging deliveries of Whitty and Kelleway. At 5 for 70, Matthews bowled Taylor, caught and bowled Schwartz with the next ball, and then completed his second hat-trick by bowling Ward, who as third victim in both hat-tricks bagged a 'king pair'. Matthews' 20 overs in the match brought 3 for 16 and 3 for 38. After he emerged from a swarm of back-slapping team-mates, the pocket-sized Matthews explained that all six wickets fell to topspinners that deceived batsmen expecting googlies.

Matthews could not repeat this magic but he took a further nine wickets in the tournament and completed the 36-match tour with 85 first-class victims at 19.37. He also scored 584 runs at 18.25, top score 93 against Sussex at Brighton. It was a praiseworthy all-round contribution but it could not help Australia win a tournament ruined by rain and the absence of the stars who rejected the Australian Board's tour terms.

The South Africans were so impressed by the success of Matthews' 'straight breaks' they opened their bowling with Pegler's leg-spinners for the rest of the tournament. He finished with 29 wickets at 20.48 from six Tests, but looked impotent against Hobbs, Rhodes, Reggie Spooner, Fry and Woolley, all of them confident stroke-makers against spin for the winning England side.

Back in Melbourne Matthews took 5 for 25 in Victoria's surprise 1912–13 win over New South Wales, but World War I ended his career. He returned to the Williamstown ground where he began as curator, remembered more as a hat-trick specialist than for his 177 first-class wickets at 25.46. In addition to his two in one day against South Africa, he snared one in 1908–09 for Victoria against Tasmania, and on the way home from the triangular tournament—won by England—he took another hat-trick for Australia against the Philadelphians at Germantown, Pennsylvania.

Matthews' double hat-trick revived debate that had been going on since Bosanquet pioneered the googly about whether batsmen should anticipate the type of delivery they face by watching the bowler's hand or by assessing the likely break as it bounced on the pitch. Wise wrist-spinners hide their hand positions from the batsman as long as possible, but their hand action obviously provides batsmen with a fraction longer to make a judgment.

Charlie Macartney, in his youth one of the finest left-arm wrist spinners Australia has produced. As he matured, he concentrated on his batting with spectacular results.

One whose hand action fooled a lot of well-performed batsmen was Syd Emery, of 'Mad Mick' as Arthur Mailey nicknamed him on a 1913 American tour by a strong Australian team. Emery, born in the Sydney suburb of Redfern in 1885, played for the Redfern club and learnt his cricket in a tough neighbourhood with parkland never far away. He played his early cricket in a busy period for quality wrist-spin. Charlie Barnes was one of his team-mates, Gother Carlisle played for North Sydney, Les Cody for Paddington, George Garnsey for Burwood, Bert Hordern for North Sydney, Michael Pierce for Carlton, Les Pye for Central Cumberland, James Randell for Middle-Harbour, Bert Shortland for Gordon, Walter Stack for University and Arthur Mailey for Redfern, all of them

good enough to play for New South Wales and all of them students of the mechanics of leg-break bowling.

'Syd Emery on his days was probably the most devastating bowler of the bosey (googly) ever seen,' wrote Johnnie Moyes. 'He bowled at medium-pace rather than slow, spun the ball prodigiously, could make it fly back at unseemly angles and had life and fire that made him unplayable when he found his control. Unfortunately, these occasions were rare, but at Melbourne in 1909–10 he took 7 for 28 in Victoria's first innings of 93 and 5 for 85 in Victoria's second innings of 185.'

Emery had the zany streak in his make-up which some claim is indispensible to a successful wrist-spinner. He was wild in his off-the-field pranks, but endowed with the strength of a wharfie. He laughed with uncontrolled glee in 1912 when he bowled Plum Warner with an attempted googly that got out of control and bounced twice. Warner had two swings at it before it scattered his stumps. When an umpire rejected one of his exuberant appeals in a Sydney club match, Emery asked the umpire if he could borrow a match and used it to illuminate the position of the stumps.

He did not play in the match in which Matthews had his double hat-trick on the 1912 England tour, but finished with 66 wickets on the tour at 23.71, on wickets that were too wet to suit him. In 1913 he spent five months touring America with a strong Australian team that played 52 matches for 45 wins and only one loss. His 127 wickets at only 8.61 runs each was a major benefit for a happy but overworked team.

At 31, he treated the 1913 American tour as his swansong, retiring with 58 first-class matches to his credit during which he dismissed 183 batsmen at 23.79, 11 times taking five wickets in an innings and three times taking 10 wickets in a match. He was unquestionably a trailblazer when Australians were mastering the challenges googly bowling presented, but had bad luck that such skilful bowlers as Ranji Hordern and Arthur Mailey blocked his path to a more distinguished Test career.

World War I also saw the end of the controversial Victorian spinner Jack Saunders' career. For a long time Saunders bowled his spinners at medium pace and spun the ball with his fingers, but the advent of Bosanquet's right-arm boseys or googlies saw him experiment by rolling the wrist with his left-arm deliveries. He found that he lacked control at medium pace but was far more accurate bowling slowly and he ended his career of 107 first-class matches at the age of 37, advocating wrist-spin for left-handers, an intriguing admission for a bowler who had been regarded as unplayable with his finger-spin on sticky or wet pitches.

Saunders dominated slow bowling in Victoria for years, a wise-cracking dandy with a well-waxed and curled moustache who favoured formal attire off the field and never made 50 in his life with the bat. He fobbed off suggestions that he had been a chucker at various stages of his career, and was always keen to help young spinners

Jack Saunders, the Victorian spinner who persuaded Clarrie Grimmett to migrate to Australia. Saunders bowled mainly finger-spin, but occasionally rolled the wrist with impressive results.

like Warwick Armstrong. Saunders was the man who persuaded the brilliant leg-spinner and googly bowler Clarrie Grimmett to migrate from his birthplace near Dunedin in New Zealand to Australia. Saunders left Australia in 1910 after 51 matches for Victoria to coach and play in New Zealand and represented Wellington from 1910–11 until 1913–14.

The extraordinary fascination Bosanquet's delivery spread among the cricket nations was not duplicated in England, where cricket fans tend to discount events they do not witness. The impression that the fuss over the googly was a fad that would pass appeared justified when he failed to produce persistently hostile bowling on his return to England. But Ranji Hordern recorded that when he took a handful of wickets in Jamaica with the googly five black boys woke him at dawn next morning demanding to know how he bowled googlies. In South Africa, the success of their posse of googly bowlers left no doubts about the ball's value. Even in the sandhills at the back of Waterloo the impact of the googly was solemnised with a barefoot Arthur Mailey fondling an old cricket ball as he searched for the right grip. That ball was as precious in the Mailey household as the pillarbox hat his father received when he joined up for the Crimean War.

In England, the majority of county spin bowlers had a look at googly bowling and decided it was too difficult. Poor old Douglas Carr had tried it with Kent and Oxford University and, although it had won him a place in the Gentlemen and England elevens, he had finally lost control and gave up bowling the ball. The consternation Carr had caused among county batsmen despite his mature years and his dismissal of Syd Gregory, Monty Noble and Warwick Armstrong in his first seven overs of Test cricket were forgotten.

No, the googly was not a delivery a young man hoping to make a living playing county cricket should develop. Some even bounced two or three times in the nets, and others became juicy full tosses. The Hearne family, five of whom were players for England, were often cited as bowlers who produced handy spells of leg-break bowling but remained disdainful of the googly. It is true that only one of the five, John William, the youngest member of the clan, bowled the googly regularly, but it also can be argued that the others would have had more impressive Test records had they rehearsed it. Alec Hearne gave up leg-spinners to bowl off-spin because of an elbow injury, and of the others, only George Alfred Lawrence had the freedom to experiment allowed amateurs. G.A.L. played his Test cricket for South Africa, who were already overburdened with googly bowlers.

As professionals most of the Hearnes discarded wrist-spin to bowl what their county selectors wanted—and that was usually medium or fast-medium deliveries that kept scoring in check. But no such restriction applied to Arthur Alfred Mailey as he practised the googly, first with an orange and later with an old ball, flicking them in the air for a couple of metres into the hessian walls of his home. At 16, he found a job in a galvanised-iron shed as a glass-blower. His £3-a-week wages gave him money to join an art class and the job in which he had to continually spin a stump-sized pipe which held the molten glass gave him fingers of great strength and toughness.

'When bowling, my fingers never became calloused, worn or tired, and this, I feel, was responsible for the fact that I never met a bowler who could spin the ball more viciously than I, even if my length or direction were faulty,' Mailey wrote in his autobiography, *Ten For 66—and All That*. 'Persistent blowing expanded and strengthened my lungs and later allowed me to bowl for hours without

A portrait of master leg-spinner Arthur Mailey, whose appeals were said to have been delivered in an apologetic whimper. He mistrusted the occasional waves of accuracy that attacked him.

showing any sign of fatigue. Perhaps I could have made greater use of my lung power when appealing instead of asking in what Neville Cardus called "an apologetic whimper".'

Mailey took a job as a Water Board repairman when he lost his job as a glassblower because of a strike for higher wages and spent his days up to his knees in mud fixing broken pipes. He joined the Glebe Cricket Club and for a couple of summers practised after work at Redfern Oval, alongside clubmates Syd Emery and Charlie Barnes, both googly exponents. As his length and control improved he rose up through the grades and word spread around Sydney that he could bowl an occasional good ball. On 8 November 1912 Mailey made his debut for New South Wales on Sydney Cricket Ground against Western Australia, alongside the Paddington leg-break bowler Leslie Alwyn Cody and the South Australian-born Solly Hill, one of six Adelaide brothers to play first-class cricket in Australia.

It was an eventful beginning. New South Wales were dismissed for 95 on a damp pitch, despite an innings of 51 by their captain Victor Trumper, and this remained New South Wales' lowest score against Western Australia until 1985–86, Hugh Christian taking 6 for 40 with slow left-arm deliveries that kicked and reared. Mailey then took 5 for 46 and with the giant left-arm pace bowling prodigy Bob Massie (5 for 24) had Western Australia out for 105.

New South Wales reached 348 in their second attempt but time ran out with Western Australia 2 for 83 in reply. Cody did not get a bowl but a left-arm spinner named Herbie Collins took 2 for 21 from nine overs in the final innings.

In the return match a week later on the same ground Mailey took 7 for 105 and 6 for 47 to ensure New South Wales of victory by 155. This display, impressive as it was, did not save Mailey from omission when the state's seven Australian team players returned from England before the next match, but it did earn Mailey an invitation to accompany a strong Australian side to America in 1913, managed by American R.B. Benjamin, 'a small, rotund Jew wearing the biggest diamond I ever saw'. They lost only one of their 50 matches, when a slips fieldsman named W.P. O'Neill took 10 catches.

Mailey's now vastly improved control impressed Arthur (later Sir Arthur) Sims, who included Mailey in the Australian team he took to New Zealand in February and March 1914. Mailey suddenly found himself among idols like Victor Trumper, Monty Noble, Warwick Armstrong, Vernon Ransford and Frank Laver.

The Australians indulged in some remarkable hitting, which began with an innings of 658 against Auckland. At Christchurch Trumper hit 293 in three hours and at one stage added 50 in 12 minutes with Sims, who went on to 184 not out in a partnership of 433 in 180 minutes. At Temuka the Australians made 9 for 992 against Fifteen of Canterbury, Englishman J.N. Crawford scoring 298 in 69 minutes with Trumper and 213 with Noble before reaching 354, the last 100 in 60 minutes. Even the finest bowlers would have been overshadowed by such scoring.

The world went to war with Mailey a regular member of the New South Wales XI, and as it ended he was promoted to water machine cleaner. He began his bid for a place in the Australian team in February 1920 by taking 10 wickets against the returning AIF, but 129 from Collins and two centuries by Jack Gregory (122 and 102) gave the AIF victory by 203 runs. The retirement of Syd Emery made Mailey an automatic selection for the first Test against Johnny Douglas' visiting England team in 1920–21 in Sydney.

Australia won all five Tests that summer, and although he did not bowl in the second Test, Mailey's 36 wickets in the series set a record for any five-match rubber against England. His 9 for 21 in the fourth Test at Melbourne was the best-ever haul by an Australian in a Test innings. Apart from his triumph with his googlies and leg-breaks, Mailey's demeanour made him a tremendous crowd favourite, popular with opponents and team-mates alike.

Mailey wrote that success came despite two altercations, one on the field and another between his mother and the notorious barracker Yabba, who hollered 'Oh for a strong arm and a walking stick' every time Mailey went up to bowl. Mailey's mother on The Hill finally had enough of this and threatened Yabba with her walking stick. 'Blimey, lady, it was only a joke. I was only kiddin'. He'd be best bowler in the team.' The other hassle occurred when Johnny Douglas accused him of using resin and said he had seen a puff of white dust when Mailey took his hand from his pocket. Mailey calmly took Douglas' hands and examined his nails, which were cracked and cut about. 'And you, Johnny, have been using your nails to lift the seam,' he said. Douglas laughed and never mentioned resin again.

On the morning he was to attend a reception in the Australian team's honour, Mailey was called to fix a bad leak in a Sydney department store. He went into the basement and only when it was almost flooded turned the right bolt. He cleaned himself and went up in the lift to the reception where he apologised for being late. 'My dear fellow,' said one of the store directors, 'it is we who should apologise. Some damn fool from the Water Board cut the water off and we were all late.'

Mailey went to England with Warwick Armstrong's Australian team in 1921 unaware of how envious a little gnome-like New Zealander named Clarence Victor Grimmett, five years Mailey's junior, was of his position as Australia's No. 1 wrist-spinner. Grimmett had begun as a fast bowler at Mt Cook Boys' School in Wellington because he feared being punished if he bowled breaks. A teacher with the unlikely name of Hempelman saw him bowling spinners one day when he felt too tired for pace and was so delighted he advised Grimmett never again to bowl fast. From the start Grimmett fully understood the reasons why a ball gripped and turned a certain way. He could bowl a handy topspinner before he was 10 and adults who asked how he did it were shocked to find it was no fluke.

Clarrie played for Wellington in Plunket Shield matches and against visiting Australian teams, and when he completed his apprenticeship as a signwriter took the advice of Australian Test bowler Jack Saunders and migrated to Australia. He joined the Sydney district club in 1914 and, after he had overcome the fear of captains who thought he would be hammered, bowled his way from third grade to first grade in one season. He took 78 wickets in his first season in first grade but promotion to the state XI was barred by Syd Emery, Arthur Mailey, Les Cody and others.

Grimmett moved to Melbourne in 1917, but found selectors inconsistent in their attitude towards spin bowling. He made his debut for Victoria in January 1919, against New South Wales in Sydney, but despite a splendid display found himself alternating between the state seconds and the senior side. He married at the end of his third summer in Melbourne and settled in Prahran, where he took 228 wickets in four seasons for the district club. In Prahran he trained the first of a series of fox terriers to retrieve balls he bowled in backyard practice. The dogs had to wait until he completed an over and then carry all the balls back to the bowling crease.

The Australians arrived with one of their best-ever teams to find English selectors still undecided about their spinners. They appeared to have doubts about Roy Killner,

young Jack Hearne, Dick Tyldesley, Cecil Parkin, Percy Fender, Charlie Parker, 'Farmer' White and 'Tich' Freeman and likely to gamble on Cambridge University spinner Charles Stowell Marriott, later known as 'Father' Marriott, or the precocious Oxford University star Greville Stevens, who in 1919 at the age of 18 had scored 466 in a house match at University College School and in the same match created havoc among schoolboy opponents with a mixture of leg-breaks and googlies. This double was in celebration of his debut for Middlesex in which he took 10 wickets and won a berth in the Gentlemen's XI against the Players at Lord's.

The celebrated 'Father' Marriott, who learnt wrist-spin in Dublin but executed it for Cambridge University, Kent, the Gentlemen, and in one Test for England, in which he bamboozled the West Indies.

Father Marriott had learned the art of leg-break and googly bowling at St Columba's School in Dublin. He had been born at Heaton Moor in Lancashire and after graduating from St Columba's bowled impressively in his debut for Lancashire, before taking 14 wickets in his two varsity matches for Cambridge. He was well over 6 feet tall and approached the crease with a goose-stepping run from mid-off, releasing the ball with a high, relaxed swing of the arm which had been held behind his back. On hard pitches his crafty variations of flight and pace, coupled with a nagging length and sharp turn, made him difficult and when the pitch assisted him through wear or dampness every ball was a problem. His fielding was so abysmal he was the despair of captains faced with hiding him, and his aggregate of wickets exceeded the number of runs he made with the bat, in statistician Bill Frindall's calculations by 137 (574 runs, 711 wickets).

For the first Test at Nottingham in May 1921, however, the English selectors settled on Thomas Leonard Richmond, a leg-break and googly bowler with nine years county bowling for Nottingham behind him. Richmond took two wickets but was unimpressive in an overwhelming Australian victory on Richmond's home pitch. Gregory and McDonald blitzed the England batsmen to end the match on the second afternoon. For the second Test at Lord's England relied on Parkin's odd mix of off-breaks and leg-breaks but Gregory (five wickets), McDonald (eight wickets) and Mailey (six wickets) had the match won in three days. Gregory and McDonald got another 10 wickets in the third Test at Leeds to give Australia the Ashes after three straight wins inside three days.

Parkin, a competent juggler and conjurer, had his best figures of the series in the fourth Test but rain forced a draw and Armstrong allowed the fifth Test to deteriorate into a draw by fielding on the boundary and reading a newspaper. The Australian pace bowlers were so destructive Mailey only played in three Tests. Armstrong knew he could provide spin himself and had Collins' left-arm spin if required.

Although he was hardly needed in the Tests, Mailey retained his sharp wit and had the laugh over Armstrong and his co-selectors when he took 10 for 66 at Cheltenham against Gloucestershire. Team-mates said he could have dismissed Gloucestershire for less than their total of 175. Mailey also took three wickets in the first innings for match figures of 13 for 87.

Despite his limited opportunities, Mailey finished with 134 wickets from the tour at 19.37, notable figures for a bowler of his type always prepared to buy his wickets. The last major game on tour saw a shock Australian defeat by a specially chosen England XI led by Archie MacLaren. With the Australians asking why selector MacLaren had passed over Greville Stevens, Aubrey Faulkner made 153 and took six wickets.

Stevens won Blues in all his four years at Oxford University from 1920 to 1923 and played in 10 Tests for England between 1922–23 and 1929–30. He toured South

Greville Stevens, as handsome as a film hero, who helped England win the Ashes from Australia for the first time in 14 years with a splendid effort in the last two Tests of the 1926 rubber.

Africa twice with MCC teams (1922–23 and 1927–28) and the West Indies twice (1929–30 and 1931–32) but never visited Australia. His 10 for 195 at Bridgetown in 1929–30 remains the best by an overseas bowler in a Test on that ground. He twice scored more than 1,000 runs in an English season, finishing with 10,376 runs at 29.56 and 684 wickets at 26.84, taking five wickets in an innings 29 times and 10 wickets in a match five times, best analysis 8 for 38, an intriguing cricketer whose work as a stockbroker severely restricted his appearances.

Stevens played a major role in England regaining the Ashes in 1926 when he bowled Australia's great batsman Charlie Macartney for 25 in the decisive Test at The Oval. This was a bountiful match for leg-spinners, with Grimmett bowling 88 overs, Mailey 76, and Stevens 32. The two Australians took 14 wickets compared with two to Stevens but the dismissal of Macartney, who had scored three Test centuries earlier that summer, was rated the crucial wicket of the series.

Stevens' striking film-star looks and tall, slim physique contrasted strongly with that of his contemporary Roy Kilner, who, having survived World War I wounds and shrapnel damage to his right wrist, emerged after the Armistice as a left-arm spinner of quality. Coached by Wilfred Rhodes with whom he often bowled in tandem, Kilner did not allow excess weight to upset his accuracy as he developed into a major threat whenever Yorkshire took the field. He played 365 matches, taking 1,003 wickets at 18.46, including 100 wickets in a season five times, and 24 wickets at 30.58 in his nine Tests for England. He also made 1,000 runs in a season 10 times in a career that yielded 14,707 runs at 30.01 with 18 centuries.

Kilner's main claim to fame, however, was that he was reported to be the first to bowl the delivery known as the 'Chinaman', a ball Australians describe as the left-hander's googly with topspin added and Englishmen as a left-arm delivery which spins in from a right-hand batsman's legs towards the slips. Kilner played twice against the 1921 Australians, both times for Yorkshire, but did not impress them as much as a balding little man (5 feet 2 inches) from Kent, with small hands that somehow managed a wide break, named Alfred Percy Freeman, who bowled to a better length than other English wrist-spinners and relied on batsmen's mistakes.

'Tich' Freeman, the little gnome who kept rocking up to the stumps and took more than 250 wickets in an English summer six times, and 3,776 in all.

5

Little Tich

Alfred Percy Freeman, born at Lewisham in Kent on 17 May 1888, took the first of his 3,776 first-class wickets in 1914 when he was 26. By then he followed a meticulous bowling drill, hitching up his trousers before each ball, moving his spare frame into the crease with a five-pace approach, and tossing up cleverly flighted leg-breaks and googlies of impeccable length. Despite tiny hands his strong fingers imparted sharp turn.

'There was something grotesque in the way this little gnome of a man came rocking up to the stumps, and flicked one ball after another, all so nearly the same and yet so vitally different, until the victim would commit some act of indiscretion, or more probably fall to his own timidity,' wrote learned critic E.W. Swanton. Another critic, Ian Peebles, likened Freeman's neat rotary action to that of 'a spring snapping'. One of Freeman's victims retired to the pavilion commenting: 'Bowling! That isn't bowling. Them's contraptions.'

Although he could sustain a perfect length through long spells, testing the patience of even the finest batsmen, sharp wits accounted for most of Freeman's victims. He claimed he secured many wickets simply by not bowling the googly. 'The batsmen knew I could bowl it, and they often became fidgety watching my hand to try and anticipate it and got out in some other way,' Freeman said.

This boast was not typical of Freeman, who was a modest, reticent man content to allow his results speak for him. And what results they were. He took more than 100 wickets in an English summer 17 times, more than 200 wickets eight times and 250 or more six times. He remains the only bowler to take 300 wickets in a season, with 304 dismissals in 1928. His career total of 3,776 first-class wickets at a cost of 18.42 has only been bettered by one bowler, Wilfred Rhodes, whose 4,204 wickets cost 16.72 apiece.

Freeman's variations of quality spin, an eye for batsmen's faults and his combination with wicket-keeper Les Ames made him the idol of cricket-loving Kent fans, but his popularity did not reach the England selectors who gave him only 12 Tests. This remains one of cricket's unsolved mysteries, for Freeman was unquestionably the greatest English leg-spinner of his time and one of the finest of all time.

Freeman joined the Kent CC ground staff in 1912, and although he impressed in club and ground matches and in appearances for the Kent Second XI, he was unable to force his way into Kent's first team until 1914. Recognition was made difficult because of the presence in the Kent XI of two famous slow bowlers, Colin Blythe and Frank Woolley, and the Test wrist spinner Douglas Carr. He had taken 29 first-class wickets at 27.55 when World War I intervened.

Resuming in 1919, Freeman became a vital part of the Kent team until his retirement in 1936, aged 48. He expected to bowl around 1,800 overs for his county every summer and looked forward to it, often opening up the bowling for Kent with his leg-breaks and regularly carrying the attack. 'Where would we be if Tich fell ill?' asked Kent captain Percy Chapman, who thought nothing of giving Freeman 30-over spells.

Freeman visited Australia briefly in 1922–23 with Archie McLaren's England team, which popped in twice on their way to and from a New Zealand tour. They played seven first-class matches and Freeman bowled in all of them, taking 30 wickets but conceding a lot of runs. His best effort was 6 for 176 in the return match against South Australia in Adelaide. In 13 appearances on the complete tour, Freeman took 69 wickets at 23.97, five times taking five wickets in an innings in New Zealand.

He returned to Australia for a full tour in 1924–25 under Arthur Gilligan's captaincy but found all the leading Australian batsmen accustomed to skilful wrist-spin bowling, with Grimmett and Norman Williams fixtures in the South Australian team, Albert ('German') Hartkoff playing for Victoria in preference to Bert Ironmonger or Don Blackie, Arthur Mailey, Bill Trenerry and Tommy Andrews in fine spinning form for New South Wales, and Charles Barstow bowling leg-breaks effectively for Queensland.

Freeman opened the tour splendidly by taking 4 for 118 in the first game, then 6 for 47 and 3 for 23 against Western Australia in Perth to set up an England win by an innings and 190 runs. He did not play against South Australia in Adelaide, where all the England batsmen had trouble facing Grimmett, who had moved from Melbourne to further his Test hopes at the end of 1923 just after taking

Clarrie Grimmett when he first came into Test cricket, bowling in a cap to conceal a bald head from selectors whom he feared would consider him too old at 32.

8 for 86 for Victoria in a Sheffield Shield match. Bowling in a cap to hide his baldness, Grimmett took nine wickets in his debut for South Australia against Victoria in November 1924 on Adelaide Oval. Grimmett was then in his thirty-second year.

Grimmett's partner in the South Australian attack was Norman Williams, a short, bald-headed Adelaide dentist who mixed right-arm leg-breaks and googlies with a sunny disposition. They formed a very hostile combination. Williams was one of the most popular cricketers in South Australia, and had strong claims to be regarded as the best locally born spinner. He had some great days for South Australia but because of the presence of Grimmett, Mailey, and to a lesser extent, Hartkoff, was never tried in a Test. He had had a satisfying time in December 1923, taking 5 for 155 and 6 for 40 in Adelaide against Queensland, South Australia winning right on time.

The hard Australian pitches, sun-parched and heavily rolled, proved a major handicap for Freeman as England swung round the states, with aggressive Australian batsmen ready to use their feet against spin. He took six wickets in the match against an Australian XI in Brisbane but at a cost of 160 runs. Grimmett fared even worse in this match, with 4 for 176, and selectors preferred Hartkoff as Mailey's spin-bowling partner when they opted for a spin attack in the second Test.

Hartkoff, a no-nonsense cricketer who received a scholarship from the Melbourne Cricket Club while he studied medicine because of his feats in Melbourne's Scotch College XI, beat Blackie and Ironmonger into the Victorian XI and Grimmett into the Australian team because of his batting. He bowled steady, well-flighted leg-breaks with a high, copybook action but it was his furious hitting that gave him the edge over two talented spinners. In his Test debut he made 80 late in the order which took Australia to 600, adding 100 for the ninth wicket with Oldfield, but his leg-spin proved expensive and that proved his only international. Grimmett came into the Australian line-up for the fifth Test and took 11 for 82, a splendid initial contribution.

Freeman made his Test debut in Sydney, where his five wickets cost 258 runs. He was tried again in the third Test at Adelaide but this time conceded 201 runs in taking three wickets. His failure to adapt to Australian conditions on the tour on which he appeared in only nine of the 17 major matches was to haunt him for the rest of his career. Australians felt that he had been outbowled by Mailey and Grimmett, both of whom took 59 wickets in the season, compared to 40 by Freeman. The truth was that he had to bowl against a superior batting line-up—Collins, Bardsley, Macartney, Andrews, Taylor and Kippax—than Mailey and Grimmett—Sutcliffe, Hobbs, Hendren and Sandham.

Despite this chastening experience, Freeman took 146 wickets for Kent in 1925, including 15 hauls of five wickets in an innings and 10 wickets in a match four times. The impression lingered, however, that in spite of his success in county cricket he could not persistently threaten Test batsmen. He missed selection in the 1926 England v. Australia series in which selectors preferred Greville Stevens for the decisive fifth Test. Stevens finished with 1 for 85 and 1 for 13. However, Freeman shared a fascinating leg-spin attack in county cricket with Father Marriott joining him at the crease in the school holidays after taking up an appointment as master-in-charge at Dulwich College.

Mailey finished the 1926 tour of England with 126 wickets at 19.34, clean bowling Jack Hobbs in his farewell Test at The Oval. Not bad for a 40-year-old. He dismissed Sutcliffe, Woolley, Chapman, Stevens and Rhodes during the rubber, but he enjoyed that full toss to Hobbs most. He had even greater pleasure out of recalling the Sheffield Shield match in Melbourne that year against Victoria, who scored a world record 1,107 runs. Mailey took 4 for 362. 'I was just finding my length when the innings finished and but for a chap in the crowd who kept dropping catches I'd have had better figures,' Mailey said.

By then his art classes had shown his talents and he had left the Water Board to become a newspaper cartoonist. Whenever he had a match off in England he joined Dr Rowley Pope in visits to the opera or famous galleries. Pope taught him how to tie a bowtie, introduced him to royalty, and showed him the difference between a steak knife and a fish knife. His transformation from a yahoo to a sophisticated member of the big match press corps was completed by visits to London tailors.

South Africans had a brief glimpse of Mailey the cricketer in 1921, when his captain Herbie Collins brought him on to clean up the tail after the pace bowlers had broken through. In the third Test in South Africa Mailey had scored the single that gave Australia victory. This run gave him far more glee than his record tenth wicket stand of 127 with Johnny Taylor against England in 1924–25, for he enjoyed his status as a batting duffer and discounted the 46 he made that day with Taylor as a fluke.

Mailey could have gone on bowling in his forties because there was no physical strain in the way he moved in to bowl off a few bouncy paces, bowling hand tucked behind his buttocks until he swung his right arm high above his head in a neat swing, wrist and fingers coordinated to impart spin that made the ball buzz. Even batsmen at the non-striker's end could hear the work he got on the ball. Often it appeared overpitched but the spin cut it down in its flight to pitch in front of batsmen who were then faced with picking if it was a leg-break or a googly.

Mailey retired because the Australian Board of Control objected to him commenting in newspapers on matches in which he played. The board asked him to choose between cricket and journalism and Mailey decided he had been hounded long enough. He took to landscape painting and organising cricket tours into the Australian bush or wherever he thought there would be a bit of fun. There was only one rule on these tours—no opponent should get a duck if it could be avoided. If he dislodged a batsman's stumps before he had scored, Mailey would turn to the umpire. 'Better call no ball. Chap hasn't scored.'

In 1932 Mailey arranged a trip to America and Canada, a joyful romp that was Don Bradman's honeymoon trip. Typically, he could not be found when American Customs officers asked for the team's passports, for he was a great organiser but a poor finisher. He enjoyed bowling in Saskatoon and Moose Jaw as much as bowling his googly to Neville Cardus at midnight in Piccadilly Circus when both were in their dinner jackets. 'There you are, Neville, I told you you couldn't pick my wrong-un,' he laughed. This same Mailey hated the solemnity that often pervaded the press-box at big matches and he once invited colleagues in the box to join him in a hymn.

Altogether Mailey took 779 first-class wickets in his 18 years of cricket fun at an average cost of 24.09 runs each. Friends lamented that he quit with 99 Test wickets at 33.91, but he enjoyed being one short of a milestone. In 1955–56 when the New South Wales Cricket Associa-

Herbert Sutcliffe survives after playing Grimmett onto his stumps in 1924–25 in Sydney. The ball hit the stumps but the bails did not fall.

tion gave Mailey and Johnny Taylor a testimonial match, the two old men went out into the middle at lunchtime. Wearing a coat, Mailey clean bowled Taylor first ball. 'Should have always bowled with my coat on,' he told us back in the stands.

In the 1920s Grimmett conferred with Mailey, who was five years his senior, on how to bowl the googly. They did not have a serious discussion again for 10 years when finally Grimmett blurted out: 'Hey Arthur, you told me wrong about the googly!' As the noted English critic R.C. Robertson-Glasgow commented: 'It was rather like Virgil tricking Horace on the number of feet in a hexameter'.

Both Freeman and Grimmett bowled with arms far lower than Mailey—Freeman often releasing the ball when his arm was in front of his body, Grimmett occasionally skidding in deliveries that were almost round-armers. But they were bowlers of contrasting temperaments. Freeman was prepared to lull batsmen into false security or bait traps that took two or three overs to spring. Grimmett was at the batsman with every ball.

Freeman reached his peak in 1928 when he became the first bowler to take more than 300 wickets in an English season. He did not again approach that 304-wicket haul, but for the next seven seasons he exceeded 200 wickets. In that incredible spell he took 2,090 wickets in eight summers. His wicket-keeper, Les Ames, benefitted in those years from Freeman's persistent ability to find the edge or beat the bat altogether. Ames made 128 dismissals in 1929 and 104 in 1932 and confessed that he could not understand the carping critics who claimed Freeman did not bowl well against top-class batsmen like Wally Hammond. 'I stumped Wally half a dozen times off Tich,' said Ames. Freeman in turn believed he was lucky to be associated with a keeper of Ames' skill. 'A slow bowler without the support of a good keeper would find that half of his work was wasted,' said Freeman. 'Les and I were a perfect combination because he knew everything I could do with the ball.'

Freeman was, in fact, punished by Hammond, Duleepsinhji, Hendren, and by leading Australian batsmen such as Ponsford, Bardsley, McCabe and Bradman, but so was every other slow bowler they met. Charlie Parker, the irascible Gloucestershire off-spinner who took 3,278 wickets in his career, suffered like Freeman from neglect by Test selectors, and only appeared once for England. But unlike gentlemanly, well-disciplined Freeman, Charlie was openly critical of England's cricket establishment and was alleged to have punched Plum Warner in a lift.

When Australia played at Canterbury on their 1930 English tour, Freeman took 5 for 78 in their first innings, with Bradman, Ponsford, Archie Jackson and Allan Fairfax among his victims. But in the Tests Walter Robins and Ian Peebles were preferred to Freeman as England's wrist-spinners. Ames believed this was because Freeman was not as good a fieldsman as Robins and Peebles and lacked a strong throwing arm if he was stationed at deep third man or fine leg. Robins and Peebles were also more

capable of scoring runs than Freeman, who had a career batting average of 9.60. The notion persisted, however, that Freeman was never given a fair go by Test selectors.

The selectors' assessment of Freeman was supported by his failure to earn a place in the Tests in Australia in 1928–29 when his county captain Percy Chapman led England. Freeman suffered a stiff neck early on the tour, was heavily punished by the glamorous state sides and only got among the wickets against Queensland and the bush teams at Bathurst (8 for 31) and Goulburn (8 for 66). One of his team-mates on that tour, Herbert Sutcliffe, was among those who questioned the selectors' wisdom in their handling of Freeman. Sutcliffe said: 'Freeman has played so rarely in Test cricket it is not possible to give a reasoned opinion of his qualifications. Judged by his record in county cricket, and with recollections of the success of Australian bowlers of a similar type in England, one is bound to say that Freeman ought to have been a valuable man for England all the time that he has been such a valuable man for Kent.'

From 1930 until his retirement in 1936, Freeman played no Test cricket at all, and he had to be content with two Tests against Australia, seven against South Africa and three against the West Indies. His only notable display in those 12 Tests was in 1928 against the West Indies at Old Trafford, when his 5 for 54 and 5 for 39 made him the first to take five wickets in an innings and 10 wickets in a match against the West Indies. His 12 Tests produced 66 wickets at 25.86. In 1930 when he had his career-best analysis of 10 for 53 against Essex at Southend he still was not called on to play in a Test. England played 100 Tests during his career and for a bowler with Freeman's record it remains an incredible statistic that he was only used in a dozen of them.

Walter Robins, one of the leg-break and googly bowlers preferred to Freeman, said: 'Against other than the greatest batsmen, Freeman was the most effective bowler I ever saw. We will never see his like again as a persistent wicket-taker. Under Percy Chapman, Freeman sometimes opened the bowling, astonishing in itself and almost unheard of among leg-break bowlers since his time.'

The county cricket Freeman enriched with his wicket-taking also benefitted in the 1920s from the presence in Oxford University teams of the Sydney brothers, Jack and Reg Bettington. Both were Rugby forwards and with the bat gave the ball a terrific whack. Both bowled leg-breaks and were noted for their vociferous appeals. Reg went straight to Oxford from The King's School at Parramatta and won his Blue in his first year, 1920. The cricket ball looked like a grape in his massive hand and on wickets that gave the slightest assistance he could turn his leg-breaks and googlies with disconcerting sharpness. In his initial year in first-class cricket, he took 7 for 47 and 5 for 42 against Somerset, 5 for 48 against Essex, and 5 for 48 against Warwickshire.

At the end of that season Reg found himself at the centre of a controversial incident in a festival match at

Australian legends in the leg-spin bowling caper: Top, Reg Bettington, who could make the ball buzz like a top, and Grimmett, who could click his fingers to deceive batsmen.

Eastbourne. H.D. Leveson-Gower's XI left Oxford to score 179 to win and the university reached that target with Reg on 99. He remained at the crease and Ernie Smith bowled another ball which Bettington struck for two runs to reach what was called a 'totally illegitimate century'. Some statisticians claimed it was a 'presentation century', a 'phoney that should be expunged from first-class records'.

Reg took over the Oxford captaincy in 1923 and distinguished himself by taking 3 for 19 and 8 for 66 bowling off his long run. This enabled Oxford to defeat Cambridge by an innings and 227 runs, the biggest margin in the history of the varsity match. He followed with 6 for 71 against Hampshire, 5 for 22 and 4 for 91 against Surrey, and a haul of 61 wickets for the summer at 16.55 each. From Oxford he went to London's St Bartholomew's Hospital, where he qualified as a doctor, and assisted Middlesex and played for the Gentlemen v. the Players. In 15 county matches he took 54 wickets at 29.44 apiece and scored 605 runs at 30.25.

Reg Bettington made the ball buzz like a top, said the famous English critic R.C. Robertson-Glasgow. 'At the moment of delivery there was a loud snapping sound. There was another even louder snapping sound when he asked for an lbw or catch at the wicket. A Bettington appeal brought all Sydney to the Oxford parks or to Lord's.'

Jack Bettington, or more correctly, Brindley Cecil John Bettington, two years Reg's senior, accompanied him from their mutual birthplace at Oatlands, New South Wales, to The King's School, Oxford University, Middlesex and the New South Wales XI. His appeals were just as noisy as Reg's, his leg-breaks and googlies just as troublesome for batsmen, but Jack was the superior golfer. Jack did not win a Blue for Rugby at Oxford, although he was just as robust a forward, because he did not kick for goal. He returned to Australia a qualified civil engineer but died at the age of 33. Reg lived until he was 69 when the car he was driving in Gisborne, New Zealand, plunged 100 feet onto a railway line.

'Length, flight, spin and persistence; Reg Bettington had them all,' wrote Robertson-Glasgow, who had had a good view of Bettington's wrist-spin fielding at first slip for Oxford. 'Years after his skill with the leg-break had declined, I saw him bowl a fellow leg-spinner, Richard Tyldesley, with his faster ball of vicious suddenness. Poor Dick; he had to disentangle the bat handle from his ample girth, and stood at the ready, blade in the air; but when he brought it down the bails had flown.'

Grimmett followed the Bettingtons' habit of never revealing his intentions. Indeed he kept his plans so completely to himself nobody to this day can be sure if he was the inventor of the ball known as the flipper, the googly with overspin that hurries it on to the batsman. Arthur Morris, Bill Brown, Keith Miller and a host of other distinguished Australian cricketers have no doubt that Grimmett introduced it to first-class cricket but the cagey Grimmett would not even confirm that he could bowl it. Robertson-Glasgow was fascinated by Grimmett, whom he said was an ageless compound of leather, patience and subtlety and, even among Australians, a champion tea drinker.

'You could not say that Grimmett was old or young, or in any known state of age at all,' Robertson-Glasgow wrote. 'He and the calendar have never reached any proper understanding. Just as Mr Pickwick was obviously born in tights and gaiters, so Grimmett surely began with a large-peaked dark green cap and ripe views on the status of the topspinner. He has always been mysterious. None can say whether his jerking round-arm action is a throw-back to George III or a projection of H.G. Wells. "Do you think you ought to do this sort of thing?" I once asked him? In tried, metallic tones he said: "Never communicate your intentions".'

Whether Grimmett invented the flipper can never be confirmed but he certainly took a lot of wickets with it. He never bowled a loose ball in matches because he rehearsed all his tricks in his backyard with those fox terriers for hours at a time before he tried them in matches. When word went round that you could expect a googly from him when you heard his fingers click, Grimmett taught himself to click his fingers with his free hand. He studied the positioning of all his fieldsmen and was always alert for incidents that could be used to fool batsmen. After he bowled Tommy Andrews with a big leg-break, Andrews spread his hands wide to show incoming batsman Allan Kippax the width of Grimmett's turn. With Kippax expecting the leg-break, Grimmett knocked back the middle stump with a fizzing straight one.

In one of Keith Miller's early first-class matches, Miller gave up trying to read Grimmett's deliveries from his hand. 'I simply played everything on the off as an off-break and everything on the legside as a leg-break for I had no idea what he was up to,' said Miller. 'No other bowler did that to me.'

Grimmett's superiority thwarted the ambitions of a long list of Australian spinners once he got the chance to show his skills regularly in the South Australian team. He took five wickets in a first-class innings 127 times and 10 wickets in a match 33 times. From the day he displaced Mailey in the Australian team, Grimmett made it hard for all types of spinners to beat him to the Test elevens. Ray McNamee, from Sydney's Randwick club, had three seasons in the New South Wales team from 1926 to 1929 bowling off-breaks critics said would win him Test status. Austin Punch, from North Sydney, had some triumphant days for the same state with his leg-breaks in the 1920s.

In the south, 'Dainty' Ironmonger had 36 five-wicket hauls for Victoria between 1914 and 1934 with his left-arm spinners, and Don Blackie's right-arm off-spinners brought him 12 five-wicket coups and 211 first-class wickets. Bowling in tandem, Blackie and Ironmonger were a formidable pair; Ironmonger had 14 Tests, Blackie three. They were fine bowlers but nobody could seriously suggest playing them in more Tests ahead of Grimmett. The same could be said of the South Australian off-spinning success of the 1920s, Arthur Richardson, and Queensland's long serving Ron Oxenham, an outstanding exponent of off-spin.

Every weekend Grimmett provided dramatic evidence of his skill. Grimmett's biographer, Ashley Mallett, calculated that between 1924-25 and 1944-45 Grimmett sent back 579 batsmen in Adelaide club cricket at an average cost of only 13.44 runs each. This was achieved in between his commitments in 37 Tests in which he took 216 wickets, 79 Sheffield Shield matches that brought him 513 wickets, and tours to England in 1926, 1930 and 1934, to New Zealand in 1927-28 and to South Africa in 1935-36. His success in England was even more pronounced than in Australia and he took more than 100 wickets on each of his three tours, with 144 in 1930 at 16.85 his best.

To Grimmett, a bowler who deliberately gave boundaries away to induce overconfidence and bad habits in batsmen was unnecessarily penalising his side. He believed he could bowl tight and attack simultaneously and never agreed to Mailey's profligate outlook. This was the source of Neville Cardus' celebrated valuation: 'Grimmett bowled like a miser, Mailey like a millionaire'.

Grimmett took all his wickets despite difficulties no present-day cricketer encounters. Payment for first-class matches was meagre, and opportunities to impress Test selectors limited in the days before Western Australia and Tasmania competed in the Sheffield Shield. The Adelaide Cricket Club induced him to quit Victoria on the promise of a £10-a-week signwriting job and £40 relocation costs, but work in Adelaide was often scarce during the Depression and sometimes he was rescued financially by collections for his triumphs in international matches. The Wolfe Schnapps company made him a special award of £10 for his 11 for 82 in his first Test, plus two shillings for hitting a boundary. The South Australian Cricket Association raised £220 for him in a testimonial among *Adelaide Advertiser* readers. The Adelaide Abattoirs got a further £9 for him by auctioning a sheep. A dancing academy raised £10 with a whip-round among patrons.

But a business venture, The Clarrie Grimmett Bag Store in Gawler Place, Adelaide, went bust. Signwriting jobs and fees from coaching at schools and from the SACA for managing the Colts XI kept him going but it was not until he collected his £600 for his triumphant 1930 tour of England that he became financially secure. After the tour, royalties from an instructional film began to dribble in and helped pay for his new home at Firle and school fees for his son Victor. Aware of their Test cricketers' financial difficulties, the SACA paid Vic Richardson £187 and Grimmett £152 in 1931-32, although the SACA itself lost money that summer.

A further threat arrived for Grimmett when Don Bradman moved from Sydney to Adelaide and enticed his St George club team-mate Frank Ward to go with him. Ward moved to Adelaide at a time when accusations that

Bill O'Reilly as a young man and about to enter a great partnership with Grimmett.

Grimmett had told fibs about his age were at their peak. One Sydney paper claimed he was 44, not 37 as he claimed. Grimmett responded by offering £500 to anyone who could prove he was over 40.

Ward made his debut for South Australia in November 1935, after taking 121 wickets in first grade for St George at 21.23 each. He proved a classy leg-break and googly bowler who could turn the ball sharply on even the most unresponsive pitches. In his first season for South Australia he took 50 wickets at 20.94. At the time Grimmett was touring South Africa with the Australian team captained by Vic Richardson and fashioning, with a school teacher named William Joseph O'Reilly, one of the finest spin-bowling partnerships known to cricket.

O'Reilly approached the crease like a windmill, arms pumping, fingers formed in a claw as if he was about to strike batsmen. He looked like a man in a rage. Grimmett moved in at a short, skippety jog, ready to vary the roll of his wrist to avoid bowling straightforward leg-breaks and googlies and produce a bewildering variety of overspinners and flippers to fool careful scrutiny of his hand. His cunning was such that he could even pretend he was losing control under punishment, creating false expectations of a run-feast to force the error that allowed him to fizz one into the stumps or pads.

Grimmett and O'Reilly lacked nothing in courage. Vic Richardson said that when Grimmett was troubled by blisters in South Africa in 1935–36 he kept bowling despite the blood that saturated his socks. O'Reilly bowled 463 balls in the Durban Test on that South African tour, wearing the skin from the knuckle of his third finger, the one with which he gave his leg-break a final flick. Bruce Mitchell dug in for a draw, taking all O'Reilly's bowling to shield team-mates. For nine overs O'Reilly bowled him off-breaks with his sound fingers, waiting for the chance to get at other batsmen. When it arrived he spun a big leg-break off raw flesh, enticing a catch. He did the same against the next man and Australia walked off winners. Team-mates who went to shake O'Reilly's hand were brushed away because he couldn't close his hand.

6
Tiger Bill

Bill O'Reilly bowled every ball in his 27 Tests as an impassioned protest against the injustices suffered by Irishmen. He went back to his bowling marker simmering hate for all batsmen, swivelled in his large white boots, and bounced in on an unusually long approach. Holding the ball in his first and second fingers with the others tucked up in the palm of his vast right hand, he reached the crease with his wrist cocked, face strained, releasing leg-breaks, googlies and top-spinners in a glorious flurry of arms and legs.

He upset purists by bending his right knee at the moment of delivery, which to them produced a grotesque dip in his shoulder. Arthur Mailey and other connoisseurs of wrist-spin tried to persuade him to eliminate the bent knee and more fully exploit his long arms and 6 foot 3 inch height. O'Reilly politely declined, believing all bowlers with individual actions should forget the coaching manuals. Despite the last-instant stoop, his right arm had a rhythmical sweep that produced exceptional bounce and he could spin the ball at a fastish medium pace that made jumping out to him not only difficult but suicidal.

Some critics mistakenly judged him as a finger-spinner who simply rolled leg-breaks that tended to come straight on, but he was the master of almost every known delivery. When he needed to he flicked his wrist and let them go from the back of his hand. The over-riding trait to his whole performance, however, was the gusto. Even great batsmen found themselves exhausted by the effort of concentrating on O'Reilly's clever variations in pace and his big mixture of spinning deliveries.

O'Reilly was born on 20 December 1905, at White Cliffs, then a flourishing opal-mining centre 680 miles from Sydney in north-western New South Wales. Three years before his birth an opal worth £150,000 had been discovered there, boosting the settlement's population enough to create the need for a school in which Bill's father was the only teacher. When the opals were all extracted White Cliffs' population declined and the school closed. The O'Reillys moved to a school at Wingello, a small town 100 miles south of Sydney. There Bill learnt to bowl with a ball he and his brothers shaped from a banksia tree root with a chisel.

He played for Wingello against other country towns, including Bowral's team, which was run by Don Bradman's relatives, the Whatmans. Bradman began as Bowral's scorer but O'Reilly frequently bowled against him when Bowral were short and recruited young Bradman as a substitute. One weekend when O'Reilly was on his way home from St Patrick's College in Goulburn he was taken off the train and thrust into the Wingello team that played Bowral in a match that lasted for several Saturdays.

On the first afternoon at the Bowral ground, Bradman was twice dropped off O'Reilly's bowling but reached 234 not out by stumps, hitting four sixes and six fours in his last 50. O'Reilly bowled Bradman round his legs with his first delivery the next Saturday on the Wingello ground, but it was Bradman who received all the publicity in Sydney papers. Bradman followed with an innings of 300 against Moss Vale in that year's country final.

Bradman's prolific scoring earned him an invitation to attend the Sydney Cricket Ground nets in October 1926, but O'Reilly was not as lucky. While Bradman was graduating from bush cricket to Sydney first grade and then to the state and Test teams, O'Reilly was shunted around remote country towns by the New South Wales Education Department. He played for North Sydney while he trained as a teacher, but once he graduated was posted 'out where the crows fly backwards' in postings that sadly delayed his entry into big cricket.

O'Reilly grumbled a lot about his isolation in the bush but he did not waste his leisure time, practising diligently, so that when he finally got his chance to play again in Sydney with the St George club he emerged as a strong, confident bowler ready to ignore suggestions that he alter his technique. He always thought coaches' talk about drift and fade and using the wind was nonsense and concentrated simply on pitching the ball precisely where he wanted.

O'Reilly made his debut for New South Wales against a New Zealand XI in October 1927, when the New Zealand leg-break and googly prodigy Billy Merritt was flogged all round the Sydney Cricket Ground. Jack Gregory (152), Tommy Andrews (134), Allan Kippax (119) and Archie Jackson (104) helped New South Wales score 571 runs in

Billy Merritt, hero of the 1927 tour of England when he established himself as New Zealand's greatest leg-spinner by taking 107 wickets at 23.64 apiece.

283 minutes on the first day and Merritt finished with 5 for 218. The New Zealanders were on their way home from their initial tour of England where Merritt had taken the bowling honours with 107 wickets at 23.64, a remarkable feat for an 18-year-old who had previously played only four first-class matches. Watching Merritt being mercilessly hammered, spectators could scarcely believe this was the best-ever New Zealand wrist-spinner.

O'Reilly was far more impressed with the leg-spin of McNamee, who was relieved by Arthur Mailey after taking 1 for 54. Mailey had 2 for 64 before O'Reilly finally got the ball and took 2 for 37. New South Wales won by 10 wickets by bundling New Zealand out for 286 and 292. A month later O'Reilly failed to take a wicket in 13 overs in Brisbane against Queensland, for whom Frank Gough provided the leg-spin. Neither O'Reilly nor Gough took a wicket in a drawn match. O'Reilly was immediately dropped and for the next four years had to be content with teaching appointments in the country towns of Griffith, Rylstone and Kandos and with matches for country teams at Young and Grenfell, well away from the state selectors' eyes.

He devoured reports of England's 1927–28 Australian tour in which Bradman made his Test debut against Chapman's side. He read of the sad fate of Henry Promnitz, the latest topspin and googly bowler in South Africa, who took 5 for 58 at Johannesburg against England, but disappeared from international cricket after just two Tests. And he envied the high opinion critics had

of 'Tuppy' Owen-Smith and Quentin McMillan, the two leg-spinners who took over from Promnitz. Owen-Smith made his reputation in England in 1929 with the South African team after only five first-class matches for Western Province, but soon returned to England as a Rhodes Scholar, winning three Blues at Oxford in cricket, boxing and Rugby, and playing cricket for Middlesex. He bowled slow leg-breaks that were to earn him a career total of 319 first-class wickets at 23.23. McMillan upheld the great traditions of South African googly bowling in his four years of big cricket, taking 91 wickets on the 1929 tour of England—at 25.45 apiece—retiring in 1932 to concentrate on business.

Another googly bowler who grabbed his chance was Cyril ('Snuffy') Browne, who on his second tour of England in 1928 took 32 wickets, including 8 for 81 against Derbyshire. Browne, a magistrate from Barbados, became the first black West Indian to be made an Honorary Life Member of MCC. In 1937–38, when he moved to British Guiana, he took 7 for 13 in dismissing Barbados for 99. The intriguing feature of Snuffy Browne's cricket was that he bowled his leg-breaks and googlies at a brisk medium-pace just as O'Reilly was trying to do.

By 1930 the Education Department agreed to end O'Reilly's long exile in bush towns and appointed him to Kogarah High School in the St George area of Sydney. He proceeded to take wickets in Sydney club cricket on a scale that has never been matched. Between 1931 and 1946 he took an amazing 921 first-grade wickets at fewer than 10 runs each, heading the first-grade averages 12 times. No other bowler has ever averaged fewer than 10 runs per wicket more than once.

His phenomenal success for St George forced selectors to reinstate him in the New South Wales team after Reg and Jack Bettington, Syd Hird, Norval Campbell and Hughie Chilvers had all had turns supplying the state's leg-spin. The Bettingtons were well known for their success at Oxford and retired from cricket to concentrate on golf, Reg adding to his honours by winning the Australian amateur golf championship.

Chilvers, who had migrated from his birthplace at Sawbridgeworth in Hertfordshire as a small boy, was a fine exponent of wrist-spin, whom O'Reilly rated the best of the breed never to play for Australia. He had a curious bouncing gait that seldom failed to make spectators laugh but had exceptional whip off the pitch. When he won state selection in 1929–30 he took 4 for 57 and 4 for 38 in his third match against South Australia. The next season he took 5 for 58 and 2 for 81 against South Australia, and in two matches against the touring West Indies captured 15 wickets 4 for 84, 5 for 73, 3 for 56 and 3 for 53. He was an outstanding fieldsman of happy disposition who had come up the hard way from the unfashionable Pennant Hills club in Sydney's Northern Districts, and could score useful runs with the bat, but O'Reilly's sheer weight of wickets brought Chilvers' omission and O'Reilly's return to the state side.

O'Reilly in his prime shown in his delivery stride. He seldom concealed his contempt for batsmen, nor his desire to bring them undone immediately they hit him to the boundary.

At Melbourne, over Christmas 1931, O'Reilly snared 5 for 22 against a Victorian line-up that included six Test players and four future Test players—his first five-wicket haul in inter-state cricket. That performance clinched a place in the Australian side for the fourth Test against the visiting South Africans. This match in Adelaide was the first in which Grimmett and O'Reilly bowled in tandem and they immediately emerged as a match-winning combination. Grimmett had 7 for 116 and 7 for 83, O'Reilly 2 for 74 and 2 for 81, and their 18 wickets enabled Australia to win by 10 wickets. Bradman ran out his last partner attempting a single when he was 299 not out, and the Springbok googly expert McMillan went without wicket.

Bradman by then had become a national idol with a world record 452 not out in 415 minutes for New South Wales against Queensland in Sydney and a scoring splurge in England in 1930 that included 254 at Lord's, 334 at Leeds and 232 at The Oval. To curb him England introduced her infamous Bodyline tactics, and in the hurly-burly of this spiteful series O'Reilly established himself as a great bowler. His 27 wickets in the series, highlighted by 10 dismissals in the only Test Australia won, the fourth at Melbourne, had English and Australian critics agreed that O'Reilly's performance for Australia matched Larwood's for England. Larwood had 10 wickets in the first Test, which England won; O'Reilly 10 in the second Test, which Australia won. Grimmett, given limited bowling in the first three Tests, was sacked for the fourth and fifth Tests, selectors preferring Ironmonger as O'Reilly's partner. Grimmett never played in another Test on Australian soil, although he was by no means in decline. He took 55 wickets in the 1933–34 season, including six hauls of five wickets.

Despite this setback Grimmett and O'Reilly proved a lethal twosome in England in 1934, each taking 109 wickets. They combined so effectively that Fleetwood-Smith could not get into the Tests although he took 106 wickets. Arthur Chipperfield, a talented leg-spinner, took valuable wickets on the few occasions Grimmett or O'Reilly was rested and bowled in all five Tests. Woodfull's skilful handling of three leg-spinners was a key factor in Australia regaining the Ashes 2–1. Grimmett was then 43 but the oldest player in the series was Frank Woolley, who was recalled to the English XI for the crucial fifth Test at the age of 47.

South Africa defeated England for the first time in England in 1935, thanks to a memorable display by a thick-set Greek cricketer, Xenophon Constantine Balaskas, known to cricket fans as 'Bally'. From a short approach, he produced right-arm leg-breaks and a well-disguised googly, and surprised batsmen with his pace off the pitch. Bally came into first-class cricket with Griqualand West at the age of 15 in 1925, but had a disappointing Test career until the Lord's Test of 1935 when he took 5 for 49 and 4 for 54. This gave South Africa a win by 157 runs in the only Test that produced a result. Bally did not play

The presence of Grimmett and O'Reilly kept this leg-break bowler out of Test cricket, but Hughie Chilvers never grumbled. Maurice Tate could not believe Chilvers was overlooked for English tours.

Grimmett in his prime bowling in England in 1934 when he took the strain off O'Reilly. He took 25 Test wickets in a tour bag of 109 victims.

in the other four Tests because of injury but appeared likely to be a big threat to Australia when they made a full tour of South Africa in 1935–36 under Vic Richardson. By then Woodfull and Ponsford had retired and Bradman was unable to tour on the advice of doctors who had narrowly saved his life when his appendix ruptured at the end of the 1934 English tour.

Grimmett and O'Reilly combined with spectacular success and, long before the end of a series which Australia won 4–0, had all the South African batsmen demoralised. Their skill in flighting and spinning the ball accounted for 71 of the 98 wickets that fell in the Tests. On the entire tour they sent back 187 batsmen between them, while Australia's seven other bowlers managed 102 dismissals.

Grimmett was superb. His 44 wickets in the Tests was the best-ever haul in a series by an Australian and took

him to an aggregate of 216 Test wickets, surpassing the world record of 189 wickets by England's S.F. Barnes in the career that ended in 1914. The Grimmett–O'Reilly partnership and the batting of Fingleton, who made centuries in three successive Test innings, gave Australia 13 wins in 16 matches, with 10 of the victories achieved by an innings.

O'Reilly's 95 wickets at 13.56 gave him slightly better figures than Grimmett, who took 92 wickets at 14.80, but their presence allowed Australia to easily overcome the injury to Fleetwood-Smith, who played in only seven matches. They also deprived Chipperfield of a long bowl in the Tests. His nine overs cost 28 runs without a wicket.

Balaskas was a major failure, paying heavily for his Test wickets. He took 4 for 126 in the third Test, 4 for 165 in the fourth Test and 1 for 157 in the fifth Test. Thereafter

One of the few bowlers O'Reilly admired for his ability to impart spin to the ball, Leslie O'Brien Fleetwood-Smith, a master of left-arm wrist or finger-spin and a wide range of birdcalls.

Frank Ward, who played with O'Reilly with the St George club in Sydney. O'Reilly could not believe it when Ward was preferred to Grimmett for the 1938 tour of England.

he concentrated more on his batting, finishing with six first-class centuries. In one Test in England in 1938–39 he failed to take a wicket in conceding 115 runs, a sad end for a bowler with 276 first-class wickets to his credit.

O'Reilly was elated with the assistance he received throughout the tour from Grimmett, who returned home to find Frank Ward entrenched in the South Australian team. He thought he was bowling better than ever and those who saw him in his backyard, in the nets or in Sheffield Shield matches over the next two seasons agreed.

He did not get a Test against England in 1936–37 with the vastly improved Fleetwood-Smith and Ward providing the support for O'Reilly. He watched from the stands when Fleetwood-Smith scattered Hammond's stumps with a superb delivery early on the fourth morning of the Adelaide Test. In retrospect, it's obvious that Fleetwood-Smith's 10 wickets in that match, coupled with Ward's eight wickets in the first Test and 10 wickets for South Australia against England that summer, spelt the end of Grimmett's international career. But on what grounds? Old age was the only possible reason, yet he remained as spry as ever, powers undiminished.

Grimmett's failure to win a place in a happy Test series adorned by quality spin from both sides angered team-mates who saw him bowl the previous season in South Africa. England played the ever-scheming left-arm finger-spinner Hedley Verity, and right-arm wrist-spinners, sprightly Walter Robins and the tall, string-bean former electrician, Jim Sims; Australia O'Reilly, Fleetwood-Smith and Ward.

At Sydney England lost a thriller by 135 runs when O'Reilly took 4 for 4 for New South Wales in the last possible over to steal the match with two balls to spare. As in the west, Sims' eagerness to smash the ball out of the park had spectators laughing. His aggression sat oddly with his solemn, lugubrious demeanour. Team-mates said he hummed sea shanties to boost his morale when hit for four. He needed a big repertoire of songs as his two Test wickets cost 80 runs each. Robins' four Test wickets were cheaper at 50 runs apiece, but like Sims his batting aroused guffaws. Often he ventured so far down the pitch to slow bowling that he was nearer his partner than his crease when he made contact or was stumped.

For the more serious-minded the duels between Bradman and Verity, like those when Bradman faced O'Reilly, reached a very high level of skill. The concentration these duels drew was intense, and certainly no laughing matter for batsman or bowler, before Bradman emerged triumphant.

O'Reilly, who always believed Ward reacted badly to punishment, was furious when Grimmett was omitted from the 1938 tour of England. Grimmett's absence meant that his workload would multiply. At 47, Grimmett was bowling as well as ever in O'Reilly's view, and he regarded suggestions that Grimmett could no longer bowl leg-breaks as absurd. The selectors in turn could point to the best bowling aggregates for the 1937–38 season. O'Reilly was on top with 64 wickets at only 12.25 runs each, followed by two members of the team for England— Fleetwood-Smith (64 at 24.43) and Ward (51 at 21.56)— whereas Grimmett had taken 41 wickets at 20.60.

O'Reilly said he would have much preferred Hughie Chilvers, who struggled to get a game in the New South Wales team, to provide leg-break support in England than Ward, whose career-best figures, 7 for 62, had been achieved against a weak New Zealand team in 1937. O'Reilly's protests failed to win a reprieve for Grimmett, though they won wide support from critics aware of Grimmett's great record in England. Grimmett missed the English tour with his wicket-keeping partner Bert Oldfield. His 216 wickets in 49 Tests comprised 106 against England, 77 against South Africa and 33 against the West Indies.

The omission of Oldfield in favour of Victorian Ben Barnett and South Australian Charlie Walker had major repercussions for the 1938 Australian team in England. Walker broke a finger early in the tour and had to wear a special fingerstall in the nine matches in which he appeared. Barnett made a series of crucial errors in the major matches that cost the team and its slow bowlers dearly. At The Oval when England reached 7 declared for 903 and Hutton made a world record 364, Barnett dropped the ball when Hutton was stranded metres down the wicket on 40 after missing an attempted drive off Fleetwood-Smith. Similar stumping chances went begging, allowing star English batsmen to escape against O'Reilly.

O'Reilly found plenty to interest a leg-break bowler as the Australians spun round England's counties. Jim Sims was still trying to hit sixes for Middlesex. The bespectacled former coalminer Tommy Mitchell was well on the way to taking more than 100 wickets for the tenth time for Derbyshire, a merry-hearted spinner of great resource. The Australian spinners Sid Hird and Bill Hunt were doing well in the Lancashire League, although Hird had given up leg-breaks for off-spinners ('They're less likely to end up in the crowd than my googly'). The Australians Vic Jackson, off-spin, and Jack Walsh, left-arm wrist-spin, were qualifying for Leicestershire. Another Australian leg-spinner, Harold Mudge, had joined the elite eleven run by eccentric furniture baron Sir Julien Cahn after one match for Leicestershire.

England picked two new spinners for the first Test at Trent Bridge, a bounding leg-spinner who approached the crease with a kangaroo-style hop named Douglas Vivian Parson Wright, who since 1932 had furthered Kent's great traditions in leg-spin and googly bowling, and a right-arm medium-pace Gloucestershire off-spinner who tossed up occasional leg-breaks and always bowled in a cap, named Reginald Albert Sinfield.

Four batsmen scored hundreds for England in their first innings of 658, Barnett (126), Hutton (100), Paynter (216 not out) and Compton (102), before Stan McCabe produced one of the most exciting innings in history by scoring 232 in even time. He did not give a chance until he was out, adding his second 100 in 84 minutes and his last 50 in 24 minutes. Last man Fleetwood-Smith, a noted bunny, made five not out while McCabe added 72 of the last 77 runs. Wright bowled steadily in this onslaught but poor Sinfield wilted and was not seen again in Test cricket, leaving Verity to provide the spin for the rest of the series with periodic help from Wright.

O'Reilly clinched the series for Australia by taking 5 for 66 and 5 for 56 in the fourth Test at Leeds to give Australia an unbeatable 1–0 lead. On the way to this 10 wicket coup he produced one of the most memorable deliveries in cricket history to clean bowl Joe Hardstaff in England's second innings. Hardstaff hit him for four, which produced no word of congratulation, but a testy command to the Australian fieldsmen to give him the ball quickly. He went back to his marker simmering with rage and came bobbing in to deliver a medium-pace leg-break which, bouncing high, turned right round Hardstaff's body and flicked off the leg bail.

O'Reilly received splendid support from Fleetwood-Smith, who took seven wickets in this match, with Australia compelled to rely on a spin attack because of the problems of fast bowler Ernie McCormack, who was no-balled 35 times in the first match and sent down 54 no-balls in his first 48 overs of the tour, passing a century of no-balls in the tenth match.

At Lord's against Middlesex the Australians found themselves on a well-prepared pitch alongside the Test match strip or just off dead centre. O'Reilly tossed up his googly, which came out higher and slower than his leg-break, twice in three overs. Walter Robins spotted them and each time went down on his right knee and hit them into the Tavern. O'Reilly hollered impatiently for the return of the ball, and as he passed the umpire commented: 'You'd have thought they'd play a match like this in the middle'. Off the field he believed in the restorative effects of a few ales and enjoyed prankster Lindsay Hassett's jape in releasing a goat that licked Bill's face in the middle of the night in Derbyshire, but he objected strongly when Fleetwood-Smith took the field smoking a cigar.

Ward had to be dropped after an unimpressive display in the first Test at Nottingham. He still had some good days, finishing second in the tour bowling averages to O'Reilly with 92 wickets at 19.27 compared to 'Tiger Bill's' 104 wickets at 16.59. Bradman made very little use of the handy wrist-spin of Chipperfield, who bowled only 54 overs on the tour and took six wickets at 25.83 apiece.

O'Reilly returned home muttering dark thoughts about boofheaded selectors who had callously dropped his little mate Grimmett and left him to work his way through the tour like a navvy. Grimmett gave validity to this argument by clean bowling Bradman with a perfect leg-break at practice a few weeks later. 'There y'are, who said I couldn't still bowl a leggie,' he said as Bradman departed. On Adelaide Oval in December 1938, Grimmett underlined the point by taking 7 for 116 and 4 for 59 to give South Australia an innings and 55 runs win over the powerful New South Wales team. On the same ground four days later he took 6 for 33 and 3 for 96 to set up an innings and 20 runs win for South Australia over Queensland.

In 1939–40 he took 73 more wickets at 22.65 to head the Australian bowling averages, including 11 against New South Wales in January 1940 and 11 against Western Australia at Perth in February. He played his last first-class match for South Australia against New South Wales from 21 to 24 February 1941, taking 1 for 128 when a young leg-spin bowler named Bruce Dooland could not get leave from the army to play. New South Wales won by an innings and 45 runs, using no fewer than four leg-break bowlers, Ken Gulliver, Cec Pepper, Colin McCool and O'Reilly who naturally took all the bowling honours with 5 for 28 and 2 for 61. Grimmett retired reluctantly at 49 with 668 wickets for South Australia, a record for any bowler for any Australian state. Altogether Grimmett took 1,424 first-class wickets, 216 of them in Tests at 24.22, the first bowler to claim more than 200 victims in a Test career.

He was, of course, right in his argument that while he was taking wickets his selection should have been automatic whatever his age. The Indian slow bowler Cottari Kanakaiya Nayudu kept going until he was 68, when he turned out for Maharshtra Governor's XI. His brother Cottari Subbanna Nayudu bowled googlies and leg-breaks in first-class cricket from 1934 until 1961 and had a splendid record in the Ranji trophy competition, once taking 14 wickets in a match and twice exceeding 30 wickets in a season. C.S. Nayudu holds the record for bowling more balls in a match than any other bowler, 152.5 overs (917 balls) for Holkar against Bombay in 1944–45. When he retired at 47 he had bagged 647 wickets at 26.54, and had the distinction of dismissing one of the great players of spin bowling, Lindsay Hassett, and trapping Keith Miller lbw one run later in the match between India and the powerful Australian Services XI at Bombay in November 1945.

Grimmett rated Hassett the greatest player of spin he bowled against, adding: 'Bradman was a relentless, run-making machine, but I never minded bowling to him because good-length wrist-spin bowling always worried him. It was a flaw in his batting. On the other hand Hassett's footwork was almost perfect. He used his feet magnificently in any duel with bat and ball. In addition, he was a great fighter.'

Hassett confirmed this assessment by hitting 29 fours in two knocks for Victoria against New South Wales in Sydney in January 1940, judging how every delivery from O'Reilly would behave and repeatedly lofting him back over his head to the boundary. His 122 in each innings were as audacious as they were frustrating for a great bowler, with Hassett often completing his shots nearer to O'Reilly than to his batting crease.

'You, you little bastard, you don't know a googly from a leg-break,' said O'Reilly as they watched another daring drive hit the fence.

'With you, Bill, I don't need to,' said Hassett.

The end came for O'Reilly at Wellington, New Zealand, in March 1946, after he took 5 for 14 and 3 for 19 to give Australia a win by an innings and 103 runs in just two days. He had taken his Test wicket haul to 144 wickets at 22.59, but he realised that at 41 his legs could no longer take the strain. He took off his boots and purposefully threw them through the dressing-room window. 'That's it for me,' he said. 'Maybe some kid will find my boots and get some fun out of them.'

Today some historians suggest O'Reilly was an inferior bowler against left-handers. He certainly considered they should have been done away with at birth. Maurice Leyland, Frank Woolley and Eddie Paynter had no blind spots to leg-spin but he taught himself to bowl well at them. Ray Robinson calculated that he dismissed top-class left-handers 12 times in his 19 Tests against England. Victoria often fielded half a team of left-handers but O'Reilly still took a hatful of wickets against them.

7

The Left-Armers

Leslie O'Brien Fleetwood-Smith got up to mischief all his life, squandering a family fortune, attracting hordes of women with his charm and handsome black-haired looks, swilling grog, sleeping in the gutter or under bridges, and using cricket fields as a stage. Bill O'Reilly regarded him as the greatest spin-bowling talent cricket has known. 'If I had managed what he could do with a cricket ball, I would never have minded bowling to eleven Bradmans,' O'Reilly said.

On the 1938 English tour Fleetwood-Smith appeared to critics to bowl more slowly than Grimmett and with less subtlety, though they conceded he sometimes bowled unplayable deliveries. His stock ball, the left-hander's off-break to a right-hand batsman, was accurate and controlled, but when he rolled them out of the back of his hand the result either bamboozled batsmen or ended up in the crowd.

He was a complex man who sang popular songs on the field and offered fielding team-mates a range of bird calls, or encouraged them with cries of 'Up, North Melbourne!' He was an expert in imitating the magpie or whipbird and rendering music hall arias, and when the mood struck him bagged 11 for 77 against Essex, 8 for 53 against Derbyshire, 10 for 64 against an England XI at Lord's and 7 for 112 against another England XI at Folkestone.

Team-mates could not settle on a nickname for Grimmett; some called him 'Scarlet' after the Scarlet Pimpernel, others 'The Fox', 'Grum' or 'The Gnome'. But from the time Fleetwood-Smith came into big cricket in the 1931–32 season he was known as 'Chuck'. Over the next eight seasons he took 597 wickets at 22.64 and gave frequent glimpses of a bowling genius that should have put him at the top of Australia's short list of left-arm spinners, but sadly left him the biggest disappointment. 'Too many parties, too many friends, and too many social drinks,' was his later summation of his career.

His biographer Greg Growden said the spectacle of Fleetwood-Smith becoming a bum in the conservative world of big cricket all began with lost weekends of boozing, benders, falling asleep in bushes or in unknown railway goods yards. He was the first Australian of his type, the pioneer of the left-arm wrist-spinner's ball known as the 'Chinaman'—the googly that hurries on—and from right-handed bowlers is known as the flipper.

Fleetwood-Smith was born on 30 March 1908, in Stawell, the Victorian country town in the Wimmera region where they run Australia's richest professional footrace every Easter and where his family owned the local newspaper. He first tried his animal calls rounding up goats in the nearby hills with his brother Walter. The family sent him to Xavier College, an expensive private school in Melbourne, where Leslie wanted to concentrate on tennis and Australian Rules Football.

The legend is that he was naturally right-handed and began bowling with his left hand when he broke his right arm and had it in plaster. His sister, Mrs Pauline Morname, insisted, however, that this was a cricket reporter's invention and that he never broke his arm but was simply ambidextrous. A Stawell dentist, Dr W.S. Cranston, entertained Fleetwood-Smith one night at the golf club by flicking golf balls into his pocket from various angles. Chuck asked the doctor to teach him these hand movements and this was the origin of his remarkable dexterity with golf balls, tennis balls, oranges and cricket balls.

At Xavier he found future Test player Leo O'Brien among his classmates and bowled in tandem for the First XI with the gifted left-hander Karl Schneider who played for Victoria at 17, transferred to South Australia, won a trip to New Zealand in 1928 and died of leukaemia three weeks after his twenty-third birthday. Schneider was no more than 5 feet 2 inches, but with Fleetwood-Smith formed perhaps the best spin bowling pairing known to Victorian Public Schools cricket. In 1924 the partnership came to an end when the headmaster of Xavier—the school that produced one of Australia's Catholic captains, Percy McDonnell—was forced to expel Fleetwood-Smith. The reasons have disappeared in Xavier archives, but a relative suggested a girl was involved. Others claimed he had been caught swigging booze and refused to give up smoking a pipe.

Back in Stawell, Fleetwood-Smith had three years of bush cricket in which he took more than 300 wickets

Cartoonist Alex Gurney's impression of Fleetwood-Smith rolling up his sleeves after taking a wicket.

Chinaman. In 1931–32 he was recruited to the state training squad and went to Hobart with the Victorian Second XI. He took 10 wickets in the Hobart match and six more two days later in Launceston, performances which guaranteed his first-grade spot at St Kilda when Ironmonger and Blackie returned from state duty. He took 47 wickets at 14.3 that year and helped St Kilda win the first-grade premiership.

On the Melbourne Cricket Ground between 6 and 10 February 1932, Fleetwood-Smith pressed his claims for Test selection with his fourth five-wicket haul in three matches for Victoria, taking 6 for 80 against the visiting South Africans. This display won him front-page reviews in one of which Arthur Mailey predicted that, because of the strangeness of his delivery, Fleetwood-Smith 'might easily do to the Englishmen what Bosanquet did to Australian batsmen years ago'.

In the Australian winter of 1932 Mailey organised a 51-match tour of the United States and Canada and invited Fleetwood-Smith to join the team. Mailey, then 46, realised that he needed a bowler who could take a lot of wickets because the Australians would have to dismiss around 1,000 batsmen in 100 days. Knowing the American weakness against spin, he sent a telegram to his team captain Vic Richardson in Melbourne: 'If Fleetwood-Smith any good invite him to come to America'. Richardson had watched Fleetwood-Smith take 7 for 101 against his South Australian team the day before on a perfect batting strip at the MCG. Chuck jumped at the chance of joining a side that included Bradman, McCabe, Kippax and Mailey, his mentor.

Fleetwood-Smith had long stints of bowling with Mailey advising him and ended the tour with 249 wickets at 8.00 each and two hat-tricks compared with Mailey's 240 wickets at 6.5. But it was Fleetwood-Smith whose snappy dressing and good looks made him the team's glamour boy. One paper called him cricket's Clark Gable and there certainly was a similarity in their attraction to women. On the set in Hollywood, with Fleetwood-Smith sporting a cravat, trimmed moustache and well-oiled black curly hair, he filled the Gable role chatting to Jean Harlow, Myrna Loy and Jeanette MacDonald.

The Australians returned from this fun-filled North American jaunt with Mailey a fervent admirer of Fleetwood-Smith's spinning ability. 'He was probably the best of his type cricket has known,' said Mailey. 'A man who could spin the cover off the ball if he wished.' Although he was on his honeymoon, Bradman played in 49 matches on that tour, scoring 18 centuries and taking 26 wickets from his 52 overs of tidy leg-spin. He, too, remained a strong supporter of Fleetwood-Smith's exceptional skills thereafter.

The path to a place in the Australian Test team was complicated, however, by the excellence of Grimmett and O'Reilly and some freakish figures by that strange left-armer Bert Ironmonger, who held the ball on the stub of a finger damaged in a chaffcutter. Ironmonger took

cheaply. When he returned to Melbourne in 1930 he put his age back from 22 to 20 and joined the St Kilda club, which already had Bert Ironmonger and Don Blackie achieving spectacular results with spin bowling in support of the club's high-scoring batsman, Bill Ponsford. Blackie did not make his Test debut until he was 46 years and 253 days old. Ironmonger claimed he was 41 when he began in Tests but in reality was 46. So two years of an aspiring young spinner's life went unnoticed.

Fleetwood-Smith quickly won a first grade spot despite the presence of Blackie and Ironmonger. His selection attracted Melbourne cricket writers who went to some lengths to explain to readers how Chuck bowled the

5 for 6 and 6 for 18 against South Africa in the fifth Test of the 1931–32 series and this gave him the edge over Fleetwood-Smith in the Bodyline Tests against England in 1932–33 when support was needed for O'Reilly or Grimmett. Plum Warner, England's manager in that bitter rubber, found time to praise Fleetwood-Smith's bowling. 'To our secret delight, Fleetwood-Smith was not selected in any of the Tests,' said Warner. 'But I shall be surprised if we don't see him in England in 1934.'

This proved an accurate forecast and Fleetwood-Smith went to England with Bradman's 1934 team. As in America on his initial overseas tour, Chuck found women in England responsive to his wiles, but the continued fine form of Grimmett and O'Reilly denied him a Test place. Early on the tour he overdid his womanising, his on-the-field birdcalls and his congratulatory handclaps for batsmen who hit him for four. 'Great shot, old man,' he would call, affecting a well-bred Pommie accent.

English critics at first completely misjudged his nonconformity and wrote him off as a vastly over-rated bowler who, they suggested, would be harshly treated by any batsman with passable footwork. He took 41 wickets in eight matches to the end of June but in the 12 matches that followed settled down to take his tour aggregate to 106 wickets at fewer than 20 runs apiece. This was only three short of the 109 dismissals achieved by Grimmett and O'Reilly, a fine performance for a bowler of his type on his first tour of England.

Watching him take 10 wickets against Sussex at Brighton and 10 against Leveson-Gower's XI at Scarborough, admirers of cricket unorthodoxy remained puzzled about his continued omission from the Test team. Plum Warner believed it was because of Australia's obsession with containing Hammond, then at the peak of his powers, and the fear that he would slaughter Fleetwood-Smith.

The long wait ended when Fleetwood-Smith went to South Africa with the Australian team in 1935–36. He made his Test debut at Durban on 14 December 1935, and over the next four days did well enough to hold his place, taking 4 for 64 and 1 for 101, but just after the third Test he badly injured his bowling hand, stopping a firm drive off his own bowling at East London against Border. The injury worsened through inefficient medical treatment and he took no further part in the tour except to bowl a few down in the nets to team-mates.

The injury left him free to demonstrate his astounding appeal to women. O'Reilly used to advise homesick young players eager for companionship to simply follow Fleetwood-Smith around and talk to his cast-offs. It is said that the average cricketer contents himself with picking out one attractive woman at the innumerable functions touring teams attend. Fleetwood-Smith had no trouble slotting in four or five. A team-mate found him one night in the toilet leaning against a wash basin. 'Just resting before the next one,' said Chuck.

As he built his reputation as Australian cricket champion pants man, he left team-mates perplexed over the reasons for his success. O'Reilly said: 'It was strange, as he had no line of conversation when he first met a woman. You would look on horrified at the low level of gibberish he would spray at these giggling, but well-endowed females. However, they always fell prostrate when they looked at him.'

Fleetwood-Smith took one break from lovemaking to go out into a park with wicket-keeper Bert Oldfield who had been having trouble taking his spinners cleanly. There in street clothes he sent down a selection of googlies and Chinamen until Oldfield, in gloves and a tailored suit, got the knack of them. Oldfield later wrote in the book *Behind The Wicket* that Fleetwood-Smith was the trickiest bowler he ever kept to, and compared with other spin bowlers absolutely freakish. 'Having to keep wicket to Fleetwood-Smith spinners at one end and Grimmett at the other, both of them bowling googlies, was at first puzzling,' said Oldfield. 'Never had I been called on to be so wide awake, so alert.' The resourceful Test batsman Keith Rigg believed Fleetwood-Smith capable of unplayable deliveries even O'Reilly could not match. 'He spun the ball so much it was a waste of time practising in the nets against him.'

In the spring of 1936 Chuck's damaged tendon in his bowling hand required surgery. He was impatient to resume playing as he knew he could not be absent for too long while Australia boasted a surfeit of spinning talent, but he was forced to take doctors' advice and not return prematurely. He planned his comeback so that he was available for the fourth Test in Adelaide against the touring Englishmen, but he was recalled for the third Test in Melbourne.

He could not have timed it better. Australia lost the first two Tests without Fleetwood-Smith and selectors had no choice but to include him after he had proved his fitness by taking 7 for 17 and 8 for 79 in an extraordinary display of his powers against Queensland. Seven of the 15 wickets he took in that match on a hard MCG pitch were leg-before-wicket.

For years Mailey and his pal Hanson Carter, the former Test keeper who arrived for big cricket in a hearse, fresh from funeral services in his Bondi parlours, had been suggesting that one day Fleetwood-Smith would win a Test match for Australia. Melbourne Cricket Ground in January 1937 provided the perfect setting to end the fear that Hammond was his master, with Fleetwood-Smith's friend and bridge partner Don Bradman under intense pressure, amid reports that his first series as captain lacked the cooperation of the Catholics in the Australian team.

The showdown with Hammond did not immediately eventuate. Instead Fleetwood-Smith found himself at the centre of a desperate tactical ploy by Bradman. The pitch was a gluepot, with a fierce sun beating down on it after heavy rain. Australia struggled to 9 for 200 before Bradman declared. Then England slithered about, with Bradman urging bowlers to keep England in to ensure Australia did not have to bat again that day. 'Gubby' Allen thwarted him by declaring at 9 for 76, leaving 40 minutes left of the second day. When Bradman stunned the Australian dressing-room by ordering batting duffers O'Reilly and Fleetwood-Smith to open the second innings, Chuck was astonished.

'Look, the only way you can get out on this pitch is to hit the ball,' said Bradman. 'You can't hit it on a good pitch so you will have no chance on this sticky.'

O'Reilly was quickly dismissed for a duck but Fleetwood-Smith somehow managed to remain until stumps. Another batting novice, Ward, made an invaluable 18. Fingleton came in at No. 6, Bradman at No. 7 after the pitch had dried out, and together they put on 346, a world record for the sixth wicket, Fingleton reaching 136, Bradman 270. Australia were all out for 564 and won by 365 runs when they dismissed England for 323 in the final innings of a famous match. The attendance of 350,534 was a record for any cricket match.

Four players were summoned from the jubilant Australian dressing room to meet the chairman, Dr Alan Robertson, in the Australian Board of Control rooms nearby. There Dr Robertson read a statement to Stan McCabe, Leo O'Brien, Fleetwood-Smith and Bill O'Reilly, urging them to pay more attention to fitness and less to their beer drinking. Don Bradman was not present and as the players listened to this diatribe they realised they were all Catholics. The harassed Dr Robertson insisted they were not being reprimanded but instructed them not to mention the meeting to the media. O'Reilly looked out of the window into the street and saw a *Melbourne Herald* poster that read: 'Test Players Carpeted'.

Jack Fingleton said he was surprised he had not been among those lectured by Dr Robertson as he was the only other Catholic in the team but his confusion was mild compared with that of Fleetwood-Smith, who had no part in the first and second Test defeats and had his match fitness monitored by his doctor. He went to Adelaide Oval three weeks later for the fourth Test puzzled by his treatment, and mindful of the hammering Hammond had inflicted on him in 1932 in the Victoria–England match, just before the Bodyline series. That flogging—in which Hammond hit a six and 23 fours, mostly off Fleetwood-Smith's bowling, in scoring 203 to set up England's victory by an innings and 83 runs—also delayed Fleetwood-Smith's entry into Test cricket for three years. Now was the time to settle acounts.

England took a first innings lead of 42 runs, thanks to 129 from Charlie Barnett, with Fleetwood-Smith taking 4 for 129 off 41 overs. Bradman swung the match Australia's way with his second double century in successive Tests, 212. Set to score 392 to win in the fourth innings, England required 244 at the start of the last day with seven wickets left and Hammond still at the crease. Fleetwood-Smith spent the night well away from women and wine and hardly needed the reminder from Bradman, as Australia took the field next morning, that now was the time for an unplayable ball.

Fleetwood-Smith responded with the finest ball of his career, a delivery that dipped sharply in the air away from Hammond, pitched on a worn spot outside his off-stump and spun between bat and pad onto the stumps. O'Reilly always said it was the greatest delivery he ever saw bowled, and Bradman agreed, saying 'It won the match for us and paved the way for us to win the rubber'. Neville Cardus said Fleetwood-Smith had been suddenly visited by genius. Billy Brown, fielding at fine leg, described it as an incredible delivery that drifted away from Hammond and then came back as he played defensively and went through the gap. Australia won by 148 runs to level the series and went on to take the fifth Test to retain the Ashes. Fleetwood-Smith's 10 wickets on a fast, dry Adelaide pitch remained his career best.

In England in 1938 Fleetwood-Smith lacked any motivation and his customary philandering on such tours was inhibited by his wife Mollie's presence. Percy Fender, former England captain, wrote that Bradman was afraid to let Fleetwood-Smith loose because he might bowl away so many runs it would upset his best bowler, O'Reilly. With 14 Test wickets at 51.9 he did not fail, but he was far from the match-winner Mailey and others expected him to be. Increasing weight, and the old lack of concern over being hit saw him decline to a stage where his 1 for 298 in the fifth Test was greeted as reasonable justice.

He played for two more seasons in Australia but with war approaching his mind was not concentrated on winning the Sheffield Shield for Victoria. He retired at the end of the 1939–40 summer with 597 wickets in first-class matches at 22.64 each, the cheapest by any Australian over the 500 mark. He was Victoria's highest wicket-taker with 295 at 24.3. His match-winning value lay in his extraordinary feats of taking five wickets in an innings 57 times, and 10 wickets in a match 18 times. His penetration was further emphasised by his performance in taking a wicket every 44 balls, compared with Grimmett's 52 balls, O'Reilly's 49 and Mailey's 46. One-third of all his victims were bowled.

At Test level Fleetwood-Smith was not as effective, taking 42 wickets at 37.4. With the bat he upheld the tradition of genuine No. 11s by scoring only 617 first-class runs at 7.34, and most of them were off the edge. The army took pleasure in welcoming him into the infantry, but he remained the determined individualist, refusing to attend parades, sporting a snappy cravat instead of the tie army regulations required, and refusing to wear headgear. He spent most of the war as a physical training officer at Frankston, and was lucky to be cited as the co-respondent in only one divorce case.

He thought about returning to cricket after his discharge from the army but all his enthusiasm had gone, though he did attend net practice to help youngsters like Keith Miller, Ian Johnson and George Tribe. Two marriages broke down while old school friends and team-mates did their best to keep him in casual employment, but he was too unreliable to hold a full-time job. His good looks faded with every drinking binge and he gave up attending Test cricketers' reunions knowing how he looked after nights of dossing in the park. He was always short of cash and when he went back to Stawell old friends avoided him because they knew he would be after them for money.

Len Hutton, the first professional to captain England, told how on a visit to Australia he was approached by Fleetwood-Smith, down on his luck, for a hand-out. 'I remembered how the Australian had pressured me in 1938 as I neared Don Bradman's world record,' said Hutton. 'Every time I looked up there were the Aussie fieldsmen creeping closer and closer. In the end Fleetwood-Smith bowled a long hop which I gratefully chopped through the slips and I had passed Bradman and was on my way to 364. I remembered that long hop when Fleetwood-Smith approached me and reckoned it was worth a fiver of anybody's money.'

After years on skid row, Fleetwood-Smith was arrested and charged with vagrancy in March 1969, and appeared in the Melbourne City Court, haggard and scared, his black hair turned grey. The magistrate, a cricket lover, remanded him for two weeks and in that fortnight a Fleetwood-Smith Recovery Fund was launched. The premier Henry Bolte, old Test cricketers, sportswriters, ex-prime minister Bob Menzies and relatives rallied to support the fund and buy him a new suit and get him cleaned up for his court appearance. Famous barrister Frank Galbally defended him and Test team-mate Leo O'Brien appeared as the only witness for the defence, suggesting that 'it was in our hearts to bring him back to his former self'.

The magistrate released him under the care of the doctor in charge of St Vincent's Hospital's alcoholic clinic and Fleetwood-Smith vowed never to take another drink. His first wife Beatrice Collins took him back into her home and for the last two years of his life Fleetwood-Smith kept his promise not to touch the booze. But his lost years had robbed him of his robust health and he died of major chest ailments in St Vincent's Hospital, Melbourne, aged 62. His marriage had been restored, he had a gardening job, and he did not die a derelict, but from the damage that had been done when he was one.

Fleetwood-Smith's bowling in his heyday inspired dozens of young left-arm bowlers around Australia, among them a dedicated bowler from the Glebe club in Sydney named Jack Walsh. He began as an orthodox finger-spinner but when he saw the back-of-the-wrist-spin Fleetwood-Smith imparted to the ball switched to developing his own Chinaman delivery. Despite the presence of O'Reilly, Chilvers and other wrist spinners he graduated from New South Wales Colts to the State Second XI until in 1937, at the age of 25, he realised the path to Test honours was littered with other talented spinners and opted to join Sir Julien Cahn's team at its headquarters in Nottingham.

Walsh had two successful years with Sir Julien's crack eleven and when war forced its abandonment returned to Sydney for a few happy matches with the Petersham club. He appeared twice for New South Wales before he joined the RAAF and for the next five years his cricket was confined to services' pick-up matches on pitches of ground coral in the South Pacific.

Discharged in 1946, he did not try for a place in the Australian team but headed straight for Leicestershire with fellow Australian Vic Jackson. They formed the spearhead of the county's attack for years, Jackson bowling accurate off-spinners, Walsh dispensing left-arm wrist-spin which the best batsmen in England had trouble reading. No other bowler has matched Walsh's mastery of the deadly Chinaman. Len Hutton, Denis Compton, Cyril Washbrook, Bill Edrich and dozens of others all looked foolish at times facing Walsh's special brand of wizardry. Moreover, he was one of the few Australians who did not mind playing cricket six days a week as a county professional. 'I love it,' he said. 'Fancy being paid to do what you love.'

Other Australians spoke of the bizarre distinctions between amateur and professionals in the 1950s and 1960s in English cricket. Captains changed in their own rooms, separated from their teams, and although amateurs and professionals did not go onto the field through different gates as they did between the wars, the snobbery and bigotry remained among Englishmen who considered professional cricketers a lesser breed. Jack Walsh took it all in his stride, playing under captains who knew far less about the game than he did, happy just to get five wickets in a match.

I have vivid memories of Walsh bowling to Bill Alley at the Sydney Cricket Ground nets during a coaching class conducted for aspiring youngsters by state selector Dudley Seddon. Alley, a super stroke-player, was supposed to show us teenagers his shots but Walsh turned the ball the best part of a metre each way, buzzing the ball through the air and achieving so much bounce poor Alley could hardly get a bat on ball. Alley, former prize-fighter and night club bouncer, let fly with some impressive expletives, but Walsh just stood and grinned at him.

Walsh bowled with relaxed swing of the left arm from a slightly stooped stance and at the instant of release his wrist snapped like a steel spring. The flexibility of his hand made what to other bowlers is a difficult movement look easy and controlled. *Wisden* was not exaggerating when it said that for many years he was the most dangerous and controlled bowler in the world.

He played for Leicestershire in 279 matches between 1937 and 1956 and was the mainstay of their attack in all of those years after touring Sri Lanka and New Zealand with Sir Julien Cahn's XI. He was also an outstanding slips fieldsman and with the bat had a full range of left-handed strokes with which he would have scored more runs had he restrained a passion for straight-driven sixes. He hit 7,247 first-class runs with a highest score of 106 against Essex at Loughborough in 1948, when 82 of his runs came in boundaries (seven sixes and 10 fours). Wal

Jack Walsh, rated by Wisden as the most controlled and dangerous bowler in the world, delivers one of his left-arm wrist-spinners.

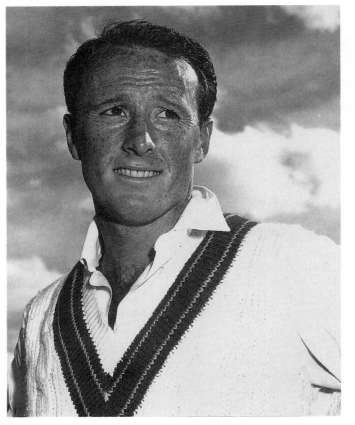

David Hourn, above, anxiously awaits the fate of one of his left-arm spinners, and David Sincock, below, who imparted so much spin to the ball his deliveries hummed on their way to the batsmen.

George Tribe, one of a highly talented group of Australian left-arm spinners, forced to win recognition in England. He took five wickets in an innings a remarkable 93 times.

Walmsley, the Sydney-born leg-spinner who took 96 wickets with leg-breaks for Queensland, could not believe it when he first saw Walsh spin the ball, but he was even more surprised when he saw Jack hit a six straight back over the bowler's head about 25 rows into the crowd.

After Walsh retired at 44 he coached in Scotland, South Africa, Tasmania and Pakistan. He died at 67 in Wallsend, near Newcastle, N.S.W., in 1980, near the ground where he often taught small boys the technique of the googly. In fact he bowled two googlies, the first designed to be easily detected and lull the batsman into a false sense of security and the other ball that defied detection and spun fiercely out of the hand just as a juggler unveils a trick to climax his act. Apart from his two matches for New South Wales, the closest he got to representative cricket was in his appearance for the Players against the Gentlemen at Lord's. One of his admirers, Denis Compton, said he was the greatest bowler never to play in a Test.

Walsh took 1,127 wickets for Leicestershire at 24.25. He excelled even his idol Fleetwood-Smith by taking five wickets in an innings 98 times and 10 wickets in a match 26 times. He also held 209 catches in first-class matches, but his batting average of 17.76 and his two centuries were not a true guide to his value as an all-rounder. Some critics believe he spun the ball too much for his own good and suggested he would have taken more wickets and not

Lindsay Kline, left, shows the high leaping delivery style that brought him a Test hat-trick against South Africa, and right, Garfield Sobers shows a similar loose-limbed action. This one looks like a finger-spinner, but Sobers mixed in a lot of wrist-spinners when bowling slow like this.

forced his wicket-keepers to concede so many byes had he reduced the spin that inspired other Australian left-arm bowlers like George Tribe, Johnny Martin, David Hourn, Lindsay Kline and David Sincock.

They were a talented bunch, all of them dangerous to even classy batsmen, and all produced some marvellous hauls that swung matches for their teams. They were members of an exclusive club, with membership taken for a time by Yorkshireman Johnny Wardle and the great West Indian master Gary Sobers.

Judged on his performance six days a week, Tribe was probably the best of this group of Chinamen bowlers, but he had the bad luck to be born at the wrong time. He only played three times for Australia and his two wickets for 165 runs in those 1946–47 matches against England gave no hint of his quality. He went off to England to break records for Milnrow in Lancashire League matches and after a tour of India with a Commonwealth XI in 1949–50 joined Northants, with whom he stayed for eight years. The Commonwealth side included master spinners Jim Laker, Sonny Ramadhin and Bruce Dooland as well as Tribe.

Tribe was born at Yarraville, Victoria, on 4 October 1920 and began playing cricket in the family backyard with his brothers. Bowling finger-spin he graduated from his school team to Yarraville Seconds at the age of 14, occasionally getting a bowl for the firsts. At 18, he made a major change by changing to wrist-spin, reasoning that under the amended lbw law he had a better chance with deliveries spinning in from the off to right-handers. By then he had overcome his lack of height (5 feet 7 inches) and learnt that his exceptionally large hand imparted wide turn. Within a year of the switch to wrist-spin he won a regular place in North Melbourne firsts.

The war interrupted his bid for first-class honours, but he managed to play for several years as a professional Australian Rules footballer because of his job as an engineer, a reserved occupation. He took 6 for 101 on debut for Victoria in 1945–46 against Queensland and within hours the word swept round Australian cricket clubs that here was a bowler who really gave the ball a tweak, a left-hander in the Fleetwood-Smith mould who bowled a Chinaman that literally buzzed as it left his hand. He ended that season with 40 wickets, a bag that positioned him with Bruce Dooland, Ian Johnson, Colin McCool, Doug Ring and Ernie Toshack, all of them challenging for Test selection.

He played in the first, second and fifth Tests of the 1946–47 rubber against England, but on hard, flat pitches that suited Miller and Lindwall found wickets hard to get. Bruce Dooland replaced him in the third and fourth Tests, but he also failed to secure significant results. Both decided they could not make a living from cricket in Australia and went off to England, where their performance over the next 20 years persistently demonstrated what a sad loss this was to Australian cricket.

Tribe did not spin the ball as much as Walsh but he had more control. He took 1,378 first-class wickets at 20.55 apiece, had five wickets in an innings 93 times and 10 wickets in a match 23 times. He also achieved the double (100 wickets, 1,000 runs) seven times in an English season. Dooland's right-arm leg-spinners and googlies brought him 1,016 wickets at 21.98, and he took five wickets in an innings 84 times, 23 times finishing with 10 wickets in a match.

Dooland, Tribe, Walsh and fellow wrist-spinners Ken Grieves and Cecil Pepper, who joined the exodus to England immediately after the war, all kept their feet on the ground in dispensing leg-breaks and googlies. But around the world some of the most successful exponents of the style introduced high leaps and bounds to their deliveries. Technical reasons for this aerial work escape me but several of the leading wicket-takers actually released their wrist-spin two feet in the air in their delivery stride. The big name in the googlies and leg-spin group when the Australians arrived in England was Douglas Vivian Parson Wright, whose action was so full of kangaroo hops and leaps for the crease that he made spectators laugh. On his best days Wright's bowling could be devastating, following Kent's great tradition of supplying match-winning spinners that had been underscored by Woolley and Freeman, but when his 10 paces of high bounding did not work no-balls and runs came in profusion.

8

Stepping Over Puddles

'I was never happy facing Doug Wright. He always seemed capable of producing a playable ball which completely shattered one's defence, not by guile or deception, but sheer skill. I can still picture his most beautiful delivery, the half over-spin leg-break which curved sinuously towards the leg stump and then turned to the off bail. It was one of these that should have won a Test in Sydney in 1947, but then Doug always seemed to be unlucky. If there is such a thing as luck in cricket, Wright was not blessed with it.'

This was Don Bradman writing in the booklet published for Wright's testimonial, a revealing recitation of Wright's seven first-class hat-tricks, the six occasions that he took 13 wickets or more in a match, and his massive aggregate of 2,056 first-class wickets.

Wright remains one of cricket's enigmas, clearly a master spin bowler to all who watched his uncanny range of leg-breaks, googlies, topspins and deliveries that defied description, but to some a Test match failure because his 108 wickets in international contests cost 39.11 each. None of the Australians who fell to him would agree. Bradman, Hassett, Fingleton, Brown, Badcock, Barnes, Morris, Miller and McCool all would have liked Wright in their side.

Bradman suggested that Wright was too reticent and modest and would have benefitted from some of the ferocity O'Reilly showed to unsettle opponents and set them up for the kill. Others said he bowled too fast or that he was too intense in a caper that demanded occasional appreciation of the outrageous. Whatever the flaws in his technique or temperament, no bowler has beaten the bat as often as Wright and failed to set up victories. The trouble was that his best balls beat the batsman, the stumps, and his wicket-keeper.

He was born in Sidcup, Kent, on 21 August 1914 and grew into a sparely built teenager, 5 feet 11 inches in height with long, sinewy arms. When he left school he became a solicitor's clerk. At 17 he had a game for the Kent ground staff and joined the county professionals the following year. Opportunities were few because of the success of Tich Freeman in the county firsts and he was considering concentrating on law when he wandered into Aubrey

Faulkner's London cricket school. Faulkner noticed his bowler's fingers and offered him a job. 'Work with me and I'll teach you to play cricket,' Faulkner said, but he could not eliminate the approach-run that made Wright look like a man stepping over puddles.

Wright's parents were divided about whether he should play cricket as a career, but Faulkner's enthusiasm attracted him to try his luck as a leg-break and googly bowler like his employer. However, when he bowled slowly even deliveries that spun proved easy to hit, so he quickened his pace to medium to avoid so many short balls.

From the start he needed a team of surveyors with theodolites to help him mark out his approach run. He varied the length and direction of his approach, coming in from mid-off one week and from straight behind the umpire the next. In 1935, he improved his run enough, despite the hops and starts, to play in half Kent's matches as support bowler to Freeman. When Freeman retired in 1936 Wright became the spin-bowling spearhead for the county.

Two years later he was invited to play in a Test trial at Lord's and although he took only three wickets for 134 runs, the six chances missed off his bowling did not go unnoticed. England's captain-designate Wally Hammond verified Wright's potential and he appeared in four Tests before a split finger forced him out of the fifth.

He could have won the crucial fourth Test at Leeds but with the rubber in the balance Hammond waited too long to bring him on, with Australia chasing only 105 to win in the final innings. Even then he disposed of Bradman and McCabe and had Hassett dropped. With rain clouds threatening Hassett made the most of his escape in an aggressive match-winning innings of 33. Just before Australia reached her target and clinched the Ashes, Wright had Hassett caught by Edrich.

Wright toured South Africa in 1938–39 with the England team led by Hammond and appeared in the notorious timeless Test at Durban, which had to be declared a draw after 10 days play because England had to make a two-day train trip to Cape Town to catch their ship home. Left to score 696 to win in the last innings

Douglas Wright approached the crease with the curious skipetty-hop run from which he unwound medium-pace leg-breaks that made him the most dangerous bowler in England.

after South Africa had made 530 and 481, England were only 42 runs from victory with five wickets down when rain during the tea interval curtailed further play.

Wright bowled 37 overs in the first innings for his 2 for 142 and 32 overs in the second innings for 3 for 146, and returned to England convinced he had to shorten his run because it was too exhausting in the heat. He had only just begun experiments with it when war interrupted him, but during service with the RAAF he was often seen in his leisure time leaping and bounding, marking out his strides with tent pegs.

Despite all these rehearsals he could not prevent persistent no-ball problems—regarded as unforgivable in a spin bowler—when cricket resumed after the war. From the same crazy run, bounding, skipping, as if coiling a spring to be released when the ball left his hand, he conceded more than 100 runs in six of the eight innings in which he bowled in the 1946–47 Tests in Australia. Yet he still baffled with wristy, spinning deliveries that bounced high off the pitch. Hassett continually had to play him off his breastbone and he often hit tall batsmen like Miller on the fingers.

Wright was at his best in the second big match of the tour when he took 10 for 121 against Victoria on the MCG, getting more spin from the flaking turf than Tribe or Ring. At Brisbane in the first Test he took 5 for 167 off 350 deliveries in an Australian innings of 645, and when noted cricket writer Ray Robinson congratulated him on his bowling, he said: 'But what about my batting?' Wright had finished with 10 not out and was to score 14 runs in five innings in Australia. An unashamed tailender, he was more concerned with banishing no-balls and full tosses from his bowling than with his batting.

Wright's plan was to bowl at a brisk medium pace that prevented even quick-footed batsmen moving out to check his spin. He needed to pitch the ball short enough to give topspin and leg-spin a chance to beat the bat, but at the pace he sought to bowl his back foot crossed the line, and 15 times in five Tests he was no-balled. The extra run each no-ball cost mattered little but at a time when no-balls offered batsmen a free swing the sixes Miller, Lindwall and Morris clouted from them savaged England's morale.

The Australians acknowledged that luck turned savagely against Wright in all five Tests and that, given a reasonable break, he could have far exceeded his 23 wickets in the series. Normally safe fieldsmen like Hammond and Edrich missed catches off him, confident stumping and lbw appeals were rejected, deliveries that beat the bat passed over the top of the stumps, and with two slips in position batsmen foozled a leg-break over their heads.

Retribution should have come in the fifth Test when he had Bradman out for 12 in the first innings and then hit him on the leg in the second innings when the great man was on three. Keeper Evans held his gloves aloft in supporting Wright's confident appeal but umpire Jack Scott shook his head, leaving Wright gawking at Scott

in disbelief. Watching Wright take 7 for 105 in Australia's first innings, the best in Wright's 34 Tests for England, former Australian captain Bill Woodfull rated him the best bowler England had sent to Australia in 25 years. With O'Reilly and Grimmett gone, he was the world's top wrist-spinner.

England's other wrist-spinner on that tour, dapper, moustached Peter Smith also indulged in fancy footwork, kicking his right leg up stump high in the delivery stride. Smith's two Test wickets cost 109 runs each, leaving Australians puzzled over why he had been chosen at all.

Although widely acknowledged as England's most hostile bowler in Australia, Wright was made twelfth man for the first Test of the 1947 series in England against South Africa. South Africa made 533, thanks to a record 319 stand by Melville and Nourse. Wright was back for the second Test and took five wickets in each innings to set up an easy England win. Despite a poisoned toe he headed England's wicket-takers with 19 victims in the rubber.

Australians saw little of Wright during the 1948 tour of England when he was hampered by lumbago and appeared only in the second Test. Yet again he was unlucky

A close-up of Wright's wrist action. He often beat the batsman, stumps and wicket-keeper with high-bouncing spinners.

Grimmett, in comparison to Wright, was beautifully balanced as he delivered the ball, as this shot of him bowling in England demonstrates. He always bowled with a cap on.

when Morris edged a catch to Evans at 55 and was given not out, going on to 105. Newcomers in the Australian team could not believe that a bowler firing the ball down at such pace could manage such bounce and turn when all the coaching manuals said the ball had to be given plenty of air to secure maximum turn. He was omitted from the rest of the rubber, with Australians thankful he was absent at Leeds when they had to make 404 on the fifth day. A damaged finger prevented him playing against Australia again.

Wright went off to South Africa in the England team led by Freddie Mann in 1948–49 and in the match against Griqualand West became involved in one of the most curious incidents of his career. The umpires were not amused as he took 5 for 61 by his habit of licking his fingers as he turned to move into his approach. Wright, who had been following this routine throughout his time in first-class cricket, found himself accused of wetting the ball. He seldom got his feet in the right position in his bounding run-up and now his hands were deemed to be at fault. He was omitted from two of the five Tests but still took 51 wickets on the tour, second to 71 dismissals by Worcestershire spinner Roley Jenkins.

Eric Hollies, the Warwickshire leg-spinner who had bowled Bradman for a duck in his last Test innings with a splendid googly, Johnny Wardle, the Yorkshire left-arm spinner who mixed off-spin with googlies and Jenkins were all tried in the 1950 series between England and the West Indies. However, Wright returned to favour by taking 5 for 141 off 53 overs in the fourth Test at The Oval. This, together with another 100 wickets in county cricket, saved his Test career and earned him his second trip to Australia under Freddie Brown's captaincy in 1950–51. He tore a tendon in his leg in the third Test, which was typical of his continued bad luck throughout the series.

Wisden said he and Bedser bowled magnificently on the tour, but Bedser ended the rubber with 30 wickets at 16.04, Wright 11 wickets at an expensive 45.45. Bedser's aggregate in all first-class matches was 51 wickets at 19.80, Wright's 33 wickets at 32.61. Once again normally reliable fieldsmen dropped catches off Wright's bowling and Australian umpires again rejected appeals that looked valid from the press-box. Undeterred, Wright went off to New Zealand and at Christchurch, in his thirty-third Test, took his hundredth Test wicket.

The following week at Wellington he took 5 for 48 in his final Test, which took his Test aggregate to 108 wickets at 39.11. He kept appearing for Kent until 1957, and right to the end of his career in which he played 397 county games he had trouble with his bounding run and continued to no-ball. Two years before he quit he bombarded his wicket-keeper Tony Catt with a barrage of high bouncing leg-breaks that constantly flew over Catt's shoulders and went for 48 byes.

Wright's international career may have disappointed after the dramatic start when he bowled Jack Fingleton with his fourth ball in Tests, but no assessment of the great wrist-spin bowlers can discount a man who took so many hat-tricks (seven) and more than 2,000 wickets. His match figures of 16 for 80 against Somerset at Bath in 1939, 15 for 163 v. Leicestershire at Maidstone in 1949 and his 15 for 173 at Hastings against Sussex in 1947 give considerable weight to the view that on his day Douglas Vivian Parson Wright was a match-winner, hops and licks notwithstanding.

While Wright was playing out his erratic career—some English critics claimed Australians only praised him to ensure they could score easy Test runs from him— Australian leg-spinners of much slower pace were building big reputations in England county cricket. Apart from the Chinamen bowlers Walsh and Tribe, orthodox right-arm leg-spinners Bruce Dooland and Colin McCool had regular triumphs.

Dooland was credited with restoring leg-break and googly bowling to an important place in the strategy of the game by taking 518 wickets in his first three seasons in English cricket—172 at 16.58 in 1953, 196 at 15.48 in 1954 and 150 at 23.01 in 1955. This made him the most successful orthodox leg-spinner in county cricket since Tich Freeman.

He went to Nottingham with a typical Australian background, having learnt the game in his family's back garden, where his father laid out a concrete pitch for him and encouraged him to bowl wrist-spin. From Thebarton Central School, he progressed to Adelaide High School where he did so well he attracted the attention of the West Torrens district club. In 1940–41, at the age of 18, he was invited to play for South Australia against New South Wales, but the manager of the bank where he worked would not grant him leave and his first-class debut was delayed until after World War II. Fresh from service with a Commando unit in the Pacific, he returned to take the first hat-trick in postwar Australian cricket, for South Australia against Victoria.

Dooland toured New Zealand in 1946–47 in a team captained by Bill Brown and on his return home went into the Australian side for the third Test against England. Competition for the leg-spinner's spot in the Australian team was fierce, however, with George Tribe, Colin McCool and Doug Ring all performing splendidly. He played one further Test for Australia in 1948 and then went off to play for East Lancashire in the Lancashire League while he qualified for Nottinghamshire. He made his debut in county cricket in May 1953, against Kent at Trent Bridge, and failed to take a wicket. Notts' faith in him was rewarded, however, when he took 5 for 73 and 4 for 46 against Surrey, the county champions.

From there on, it was a story of sustained success. Acknowledged as the best bowler of his type in England,

he appeared regularly for the Players against the Gentlemen, toured India and Sri Lanka with a Common-wealth XI in 1950–51 and returned to India in 1956–57 in a team captained by Bill Edrich and managed by C.G. Howard. Nottingham were disappointed when he returned to Adelaide in 1957 at the peak of his fame so that his children could be educated in Australia. He died in Adelaide in 1980, aged 56.

McCool was a different type of wrist-spinner but, on his day, just as hostile. A round-armer whose bowling hand rarely got above shoulder level, at 5 feet 7 inches, he was stockier and shorter than Dooland (6 feet). Playing for Paddington in Sydney club matches, he was almost unplayable on worn pitches, so wide was his turn. I saw him turn the ball from one side of the practice nets to the other and make even state batsmen look foolish if the Trumper Park curator Paddy Ryan neglected to roll the practice pitches hard. McCool would then walk over to a roller or catching machine and spend an hour rehearsing catching, a process that made him one of the best-ever slips fieldsmen.

He calmly flipped the ball up to the batsman with his arm almost parallel to the turf, imparting spin that made the ball dip and turn. Experts tried to get him to take his arm above the shoulder, but he lost the wide turn and felt uncomfortable so he returned to his natural style. He

An Eric Hollies googly hits Bradman's stumps in his last Test innings, dismissing him for a duck when he needed only four runs or a not-out to maintain an average of more than 100 in Tests.

Colin McCool, a big turner of the ball, bowling to Hammond in the England–Australia Test at Sydney in 1946. McCool took eight wickets in the match.

got a wicket with only his second ball in Tests at Wellington in 1945–46 to clinch victory for Bill Brown's Australian team after service in the RAAF delayed his entry into big cricket.

Success in New Zealand encouraged him to switch states and move to Queensland, where he formed a formidable wicket-taking partnership with Don Tallon. McCool's wide breaks and well-disguised googly ideally suited Tallon's lightning-fast stumping skill and he stood right up on the stumps, pressuring batsmen eager to move down to kill the spin. Both won places in the Test series against

Hammond's 1946–47 English tourists. McCool scored 95 in Brisbane before Wright trapped him lbw. He took eight wickets in the second Test at Sydney, hit 104 not out to save the third Test at Melbourne and took 5 for 44 to produce victory in the fifth Test.

At that stage McCool appeared destined for a long Test career but introduction of a law that allowed captains to take a new ball every 65 overs limited his opportunities. Bradman was able to bowl Lindwall, Miller, Bill Johnston and Ernie Toshack without any need to use McCool or his fellow leg-spinner. McCool's 1948 tour of England was further hampered by a damaged callus on the third finger of his bowling hand which allowed the ball to rub right through the skin whenever he attempted lengthy bowling spells.

After being one of Australia's heroes in the previous series, McCool did not get a Test in the 1948 rubber. The only wrist-spinner used in Australia's unbeaten run was Doug Ring, a big, burly Hobart-born six-footer who played most of his cricket in Victoria. Ring only had a chance to display the leg-spinners he pushed through at a brisk pace after Lindwall's 6 for 20 had bundled England out for 52 in their first innings. Ring's 28 overs in the second innings produced 13 maidens and he finished with 1 for 44. For much of the tour Ring led the Australian reserves in dressing-room renditions of 'Ground Staff Bowling is Our Game', sung to the tune of 'Champagne Charlie'.

McCool's leg-breaks proved extremely useful to Lindsay Hassett's team in South Africa in 1949–50. McCool played in five Tests, demonstrating yet again his all-round skills with superb slips catching, confident batting and steady leg-spin. His 51 wickets on the tour included 5 for 41 in the second Test at Cape Town. His batting at Durban in the third Test led to a remarkable Australian win after they were bundled out for 75 in their first innings. He stayed with Neil Harvey in an unbroken stand of 136 that gave Australia the 336 runs required to win in the final innings. Harvey finished on 151 not out, McCool on 39 not out.

Back in Australia Ring showed his all-round talents in the 1951–52 series against the West Indies. He took 6 for 80 in the Brisbane Test and had innings of 65, 67 and 32 not out, going in late and exploiting lofted drives over the heads of tired fieldsmen. In 1952–53, he took 6 for 72 in the Brisbane Test against South Africa.

Before the 1953 tour of England McCool joined East Lancashire and in 1956, at the age of 40, began a 138-match career with Somerset. He hit 1,000 runs in a season four times in his five summers with the county, with 1956 his best season, producing 1,967 runs at 37.82. His leg-breaks brought 34 hauls of five wickets in an innings and two of 10 wickets in a match. His best analysis was 8 for 74 against Nottinghamshire in 1958.

After 251 first-class matches, McCool returned to Australia to become a market gardener at Umina, near Gosford, N.S.W. He grew a beard, became an authority on rare blooms, and taught his son leg-break bowling that allowed young Russell McCool to appear briefly for Somerset in 1982.

Ring returned to England in 1953 but played in only one Test. This time he took 68 wickets at 19.89. He retired at the end of the tour, having taken 35 wickets in his 13 Tests at 37.29. Like Wright with his run-up, he always appeared to have trouble deciding on what pace he should bowl, but he still managed a career total of 451 wickets at 28.41. Highlight of a career in which laughter was never far away was his last-wicket stand of 38 with batting duffer

Bill Johnston, which won Australia the fourth Test against the West Indies in 1951–52 by one wicket, and gave Australia the rubber.

'Were you nervous?' said Hassett, Australia's captain.

'No, we knew we had no hope so there was no point in getting nervous,' said Johnston, who had made seven of the winning runs while Ring scored 32 not out.

Success of Tich Freeman and Doug Wright for Kent and then by Bruce Dooland for Nottinghamshire overshadowed the consistency of other leg-spinners in county cricket, best of whom were the Warwickshire leg-break and googly specialist, Eric Hollies, and the skilful Worcestershire member of the group, Roley Jenkins. Both appeared to Australians to be far superior to Walter Robins or Freddie Brown and at least comparable with Derbyshire's Tom Mitchell. On his performances against Australia in 1948 Hollies must have been desperately unlucky not to have been preferred to Peter Smith for the 1946–47 Australian tour.

Hollies' moment of glory came when he was selected for the fifth Test against Australia in 1948 at The Oval. After Hollies' selection had been announced for this Test between 14 and 18 August, Warwickshire met Australia at Edgbaston from 4 to 6 August. Warwickshire captain Horace Dollery urged Hollies not to bowl his googly but to save it for the Test. Bowling leg-breaks and topspinners, Dollery took 8 for 107 in Australia's first innings, flighting the ball splendidly.

When Bradman went in to bat in the Test accompanied by sustained applause from the moment he passed through the gate, the England team gave him three hearty cheers to commemorate the last innings in a memorable career. Bradman played one delivery and was bowled playing forward to the next, a perfect googly. Before that final innings Bradman had a Test average of 101.39 and needed only four runs or a not-out score to maintain the century average. Hollies' googly left him with an average of 99.40.

Cricket writers who turned to an examination of Hollies' career were surprised to find he had been playing for Warwickshire since 1932, and that in 1946 he had taken all 10 wickets in an innings at a cost of 49 runs and finished the season with 184 wickets at 15.60. He was a sturdily built figure who sent down a lot of overs every season without tiring, more heavily padded than Grimmett but the same height at 5 feet 7 inches. Indeed most of the leading wrist-spinners of his time had been short— Grimmett and McCool, 5 feet 7 inches, Tribe, 5 feet 6½ inches, Mitchell and Robins, 5 feet 8 inches, with Freeman the smallest at 5 feet 2 inches. Hollies was well liked for his sportsmanship and good humour and had a Staffordshire accent that you felt you could cut with a knife.

After delivery of his famous ball at The Oval, Hollies continued his triumphant run when he bowled Warwickshire to their first championship in 40 years in 1951. He captained the county in 1956, when he took 132 wickets at 18.94 in what proved his final season. In a wrist-spin sojourn that lasted for 515 first-class matches, 13 Tests

Part-time wrist spinner Sid Barnes traps Indian captain Lala Amarnath for a duck with his topspinner in Melbourne in 1947–48.

and two overseas tours, Hollies took 100 wickets in a summer 14 times. His career total of 2,201 wickets is the Warwickshire record and is boosted to 2,323 by wickets he took for other elevens. He went into the Staffordshire team when he retired, before returning to the Birmingham League where he continued to take wickets well into his sixties. He died in 1981, aged 68.

Roley Jenkins' career, not as long as Hollies', was similarly rewarding. He regarded wrist-spin bowling as an art form and was prepared to put in the hours of practice needed to master it. His enthusiasm for the job lasted from the time he joined Worcestershire in 1938 as a 19-year-old novice to his retirement 20 years later after 352 matches for the county. Unlike today's bowlers who celebrate a dismissal with embraces and kisses and hand-slapping, he celebrated each of his wickets with a jubilant clap and a skip.

He was born at Worcester in 1918, youngest of a family of 10, son of a keen Midlands runner and pigeon-fancier. Six of his brothers were good cricketers. He joined a Worcester CC nursery for promising youngsters at 16, played in the county Second XI in 1937, and in 1938 made his first-class debut for Worcestershire against Essex, without getting a bowl. At his second appearance he was thrown the ball and asked to bowl to Yorkshire Test star Maurice Leyland, a renowned master against spinners. He clean bowled Leyland within a few overs, but on the threshold of a bright career although on a salary of £2 a week war arrived and he served for five years in the Worcestershire Regiment. Discharge in 1948 saw him back in the county XI.

By then his batting had improved enough for him to be classed as an all-rounder, a label he justified by scoring 1,356 runs and taking 88 wickets, including a century against Nottinghamshire at Trent Bridge and a hat-trick against Surrey at The Oval. The MCC selectors were impressed though they doubted Jenkins' confidence in himself. Freddie Mann did his best to change this by bowling him in minor matches leading up to the Tests in South Africa in 1948–49 and it worked. Jenkins played in all five Tests and finished the tour with 92 wickets.

Maturing rapidly, Jenkins took 183 wickets in 1949 in county matches and made more than 1,000 runs for the third successive season. He was full of what *Wisden* called restless energy and had a hat-trick in each innings against Surrey at Worcester. Tossing the ball high with a round-arm action, he demanded careful watching. There were always fireworks when he had the ball. He retired at 39 in 1958, with 1,309 wickets at 23.64 to his credit, after taking 100 wickets in a season five times, the nautical roll characteristic of his bowling intact.

The feats of all these wrist-spinners in England were completely overshadowed, however, by the appearance in Australia of a slow bowler with a completely new delivery, a ball developed in wartime games with fellow servicemen in New Guinea. This revolutionary ball, delivered with a bent finger tucked in under the ball, deservedly attracted just as much attention in world cricket as Bosanquet's introduction of the googly, and for a time seemed to offer slow bowlers the chance of adding a ball that made even great batsmen play the wrong way.

9

The Bent-Finger Ball

John Brian Iverson was a cricket innocent who burst onto the world cricket scene in 1949–50 at the age of 34, after a few brief outings for the Melbourne Cricket Club. He joined the club for a bit of fun after returning from service with the army, reasoning that he could do as well as the spin-bowlers he watched from the stands of that vast, cavernous stadium, the Melbourne Cricket Ground.

Just as Bosanquet's googly had developed from games of twisti-twosti, Iverson had a ball he was eager to try out on full-length cricket pitches that had been produced in games played on a ping-pong table. He had begun with table tennis balls, flicking the ball at opponents at the other end, with a finger of his right hand tucked in behind the ball. Later he tried it on the grass with other infantrymen using tennis balls. The idea was that every ball which the players got past their opponents scored a point and Iverson quickly found himself a regular winner.

Back in Melbourne after his discharge, Iverson tried the bent-finger ball with kids in the park. He held the ball between his right thumb and middle finger, which he used to propel the ball, and by changing the position of his thumb he could deliver leg-breaks and off-breaks and even googlies with little discernible change in his action.

He was 6 feet 2 inches and 15 stone and despite his utter lack of experience took 46 wickets at 16.52 in his debut season for Victoria, with all Australia's leading batsmen away in South Africa with Lindsay Hassett's team. There were no development programs at the time, nothing to prepare cricketers for the first-class game except their own powers of observation and occasional advice from retired players. There were reports that Iverson was so green he did not comprehend when the umpire asked if he wanted to take block first time he batted for Victoria. He was an indifferent fieldsman, a genuine No. 11 batsman, with only his newfangled delivery to justify his place in first-class cricket.

Hassett realised how raw Iverson was but the moment he saw him bowl on his return from South Africa decided Iverson was a potential match-winner. A noted player of all the slow bowling masters from Grimmett to O'Reilly, from Fleetwood-Smith to Cec Pepper, Hassett found himself playing the wrong way in the nets against Iverson when the 1950–51 season began. Word spread quickly on the Test players' grapevine about the threat of Iverson's bowling, but none of the stars from other states was concerned. After all, they had heard similar reports about Doug Wright and Jim Laker in the last series against England and had sent them packing.

With Dooland, Tribe, Pepper, Walsh and Grieves in England, nobody was surprised when Iverson was picked in the Australian team for the first Test against England in 1950–51. There were heated words in the nets, however, before the first Test when Hassett relieved Iverson from bowling when Arthur Morris and Keith Miller had their turn with the bat. Disgusted that Iverson was removed Miller called out: 'What is this, Lindsay? An Australian team practice? Or is this Victoria versus New South Wales?'

Hassett's protection of Iverson did not help England as the raw recruit took 4 for 43 on a traditional Brisbane 'sticky', setting up Australia for a 70-run win. At Melbourne in a close, tense match on a hard, dry pitch, Hutton, Washbrook, Brown and Close all had difficulty judging which way the ball would turn facing Iverson and Bailey confessed he was nonplussed by Iverson's high bounce and the amount of over-spin he put on the ball. Iverson took a further six wickets without England attempting to upset his rhythm, and in Sydney gave Australia a 3–0 lead and the Ashes by taking 6 for 27 in England's second knock. Five more wickets in the last two Tests gave Iverson 21 wickets in the series, an outstanding feat by a bowler who sustained a good length because no Englishman was prepared to hit him.

There was no such diffidence by Miller and Morris when they faced Iverson in the New South Wales v. Victoria match in Sydney, however, and they gave him a severe hammering. Aware of his cricket innocence, Miller took guard outside the leg stump. This confused Iverson and his 20 overs cost 108 runs.

Iverson made two further appearances for Victoria in Shield cricket after asking the Victorian selectors for time off to practise. He retired in 1951–52 after conceding 214 runs in taking five wickets at Melbourne against

Gleeson traps Geoff Boycott for 36 in the Edgbaston Test in 1968. He was a very difficult bowler to 'read' although he did not spin the ball a long way, just enough to beat the bat like this.

Queensland, when he was freely hit, and ever since has been judged as a spinner who could not take the hammering all sophisticated bowlers of his type know they must periodically accept.

Iverson's fate was unfortunate considering he took 157 wickets at 19.22 in fewer than four summers, including nine hauls of five wickets in an innings. Trevor Bailey, normally a fine player of spin, wrote in 1988: 'Iverson was a bowler nobody wanted to encounter for the first time. Along with my colleagues, I was unable to decide which way the ball would turn, and we never worked out a satisfactory method of dealing with him. I found him more difficult to face than Sonny Ramadhin. He never really recovered from the hammering Miller and Morris gave him and his first-class career was over before it had really begun.'

Iverson's bent-finger grip was copied by captivating bush cricketer John ('Cho') Gleeson, a telephone technician whose fingers were strengthened by his daily round of fiddling with hundreds of wires. He came into big cricket with a solid background, thanks to his tours overseas with the Emus, who regularly sent strong sides to Singapore, New Zealand, Malaya and Hong Kong. He was on the Emus' first two round-the-world tours as a wicket-keeper but Iverson's grip fascinated him and he mastered it bowling at trees in Tamworth parks, starting a few metres out and gradually moving out to cricket-pitch distance as his control improved.

Gleeson was born in the New South Wales country town of Wiangaree, near Kyogle, and always remained a countryman in his happy, homespun attitude to cricket. He took his nickname 'Cho' from his habit of disappearing into famous art galleries and churches to study art and architecture rather than sit around the bar. Team-mates saw him in 'Cricket Hours Only'. He never turned the ball as sharply as Iverson but used the bent-finger grip far more subtly, sometimes discarding it altogether to hoodwink batsmen awaiting his tricks.

When word of Gleeson's success with his bent-finger technique reached Sydney clubs, Western Suburbs approached him to join them but he finally went to the Balmain club in 1965–66 because Balmain—who got the money from their local Leagues' Club—paid his weekly air fares to and from Tamworth in the state's north. His postal worker's wage was too low to pay such fares. Balmain's enterprise paid off the following summer when Gleeson helped them win the Sydney premiership.

His performance for Balmain won him selection for New South Wales in 1966–67, ushering in a first-class career which lasted for 116 matches and ended in 1974–75. He took 430 wickets in that time, most of the dismissals leaving batsmen puzzled over how they came to misread him. He would have taken a lot more wickets had Bill

Below: The grips used by Jack Iverson, left, and Johnny Gleeson, right, were very similar, and both demanded long fingers. Both flicked the ball with the finger that was bent behind the ball.

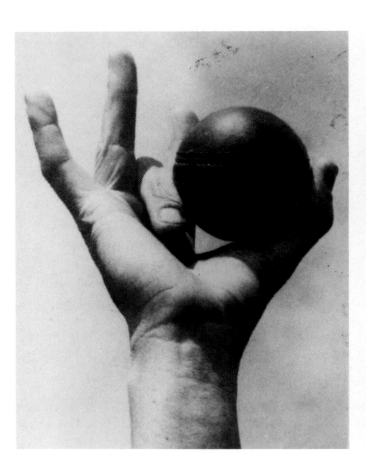

Johnny Gleeson bowling in England, where he had the handicap of a captain who lacked understanding of spinners.

Lawry, his captain on his initial tours to England (1968), Sri Lanka, India and South Africa (1969–70), shown a better understanding of his bowling. Too often Lawry's field placings were awry and he had a habit of taking his slow bowlers out of the attack immediately they were hit for a boundary or two.

Gleeson was happy at Balmain, for whom he took a wicket every five overs, finishing with 40 wickets at 17.03 in his first season. His 6 for 55 that summer of 1965–66 against Randwick included a hat-trick. In only his second season with the club he won state selection and topped the Sheffield Shield averages with 23 wickets at 18.22. This won him a place in the Australian team that toured New Zealand that year and in eight matches there he took 26 wickets at 28.61. By then every cricket clubhouse in Australia buzzed with theories about how best to play Gleeson.

He came into Test cricket late—at the age of 29 in December 1967—against India at Adelaide Oval. His Balmain team-mate Dave Renneberg had his career-best analysis of 5 for 39 in that match to clinch an Australian win. Gleeson did well enough to retain his place for all four Tests in that series, Australia winning 4–0.

He did well in England in 1968, taking 58 wickets at 20.65, but had only moderate success in the Tests. By then he had shown an ability to score runs late in the order and he was retained for the rubber against the West Indies in Australia in 1968–69. Against a batting line-up that included Kanhai, Sobers, Butcher, Nurse and Lloyd, he took 5 for 122 from 33 overs in the first Test, 5 for 61 from 26.4 overs in the second Test, 4 for 91 in the third Test, and 26 wickets altogether in the five Tests, which was by far his best series. Critics praised his part in Australia's 3–1 triumph, but said that his lack of deceptive flight placed him below Mailey, Grimmett, O'Reilly and the best Australian spinners.

Gleeson went off to Sri Lanka, India and South Africa in 1969–70 with less of an air of mystery about him, but still a fine all-round cricketer. Indian batsmen prodded and groped against him without making contact or had their snicks put down. This frustration increased for Gleeson in the face of some diabolical umpiring. In the match against North Zone when wicket-keeper Brian Taber held an edged catch from Gleeson, the entire Australian eleven appealed but the umpire froze. Two fieldsmen ran in from mid-off and covers to put the question to him again. Up went the umpire's finger. As the batsman disappeared the umpire apologised and said there was such a strong wind blowing it had taken time for the sound of the snick to reach him.

On the South African section of that tour Gleeson took 19 Test wickets in a soundly beaten Australian side (4–0). He retired at the end of that tour amid arguments about how many Tests he had played. The Australian Board of Control said it was 30 and paid him his Provident Fund money, due when players reached that mark. Statisticians around the world credited Gleeson with only 29 Tests,

however, pointing out that in the 1970–71 Test at Melbourne for which Gleeson was picked, not a ball was bowled because of rain. The ACB said the Test counted in players' record because the captains had tossed before play was abandoned.

Nobody could begrudge such a likeable cricketer whatever money the ACB paid him. Gleeson returned to South Africa in 1973–74 with Derrick Robins' international team, heading the bowling averages with 18 wickets at 20 runs apiece in his four matches. He liked the place and returned for a third time in 1974–75 for a happy summer with Eastern Province in the Currie Cup competition.

Technically, Iverson and Gleeson were not bona fide wrist-spinners because they achieved their deviation and spin with their fingers and not by rolling their wrists. But for a fascinating period they gave cricket a new delivery, although it was a ball which unhappily could not be bowled by anyone with small fingers. Both men had long, sinewy fingers and hands that could withstand the strain of the bent-finger grip.

Others who have tried it have damaged ligaments in their fingers and coaches should be warned that the method is for mature players only. The Sydney-born spinner Peter Philpott, always a deep thinker about his cricket, was attracted by the possibilities of the bent-finger method but badly damaged tendons in his hands in

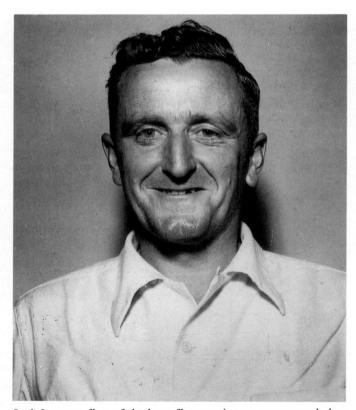

Jack Iverson, first of the bent-finger spinners, was regarded as a cricket innocent, rushed into Tests without any experience. He fooled great batsmen, but reacted badly to heavy punishment.

experimenting with it. This put Philpott out of cricket for a spell but he returned to win Australian selection, using orthodox bowling grips in all his eight Tests.

Philpott was a brilliant gully fieldsman, a first-class century-maker, and a clever leg-spinner who must rate as cricket's most nomadic player. He began in the Sydney seaside suburb of Manly, played for North Sydney Boys' High School with Ian Craig as his vice-captain, scored a century or took six wickets or more in an innings against each Australian state, coached in South Africa during English winters and, when League team duties permitted, ran coaching clinics in New Zealand and all over South-East Asia. Outside of cricket his skills as an English and history teacher earned him appointments at Sydney Church Of England Grammar School (Shore) and The King's School at Parramatta. At both these Great Public Schools he organised overseas trips for their best Rugby and cricket players.

He announced his retirement at the age of 29 without winning Test selection, but changed his mind and returned the following year to win a place in the Australian team that toured the West Indies in 1964–65. His 49 wickets in all matches remains the best by an Australian in the Caribbean, where he bowled with consistency and rare guile, and became Garfield Sober's hundredth Test victim at Sabina Park, Jamaica. He had his best Test figures, 5 for 90, in the Brisbane Test against Mike Smith's England team in 1965–66, but lost his Test spot after three Tests.

Philpott's 12 seasons in first-class cricket provided Australian fans with dozens of superb, diving catches, three centuries, and seven five-wicket hauls with the ball. At Test level his leg-spin bowling was clever, but seldom penetrative enough to swing matches. He quit in 1966–67 with 245 first-class wickets at 30.31 to his credit and 2,886 runs at 31.36.

His experience as a coach in South Africa, New Zealand and England proved of great value to Australia after his retirement. In 1978–79 he became the New South Wales coach and later became the first man to officially coach Australia in England. In 1980, when he had open heart surgery, it was discovered that he had always played with a weak heart because of rheumatic fever when he was a child. His coaching prowess, apparent in coaching clinics and instructional books, and in his work at Great Public Schools, won him the appointment as coach to the South Australian Shield team.

Philpott played in the Lancashire League in the 1960s when Australian leg-spinners dominated that competition. Wal Walmsley played for Stockport, Ken Grieves for Rawtenstall, Cec Pepper for Burnley, Radcliffe, Oldham, Royton, and finally for North Staffordshire. Pepper could be relied on for 100 wickets a season and his big-hitting made him the biggest drawcard in League cricket.

Gary Sobers said that when he played in the League while he was qualifying for Nottinghamshire, Pepper's all-round skills amazed him. Sobers rated Pepper at his best the finest wrist-spinner in the world, a rating confirmed by Pepper's former colleagues in the Australian Services XI. He was blessed with huge hands and rolled leg-breaks and googlies out of the back of his right hand at a brisk pace with rare accuracy. He had forearms like a champion axeman, developed chopping wood in the New South Wales country town of Forbes, 240 miles west of Sydney. He was an outstanding schoolboy tennis player when his family moved 50 miles to Parkes and the Davis Cup heroes John Bromwich and Adrian Quist advised him to move to Sydney after watching him play. He could get no assistance from Sydney coaching officials but found encouragement at the Petersham Cricket Club, thanks to Australian selector Dudley Seddon. For a time he lived at Sid Barnes' home.

Every morning before breakfast Pepper, Barnes and Ken Grieves went to the Petersham nets to practise. At night they practised on the road, using the space between tramlines as their pitch. When peak-hour trams drove them off, they retired to back lanes and played against wickets chalked out on the walls. Pepper was a natural games player, who took easily to skating, squash and golf, often appearing in charity matches with Barnes' mate, Norman von Nida. He was on a handicap of two at golf and had 16 matches for New South Wales behind him at cricket when he became a commando in World War II.

By then he was renowned in Australian cricket for his hitting. He could cut and pull strongly but driving with all the strength in those vast forearms and his 6-foot, 16-stone frame behind it was his special joy. Stories about Pepper bombarding the old galvanised roof of the Gabba dressing-shed in 1939–40 remain vivid among a lot of old-timers in Brisbane. At Petersham the former Test batsman Tommy Andrews often spoke to Pepper about the need to curb his natural hitting ability and settle down to long innings.

Pepper served with the AIF in the Middle East and New Guinea and when the war ended in England, played occasionally at Eastbourne for a services side stationed at High Wycombe. He took just 23 minutes to reach 100 for this eleven and, when the Australian Services team was formed, became one of the strengths of an entertaining line-up along with Keith Miller, Lindsay Hassett, Bob Cristofani, Jack Cheetham and Keith Carmody. Miller and Pepper together provided some of the biggest hitting ever seen on famous English grounds and half a century later English cricket buffs still talk of the 54 Pepper made to clinch victory at Lord's for the Services XI over an England side that included Washbrook, Hutton, Hammond, Robins, Gover, Doug Wright and Billy Griffith.

Norman von Nida had taught Pepper the value of the pound and, in a few appearances for Nelson in the Lancashire League, he was impressed by the match fees and the collections fellow players and organisers made for his big hitting and wicket-taking. The Services XI, with Miller and Pepper the outstanding all-rounders, drew the Victory Tests against England—two wins each and a draw—before playing their way through India and around the Australian states.

At Adelaide Pepper had an lbw appeal dismissed by umpire Jack Scott during Bradman's innings of 112 for South Australia, and had some forthright words to say about the impossibility of dismissing Bradman on his home pitch. Bradman, whose success in this match was vital to his comeback from injury, told Scott he should not have to put up with this abuse and Scott reported Pepper to the match organisers.

Cricket writer Dick Whitington, the Services' opening batsman, helped Pepper compose an apology to the Australian Board of Control but the board said it never received it. Pepper was aware of Bradman's influence with the board and when he missed selection with Miller in the Australian team that toured New Zealand under Billy Brown in 1946, he decided he had no future in big cricket in Australia. He took his new wife off to Lancashire where he appeared for Rochdale from 1946 to 1949, scoring 3,137 runs at 52.28 and taking 296 wickets at 10.56. In one innings at Stockport in 1946, Pepper hit six sixes and 17 fours in reaching 148, scoring his last 98 runs in 44 minutes.

He had five years with Burnley from 1950, helping them to the League championship in 1952, enjoying a whole new existence as the biggest drawcard in League cricket. His hitting became more subdued as he aged but his tongue remained sharp. Periodically critics called for his recall to Australia and his inclusion in Australia's Test side, usually when the lack of a classy spinner proved Australia's weakness in defeats. But the ACB never took the idea seriously, saying it had no eye-witness confirmation of players' good form overseas.

Pepper showed what he could do on a visit to India with a strong Commonwealth XI in 1949–50. He took 34 wickets in six matches at 15.94 apiece, including a hat-trick against Holkar at Indore, and had one innings of 95. His bowling in tandem with George Tribe was wrist-spin at its best. Umpires' rejections of his appeals, particularly when his flipper rushed on and hit batsmen's pads, multiplied, along with Pepper's noisy protests. After discussion with his team captain 'Jock' Livingstone, Pepper returned to England, though there were still 15 matches to play.

After he quit as a player in 1964 at the age of 48, Pepper became a first-class umpire, but he was removed from the Test panel following some characteristic expletives. He umpired several times in this period with countryman Bill Alley in matches that reached a high level of colourful rhetoric. He retired from umpiring in 1978 to concentrate on his prosperous packaging business in Rochdale and over the following decade became a wealthy man with a holiday home in the Riviera and new luxury cars each year. He died in 1993 at 77, his absence from Australian cricket in his great years as a wrist-spinner a tragedy for all lovers of the game.

One of Pepper's ardent admirers was the former England Test spinner Walter Robins, a bustling, lively cricketer who made things happen much as Pepper did. Robins could not spin the ball or bowl flippers like Pepper but he still managed 969 first-class wickets at 23.30 and 13,884 runs at 26.39. While Pepper was blasting sixes in League cricket, Robins served as chairman of England's selectors in London. Fellow selectors complained that when the cricket was dull—as it often was in England in the 1960s—Robins would absent himself from Test matches to go to the pictures in Leicester Square. How Robins must have pined for a little touch of the Pepper gusto.

Another Pepper fan was his old Services XI colleague Jack Pettiford, who played in the Commonwealth XIs in India and appeared in two of the Victory Tests in England. Pettiford played 16 times for New South Wales before joining the Australians in exile in the Lancashire League. He wheeled down his leg-breaks for Oldham and Nelson before joining Kent in 1954 as a professional.

Pettiford, who learnt his cricket with the Gordon club in Sydney, often rang me in London when Australia lost a Test. 'Why don't they get Pepper into the side?' he would ask. Pettiford took 194 wickets for Kent at 29.79 in his six years with the county but was always at pains to stress

New Zealand wrist-spinner Jack Alabaster, who between 1955 and 1972 took 500 first-class wickets at 25 runs apiece. He was at his peak in South Africa in 1961–62, taking 86 wickets on the tour.

that he would have taken a lot more with Pepper's flipper in his repertoire.

They were a fine bunch, Australia's cricket exiles, and had they stayed at home most of them would have figured in Test selection calculations. Apart from Pepper, one of the most impressive was Ken Grieves, who played 10 matches for New South Wales before he left to join Rawtenstall in the Lancashire League. Grieves scored 29 first-class centuries, one of them for New South Wales against Hassett's Services XI and the rest for Lancashire after he went into county cricket. Grieves was a marvellously dexterous cricketer who took 608 catches in first-class cricket. Every winter he kept goal for top English soccer teams like Bury and Bolton Wanderers.

Grieves' 22,454 first-class runs included three double centuries for Lancashire, top score 224 against Cambridge University at Fenners in 1957. His wrist-spin bowling was not as effective on soft pitches in the north of England as it was on hard Australian strips but he still managed 242 wickets at 29.78. He captained Lancashire in the 1963 and 1964 seasons and after he retired he was invited to join the Lancashire committee, a signal honour for a cricketer who was not born in the county.

Grieves toured India with the Commonwealth XI in 1950–51 and joined Pettiford and Pepper in his admiration for all the aspiring young Indian spinners he saw on that trip. Since India played her first official Test at Lord's in 1932 and her first at home in 1933–34, her international rating had been stagnant. But Australians had seen enough of Indian cricketers through the Services XI's tour at the end of the war and India's 1947–48 visit to Australia to indicate that better performances were about to come. With partition and the separation from Pakistan, Indian spinners started to play a major role in the outcome of Tests.

This was no surprise to the survivors of the unofficial tour of India in 1935–36 by the Australian side under Jack Ryder. In every match this team played they encountered bowlers eager to throw the ball high, roll their wrists and wait for dusty Indian pitches to produce bounce and turn that forced batsmen into mistakes. Arthur Allsopp, Wendell Bill, 'Stork' Hendry and 'Bull' Alexander were adamant that when India made her bid for greater recognition in world cricket it would be through the spin bowling, a style that suited India's hot climate and the Indian penchant for juggling and sleight of hand.

10

Cricket's Sorcerers

All Indian cricketers, Hindus, Muslims, Sikhs, Parsees or Christians, play the game with infectious enjoyment in stark contrast to the solemnity that often casts a pall over Anglo–Australian contests. Their best players are usually university-taught, nimble-footed, sagacious characters drawn from a small, privileged pool of the nation's 400 million people. They are resilient, smart with their hands, plucky, but have little chance to learn how to play fast bowling because in the steamy heat of Bombay, Punjab, Nagpur and the other cricket centres, to bowl fast is madness. Indian bowlers never court exhaustion with long approach runs but get to the crease with a hop, skip or bound, depending on trickery rather than pace to get wickets.

This was why three of the six men who formed the mainstay of India's attack on her first official Australian tour in 1947–48 were googly bowlers. The only genuine fast bowler in Indian cricket history, Mahomed Nissar, a tall, strapping Punjabi, had retired in 1942. India had to rely on 'Vinoo' Mankad, a personable 30-year-old Hindu who delivered orthodox, slightly round-arm left-arm spin off five side-on half steps, tossing in occasional leg-breaks; 39-year-old Muslim Amir Elahi, who bowled leg-breaks and googlies in short sleeves; and Chandrasekhar Sarwate, a 27-year-old Hindu fingerprint expert who spun the ball with a swirl of the wrist that made detection of his googly difficult.

Mankad, born on 12 April 1917, and christened Mulvartrai Himatial but always known as Vinoo, opened the batting or bowled long spells of left-arm slows as the situation decreed. He began his first-class career with Western India in 1935–36, and after coaching from visiting Sussex professional, Albert Wensley, made a striking international debut against Lord Tennyson's powerful English touring team, scoring 376 runs at an average of 62.66 and taking 16 wickets at 14.53 in five representative matches. This was the series in which an earthquake held up play during the match at Lahore.

Touring England in 1946, Mankad became the first Indian to achieve the double by scoring 1,120 runs at 28.00 and capturing 129 wickets at 20.75, including 7 for 146 from 67 overs in the second Test. On his first visit to Australia in a team lacking opening bowlers, he hit centuries in both the Melbourne Tests, 116 and 111, and took twice as many wickets as any other Indian. At Sydney in the first Test he made history by running out non-striker Bill Brown for backing up too far. He had rehearsed this dismissal in the India v. an Australian XI match earlier on the tour, when he warned Brown but did not appeal.

Only Ian Botham (21 Tests) has completed the Test double of 1,000 runs and 100 wickets in fewer matches than Mankad's 23. A few years later he joined a select band of 13 players, including Keith Miller and Wilfred Rhodes, on 2,000 runs and 100 wickets. He turned up at the Lord's Test in 1952 after securing special leave from his Lancashire League club, Haslingden, and without any practice with team-mates, made 265 runs (72 and 184) and took 5 for 231 from 97 overs.

Mankad made six overseas tours for India, appearing in 44 Tests between 1946 and 1958–59, and in between stints in the Lancashire League played for eight Ranji Trophy sides, Western India (1935–36), Nawanagar (1936–37 to 1941–42), Hindus (1936–37 to 1945–46), Maharashtra (1943–44), Gujarat (1944–45 to 1950–51), Bengal (1948–59), Bombay (1951–52) and Rajasthan (1956–57 to 1961–62). He was an enthusiastic member of the Commonwealth XI which appeared in festival matches from 1950 to 1958, and when he retired at the age of 45 he was acknowledged the greatest Indian all-rounder. He made 11,591 first-class runs at 34.70, top score 231, with 26 centuries. He also took 782 wickets at 24.53, best figures 8 for 35. His 231 came in a record opening stand of 413 with Pankaj Roy for India against New Zealand at Madras in 1955–56.

Mankad was a man of astounding stamina, who often bowled 40 or 50 overs in an innings and walked out to open the batting 10 minutes later. He was at the centre of the action in the field, too, taking 190 first-class catches. On the Australian Services team's Indian tour in 1945, Hassett's servicemen liked Mankad so much they all chipped in to buy him a wedding present. His son from that marriage, Ashok, appeared in 22 Tests, half his dad's total, but forsook googlies for medium-pace swingers.

Amir Elahi, Mankad's slow-bowling partner on India's

1947–48 tour, had played against Jack Ryder's side for the Maharajah of Patialia's XI back in 1936 when he took 6 for 164, imparting surprising turn and bounce on his googly. He was a great favourite before his home crowds because of his waggish antics, but found jokes hard to sustain because of the language problems. He was born at Lahore in 1908 and played all his 20 years of first-class cricket as an amateur.

He began in the Ranji Trophy competition in 1934–35 with Northern India at the age of 26 and later appeared for Muslims (1935–36 to 1944) and Southern Punjab (1937–38 to 1949–50). Neither of his tours for India (to England in 1936 and Australia in 1947–48) was successful but he achieved prominence through his performances in five matches for Pakistan in 1952–53. Amir Elahi took 513 first-class wickets at 25.77 but like Bombay wrist-spinner S.G. Shinde found Test dismissals hard to get. Elahi took several Test wickets in a career total of 230.

Chandra Sarwate, born in 1920 at Saugor, Vidarbha, India, was only 16 when he made his Ranji Trophy debut for Central Provinces and Berar in 1936–37. He was a genuine all-rounder who contributed runs and wickets to teams representing the Hindus (1941–42 to 1944–45), Bombay (1943–44), Holkar (1944–45 to 1954–55), Madhya Bharat (1955–56 to 1956–57), Madhya Pradesh (1958–59 to 1967–68), and Vidarbha (1968–69). He toured Sri Lanka with Holkar in 1947–48, toured England twice for India (1946, 1952), and made just one tour of Australia (1947–48). He found the jump from Ranji Trophy cricket to Tests difficult when bowling but succeeded with the bat. Altogether he took 494 first-class wickets at 23.54 but only three of them came in Tests at a cost of 124.66. He figured in a record tenth wicket stand of 249 with Schute Banerjee for India against Surrey in 1946, when he made 124 not out and followed this by taking 5 for 54 in Surrey's second innings.

For a time India's spin bowling duties were taken over by Subhashchandra Pandharinath Gupte, born in Bombay in 1929, a slightly-built leg-break bowler known through the cricket world as 'Fergie'. He bowled with rare confidence, flighting the ball cleverly, but was continually experimenting with tricks he hoped would deceive. He began in the Ranji Trophy competition with Bombay in 1948–49 and, despite an unimpressive start against England in 1951–52, when he was discarded after one Test, he won back his place in 1952–53 against Pakistan.

Gupte became an established Test bowler in the West Indies that year by taking 50 wickets at 23.64, 27 of them in the five Tests—good figures against batsmen like Worrell, Weekes, Walcott and Stollmeyer. He seemed to relish 40-over spells despite a frail physique and a high number of dropped catches off his bowling.

English Test veteran Trevor Bailey thought highly of Gupte, whose style he labelled classical and ageless. 'He was a beautiful bowler who never suffered from sore hands because his break was essentially the product of a superbly supple wrist,' said Bailey in *The Spinners' Web*. 'This explained why his googly was so hard to pick. His control was exceptional, especially for a bowler with the ability to achieve turn on plumb wickets and he was never content to be mechanical. He was forever varying his pace and trajectory, which was one of the reasons why so few batsmen were able to read the Gupte googly.'

Gupte was a sensitive fellow and when responsibility for carrying India's attack got too much for him, he was content to allow specialist batsman Chandrakant Borde take over with his leg-breaks. Borde, born at Poona in 1934, took 52 Test wickets but at a costly 46.48 runs each.

Sir Garfield Sobers said Gupte was the finest wrist-spinner he batted against and by far the best to have toured the Caribbean. Hanif Mohammad, who faced Gupte in the prolonged tussles between India and Pakistan, agreed with Sobers and rated Gupte the best leg-break and googly bowler he encountered. England batting hero Tom Graveney bracketed Gupte's bowling with Bruce Dooland's in Dooland's two golden summers with Nottinghamshire.

'Fergie' Gupte, the bowler with a 14-letter Christian name, enjoyed bowling long spells despite a frail, spidery physique and a curious little skip as he released the ball.

Fergie Gupte never toured Australia but he played three Tests against the 1956 Australians on their way home from a long tour of England under Ian Johnson. The Australian batsmen made him pay a high price for his seven wickets in those matches, although they were impressed by his googly in several long spells. He faced the West Indies again in 1958–59 and in the second Test at Kanpur became the first Indian bowler to take nine wickets in an innings. His 9 for 102 and 1 for 121 gave him 10 wickets in a match India lost by 203 runs. He retired in 1964 with 530 first-class wickets to his credit at 23.71, 149 of them in Tests at 29.55, and migrated to the West Indies.

'Baloo' Gupte, Fergie's younger brother by five years, was also a bowler of exceptional stamina who bowled splendidly flighted leg-breaks and googlies. He once bowled more than 100 overs in an innings for Bombay against Delhi, finishing this 1956–57 match with 15 for 302. Baloo took 237 wickets in Ranji Trophy matches at 22.41 but his Test appearances were restricted to three matches between 1960–61 and 1964–65.

The natural successor in the Indian team for Vinoo Mankad was a strongly built Sikh from Amritsar named Bishen Bedi, who in his prime probably was even more popular than Mankad. Bedi bowled in an assortment of colourful turbans or patkas with a high, classical action, using three fingers and his wrist, relying on teasing flight and variation of pace, and seldom trying the leg-cutter like Sonny Ramadhin. The Bedi wrist did not roll but was used to push finger-spun off-breaks through the air. He moved like a ballet dancer on the balls of his feet, pitching deliveries down outside right-hander's leg stumps that turned towards their off stumps in the manner of leg-breaks and for 12 years he was indispensable to the Indian team.

Bedi played in his initial first-class match at 16 and in the first of his 67 Tests at 20. He finished with 266 Test wickets, mostly taken in high-scoring matches at an average cost of 28.71. He was an outspoken character who had more than one nasty clash with Indian administrators. When Tony Greig let him have a barrage of bouncers in an England v. India match before restrictions on bouncers were introduced, Bedi's response was to get into the nets and rehearse bowling bouncers that he could hurl at Greig when he batted.

Bedi played for Northants in English county cricket from 1972 to 1977 and captained India in 22 Tests from 1975–6, winning six. In the Madras Test in 1976–77 he protested against vaseline gauzes used by English bowlers. At Kingston, Jamaica, he declared India's first innings closed as a protest against the West Indies' intimidatory bowling after three of his batsmen were injured. With three men in hospital, Bedi declared India's second innings closed at 5 for 97 when he and Bhagwat Chandrasekhar could not bat because of injuries sustained while fielding. All 17 members of the Indian touring party fielded at some time in the match played on a recently relaid pitch and on the fourth day Surinder Amarnath had to quit fielding

as a substitute to have his appendix removed. The West Indies won by 10 wickets to take the rubber 2–1.

Australians who saw Chandrasekhar in action in Australia in 1967–68 and 1977–78 could well understand Bedi's reluctance to risk sending him in to bat on a troublesome pitch. Chandra proved himself a consistent match-winner but was one of the worst batsmen ever to play Test cricket. He had ducks in each innings of a match, the feat known as 'spectacles' four times and in 58 Tests managed only 167 runs at an average of 4.07, which was only slightly inferior to his career batting average of 4.61.

Chandra, born at Bangalore in 1945, was lucky to play any brand of cricket, let alone Tests against all the major cricket nations. He had one arm withered by polio as a child and had to play with both sleeves buttoned at the wrists to avoid exposing his arms to sun. He was a handsome figure, always heavily bearded, just as his top-spinners and leg-breaks were heavily loaded. His brisk medium-pace deliveries popped and spun so much his wicket-keepers faced a major task just preventing byes, without executing stumpings.

He had the good fortune to bowl with Bedi and the right-arm off-spinner Erapalli Prasanna in support, and

Bhagwat Chandrasekhar, who overcame polio to become a wrist-spinner of world-class, and caused amusement when he took more wickets than he scored runs.

occasionally the fine off-break master Srinivasaraghavan Venkataraghavan, usually known as Venkat. In a variety of combinations these four bowled India to some big triumphs but it was always Chandra who was the most unpredictable and the most likely to produce the unplayable deliveries.

Chandra began his international career in 1964 at Bombay against England when he took 4 for 67 and 1 for 40 and had 10 wickets in four Tests. At Bombay the following summer his 4 for 50 and 4 for 73 was largely responsible for India beating Bob Simpson's Australian team when Norm O'Neill fell victim to stomach trouble and could not bat in either innings.

He made the first of his four visits to England in 1967, taking 57 wickets, 16 of them in the three Tests. In 1971 he took 50 wickets, with his 6 for 38 in England's second innings clinching India's first win in 22 Tests dating back to 1932. This ended England's sequence of 26 Tests without defeat and was her first loss in 20 Tests under Ray Illingworth's captaincy. Chandra was at the peak of his powers now and in 1972 he bowled India to two wins over England in India.

England won the first Test at Delhi by six wickets, despite Chandra's 8 for 79 in their first innings. Not to be denied Chandra set up victory in the second Test at Calcutta by taking 5 for 65 and 4 for 42 with Bedi taking seven wickets and Prasanna three. At Madras in the third Test Chandra had 6 for 90 and 1 for 69, Bedi supporting him with six wickets and Prasanna also taking six. The last two Tests were drawn, giving India the rubber 2–1, Chandra emerging with 35 wickets in the five-Test rubber, a record for India against all nations.

On his second tour of Australia in 1977–78 Chandra again went on a rampage, paving the way to India's wins in the third Test by 222 runs with 6 for 52 and 6 for 52, and in the fourth Test by an innings and two runs, by snaring 4 for 30 and 2 for 85. The fifth Test was a thriller which Australia eventually won, despite Chandra's 5 for 136 in the first innings, Australia taking the series 3–2.

That proved his last hurrah, for he was clearly in decline on his last tour of England in 1979–80 when India had a disastrous tour, winning only one match on the entire itinerary. Achilles tendon problems prevented his continuing after one Test on that tour and he retired in 1979–80 following a final season with Mysore-Karnataka to work in a bank. His career total of 1,063 wickets at 24.04, impressive as it is, gives no hint of what a difficult bowler he was to face on his home pitches with a ring of close-in fieldsmen. Tony Greig was one of the few to look at ease against him, exploiting his long reach to get down to the googly, which from Chandra was more frequent and turned more than his leg break.

Indian cricket has been littered with leg-break and googly bowlers who appeared full of promise on their own dry, dusty pitches, but failed to make an impact in overseas Tests, either through lack of opportunity or their problems with harder, faster wickets. Vaman Kumar, the Madras

One of the long line of Indian wrist-spinners, Sivaramakrishnan, who disappointed all devotees of leg-spin by failing to reproduce his devastating bowling in just one Test.

leg-spinner, took 25 wickets or more in five successive Ranji Trophy seasons in an impressive total of 599 first-class wickets at 19.98, but played in only two Tests, taking seven wickets at 28.85. Rakesh Shulka took 211 wickets at 23.14 in the Ranji Trophy, but did not appear in a Test despite four first-class centuries. Jayasinghrao Ghorpade, the Baroda leg-spinner, took 114 wickets, but had only eight Tests, despite hauls like his 6 for 19 for Indian Universities v. Pakistan in 1952–53.

Two Indian leg-break bowlers who have taken their opportunities, however, are Narendra Hirwani and Anil Kumble, both unlikely looking Test cricketers who first appeared wearing glasses. Hirwani, born at Gorakhpur in Uttar Pradesh in October 1968, made his debut in first-class cricket for Madhya Pradesh in the Ranji Trophy competition in 1987–88 and by the end of 1993 had taken 227 first-class wickets at 31.60. He had a sensational Test debut at Madras in 1987–88 when he took 8 for 61 and 8 for 75 to finish with a match analysis of 16 for 136

Anil Kumble, who has produced outstanding figures in the early 1990s with his wrist-spin. An unlikely customer who bowls in glasses, he has overcome a bad start in big cricket to become a match-winner on pitches that offer any help to his spin.

against the West Indies. But he was not a success in the 1992 World Cup competition in Australia, and Kumble has taken over as the No. 1 Indian spinner.

Kumble, born in Bangalore in October 1970, made his debut in the Ranji Trophy competition for Karnataka in 1989–90 and appeared in his first Test against England at Manchester in 1990. His figures (3 for 105 and 0 for 64) gave no indication of the dramatic triumphs he has since achieved in India, Sri Lanka and South Africa. He rushed to 53 wickets in his first 10 Tests and by his fifteenth Test had taken 83 wickets at 23.19, including five wickets in an innings five times.

Kumble's 21 wickets in the three-Test series against England in India in 1992–93 exposed deficiencies in the technique of leading England batsmen against wrist-spin just as forcefully as Shane Warne did on Australia's 1993 tour of England, although he did not have the benefit of television coverage of his bowling.

He began his triumphant sequence in Johannesburg in 1992–93 by taking 6 for 53 at Johannesburg, and followed with 6 for 64 against England in Madras, 5 for 70 against Zimbabwe in Delhi, 5 for 87 against Sri Lanka in Colombo, 7 for 59 and 4 for 69 against Sri Lanka in Lucknow for a match haul of 11 for 128, and 4 for 69 and 7 for 56 against Sri Lanka in Delhi in January 1994. His bowling has embarrassed the best batsmen from England, Zimbabwe, South Africa and Sri Lanka, and although he is only in his twenty-third year he appears certain to become one of the greatest wrist-spinners of all time if he can repeat these figures in England and against the West Indies, Pakistan and Australia.

The disappointment of Indian cricket followers over the recent performances of their Test team may quickly disappear with Kumble in such match-winning form. Thirteen months younger than Shane Warne, Kumble has overcome rejection by the Indian selectors after his Test debut at Manchester, a year in the wilderness, a torn ligament in his right thumb which had to be encased in plaster, and persistent charges that he does not turn the ball enough to be a great leg-spinner.

Kumble, who started his cricket education at school as a fast-bowler, laughs at the accusations that he bowls 'straight breaks'. 'I do not turn the ball as much as Shane Warne,' he says, 'but what matters to me is the taking of wickets.' Nobody can quarrel with that philosophy as Kumble boasts the best strike rate of all Indian bowlers. At Eden Gardens in Calcutta in December 1993 he took 6 for 12 as the West Indies collapsed to their worst-ever limited overs defeat. For a leg-break bowler to take six wickets delighted 100,000 Indian spectators.

Understandably, Pakistan had a frustrating time becoming established in world cricket. The nation created by the partition of British India in August 1947 made her first appearance in Tests in October 1952, and despite the efforts of accomplished cricketers, Abdul Hafeez Kardar and Fazal Mahmoud, found success elusive, but today thanks to a mixture of crafty spin bowling, efficient batting and excellent pace bowling, can face any cricket opponent with confidence.

This high ranking has been won partly by leg-break and googly bowlers Intikhab Alam, Mushtaq Mohammad, Sadiq Mohammad, and the masterly Abdul Qadir who, as Bruce Dooland did in the 1950s, restored wrist-spin to its rightful place as a match-winner when bouncer-happy pace bowlers threatened to make it extinct.

Intikhab, born in December 1941 at Hoshiapur, India, forced his way into first-class cricket in Karachi at 16 and held his place in a wide range of teams for the next 20 years. He made his debut for Pakistan against Australia at Karachi in 1959–60 and clean bowled Australia's Colin McDonald with his first ball in Tests. He was an opening

Kumble has England captain Graham Gooch stumped by keeper More at Calcutta in 1993, where Kumble rocketed to fame with a sequence of marvellous coups.

batsman at that time and it was not until the third Test against New Zealand at Karachi in 1964–65 that he established himself as a regular member of the Pakistan side by taking 7 for 92. He captained Pakistan in 17 of his 47 Tests, and was vice-captain of the Rest of The World XI in Australia in 1971–72.

Affectionately known as 'Inty', Intikhab had his most notable success in 1974 when he took Pakistan through the 17 matches of their English tour without defeat, the first side to achieve this since Don Bradman's 1948 Australian team. He played a dominant part in the three drawn Tests. Much of the experience he brought to his captaincy stemmed from his 232 matches for Surrey between 1969 and 1981. Through the 1970s he regularly showed the high quality of his leg-spin and googly bowling and the great value of his hard-hitting right-hand batting in the middle order.

In March 1973 Intikhab made 138 against England at Hyderabad, which included four sixes. He took seven wickets in that match. Two years earlier he had taken 104 wickets in an English summer for Surrey at 28.36. For most of his career he seldom played on pitches that suited his flighty back-of-the-hand style of bowling. The pitches in Pakistan were usually too slow, those in England too green. This was why he enjoyed bowling in Australia, where he achieved bounce as well as turn in the final stages of matches.

Intikhab played his last match for Pakistan in 1976–77, and his final first-class match for Brian Close's XI in England in 1982. Since then he has continued as a major force in Pakistani cricket as manager of touring teams, forming a successful brains trust with Imran Khan on several campaigns, notably in the 1992 World Cup win in Australia. Intikhab took 1,571 first-class wickets at 27.67, 125 of them in Tests at 35.95. He also made 14,331 runs at 22.14, averaging a handy 22.28 in Tests.

Mushtaq Mohammad was the most prolific of the five brothers who played first-class cricket, four of them in Tests for Pakistan. Apart from his wonderful contribution of 31,091 runs at 42.07, 3,643 of them in Tests at an average of 39.17, with 10 centuries, he had exceptional success as a leg-spin and googly bowler, taking five wickets in an innings 39 times on his way to a career haul of 936 wickets at 24.34. Only his lengthy periods at the batting crease prevented him reaching 100 wickets in Tests but his 79 dismissals at 29.22 were valuable.

Mushtaq, born at Junagadh, India, in November 1943, began his first-class career in Karachi in 1956–57, appeared in his first Test at 15 years 124 days, and hit 72 first-class centuries, highest score 303 not out. His 13 overseas tours included visits to Australia in 1972–73, 1978–79 and in 1966–67 on his way to the West Indies. Apart from his 57 Tests for Pakistan he had 262 matches for Northants.

Sadiq Mohammad, born in Junagadh in 1945, appeared in his initial first-class match at 14 years 9 months, if his date of birth is correct, when he turned out for Fazal Mahmood's XI in 1959–60. He played for Karachi from 1960 to 1972–73, for Essex (1 match) in 1970, for Gloucestershire in 193 matches from 1972 to 1982, for Tasmania in two matches in 1974–75, and for Pakistan in 41 Tests between 1969 and 1980–81. His 24,160 first-class runs at 37.51 included 50 centuries and a top score of 203. His leg-breaks and googlies brought 235 first-class wickets at 31.81, but he failed to take a wicket in Tests.

Despite their consistent dismissal of good batsmen, the Mohammad brothers never gave the impression they could demoralise an opposing side the way Abdul Qadir did in the 1980s. After a period when bouncer-happy pace bowlers had dominated big cricket Qadir gave spectators a taste of what cricket could be like without helmets, chest pads, arm guards and thigh protectors, and almost single-handedly restored selectors' confidence in picking leg-spinners.

Qadir's magic was not as appreciated in Pakistan as it was in England and Australia, where quality leg-spin has always excited cricket buffs. English critics welcomed his bowling even on days he bamboozled their Test team, for they were aware of the wonderful skill on view and the long hours of practice Qadir put in to achieve it. *Sunday Times* writer Robin Marlar labelled Qadir 'a weaver of dreams' and 'a caster of spells'. John Arlott applauded his authentic looping flight and well-disguised googly, tagging Qadir as a master of deception.

Qadir, born at Lahore in September 1955, was a stocky, fleshy figure with powerful hands and forearms who lifted entertainment to a high level as he bounced enthusiastically to the crease, spring in his heels, the next delivery all planned in advance. I sat with 'Big Bill' O'Reilly behind Qadir's arm not long before O'Reilly died and he was elated that he could not pick Qadir's flipper or googly. We peered intently at Qadir from our position high in the Sydney Cricket Ground stand, binoculars focused on Qadir's hand. 'Isn't it wonderful,' said Bill after a few

Abdul Qadir, Pakistan's eccentric wrist-spinning genius, rolls the ball around his fingers as he prepares to bowl.

overs. 'I can't pick him. I haven't a clue. What a great bowler.'

Even casual study of Qadir showed that he was a highly temperamental quirky character who required careful handling from his captains. He believed he did not get the consideration required under Wasim Bari, Asif Iqbal, Javed Miandad and Zaheer Abbass, none of whom could extract his best bowling from him. He still achieved phenomenal figures because of the vulnerability of star batsmen against wrist-spin. But under the shrewd handling of Imran Khan, unquestionably the best-ever captain of Pakistan, he was superb.

Experts have calculated that Qadir has six different deliveries—two different googlies, his regular leg-spinner, a flipper and two topspinners. His variations hoodwink gifted Test batsmen, but crowds love it. Changing the ball from hand to hand, he comes off his curling run to whip his arm over with a balanced follow-through, and he appears to enjoy his own noisy appeals as if they are part of his routine. His recent disappearance from international cricket following a falling-out with Imran is, one hopes, only a brief respite in a great career.

To tweak it the width of the pitch? Or just enough to beat the bat? Every wrist-spinner has the choice dependent

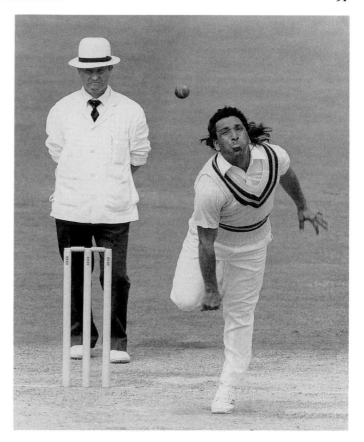

Two intriguing views of Pakistan's spinning freak Abdul Qadir. Right, he gets his tongue into play in this batsman's eye-view of his delivery; and left, a shot of Qadir from behind as he releases the ball, demonstrating how he adds fingers to the rolling wrist.

on his pace, the length of his fingers, the spread of his palm. Extravagant turn may occasionally make batsmen look foolish, but it is pointless unless it gets batsmen out.

According to Bill O'Reilly, widely acknowledged as Australia's greatest bowler, the wrist-spinner only has to turn the ball the width of the bat to take wickets if he bowls to an accurate line and length. One who followed this notion was Richie Benaud, son of a man who once took 20 wickets in a match with leg-breaks, but never in a distinguished career could be called a big spinner of the ball.

Richie Benaud giving the ball a powerful tweak as it leaves his hand in a Test match. Long hours in the practice nets paid off for Benaud, whose results were disappointing early in his career.

11

Coming up Diamonds

Richard Benaud, son of a schoolteacher who traced his ancestry back to a French family who migrated to Australia from La Rochelle, took a long time to achieve recognition as an outstanding leg-spin bowler and slightly longer to win acclaim as a captain. He seldom produced promising results on his tours to England in 1953 and 1956 and it was only on the third trip in 1961 that the benefits of his long hours in the nets appeared.

Selectors persevered with him despite all his early failures, which embittered the talented cricketers denied a similar chance. Any number of cricketers, but especially Ray Flockton, were put up as superior leg-spinners to Benaud in those lean early years. From his first-class cricket debut in 1948–49 in his nineteenth year until he finally delivered on Australia's South African tour in 1957–58, the whingeing about his continued selection in Australian teams persisted.

Neil Harvey, his close friend, but a realist aware of the anti-Benaud group's justified complaints, corrected the situation on his return from the 1957–58 South African tour, in which Benaud took 29 Test wickets, when he telephoned friends and said: 'Benaud is finally a great bowler'. Harvey's judgment was valid for the rest of Benaud's career.

On his way to becoming the first Australian to take more than 200 Test wickets and score more than 2,000 Test runs, it was hard to believe this was the cricketer who had scratched around on two extensive English tours. It was even harder to believe when he captained Australia with such subtlety and wisdom in 28 Tests that this was the bloke who scruffed about in the *Sydney Sun* business department checking on reporters' expense accounts while the management decided if they would train him as a journalist. They finally put him under the guidance of tough old police roundsman, Noel Bailey. Richie married Marcia Lavender while he was at the *Sun* and they produced two boys, Gregory and Jeffrey, before Richie's long absences on cricket tours destroyed the marriage. Richie took them all around England before his divorce on the grounds of desertion.

For most of the 12-year span which involved 63 Tests, 86 matches for New South Wales, three tours of England, one to South Africa, one to the West Indies, one to New Zealand and one to Pakistan and India, Richie was the hardest worker in cricket at the practice nets. He would be there wheeling his arm over in a high, fluent action when you arrived and you would leave him as darkness threatened still making the ball wobble as he rehearsed variations in flight and pace. Bruce Dooland taught him to bowl the flipper or the googly with topspin, requiring adjustments in his wrist action, and a heaven-sent gift as his career came to a climax. More important perhaps to his future was his decision to do the BBC course for budding commentators after his final tour.

Benaud's luck was legendary but cricket was lucky, too, that he became Australia's captain in 1958 when the game was in decline. His transformation from a shy, uncertain adolescent to a confident, aggressive leader gave him the leading role in an exciting cricket revival. He lost only four of his 28 Tests as Australian captain but it was the manner in which he achieved that fine record that was crucial to the game's prosperity. His teams attracted big crowds wherever they appeared, and tactically Benaud probably was never bested.

The sole criticism of his captaincy was that he was too lenient with team-mates who hugged bowlers or fieldsmen who had just made a dismissal, and many blame him for introducing the modern habit of embracing each other at a batsman's departure. Of Benaud's bowling, there could be no criticism because he always managed to take the vital wickets as matches or entire Test series hung in the balance. He was never as penetrative a bowler as Grimmett or O'Reilly, nor a great spinner of the ball like McCool or Warne, but he was a cagey schemer who could land the ball at will in the rough created by footmarks, and a close observer of rival batsmen's pet shots. He seldom bowled a single ball unless every fieldsman was precisely where he wanted him.

Len Hutton was scornful of Benaud's capabilities on Richie's first two tours of England and claimed there were 100 superior young bowlers in Yorkshire, but Hutton had to revise his views after Benaud's third trip in 1961. That was the tour on which England Test all-rounder David Allen gave his celebrated assessment of Benaud's luck.

'If Benordy stuck his head in a bucket of slops, he'd come up dripping in diamonds,' said Allen.

Richie Benaud was born at Penrith, N.S.W., in the foothills of the Blue Mountains, on 6 October 1930. His father, quietly-spoken Lou Benaud, bowled leg-breaks that imparted more top-spin than turn and earned him selection in the Sydney Combined High Schools XI. At 19, Lou Benaud became a legend among country cricketers by taking all 20 wickets playing for Penrith Waratah Club against St Mary's. Lou took 10 for 30 from six overs on the first Saturday, including four in successive balls in his fourth over. On the second Saturday he took 10 for 35 in 12 overs, clean bowling five batsmen and having three stumped. Local papers said he bowled occasional wrong-uns, but Lou's pace off the pitch was the factor which brought this 20 for 65.

Searching the record for other instances of bowlers taking 20 wickets in a match, sportswriters found another Penrith bowler, off-spinner Bill Howell. The beekeeper who 'made the ball buzz' took all 10 wickets for Australia against Surrey at The Oval in his first match in England in 1899.

The Benauds went wherever the Education Department decreed. Richie lived at Koorawatha until he was two years old, then spent five years at Jugiong, near Yass in southern New South Wales, where he practised in a concrete store-room adjoining the school where his father taught. Lou gave him his first bat at three and bowled to him with a tennis ball, and at the age of five Richie appeared in his first match for Jugiong Public School, scoring 11 runs.

When the family moved to Parramatta Lou rejoined Central Cumberland district club and in 10 seasons passed the 300-wicket mark. Two seasons later he reached 360 wickets, all of them in first grade. Meanwhile Richie attended Burnside School in Parramatta where he played in the Second XI at the age of seven, before going on to Parramatta High School. He captained the Parramatta High team to victory in the Sydney High school competition but had his skull fractured playing centre forward for the school soccer team.

At the age of 12 Richie became the scorer for Central Cumberland seconds and began taking his cricket gear to matches, fielding in emergencies, waiting for the off-chance that a team member would fail to show up. He batted at No. 11 when this finally happened and scored a single. In 1944–45, he played in the Sydney clubs' A.W. Green Shield competition for boys under 16 and in eight innings made 177 runs and took 20 wickets. This earned him a place in Central Cumberland's thirds in 1945–46 and the following season he hit his first century in an A.W. Green Shield match.

He impressed in his initial season in first grade in 1946–47, but at that time batting was his strength. He scored 347 runs in seven innings and his only wicket cost 190 runs. At 17, his bowling, modelled on Lou's basics of tight line and length, started to develop and at 18 he was chosen for the New South Wales Sheffield Shield team

as an all-rounder. Benaud's biographer, A.G. ('Johnnie') Moyes says that from the time Richie took over captaincy of Central Cumberland in 1953–54, the team won consistently while he was present but incurred their few losses when he was away with the state side.

The Benaud family became accustomed to Richie suffering heavy knocks. He went to St Vincent's Hospital in Melbourne after a bouncer cannoned into his face when he was playing for New South Wales seconds in 1949. Moyes lists broken thumbs, a cracked skull, a broken finger and a nasty cut in the mouth as the result of Richie's pugnacious outlook on batting. Dr Ian McDonald, who kept wicket for the Victorians when fast bowler Jack Daniel made a big dent in Richie's forehead, said he had never heard a more sickening sound than when that ball made impact. X-rays showed no fracture and the incident did not discourage him later from hooking at fast deliveries from Frank Tyson, Fred Trueman and Wes Hall.

Benaud's first big chance came when Keith Miller, an outlandish omission from Australia's team to South Africa in 1949, was flown over as a replacement when Bill Johnston was in a car accident. Benaud was promoted from twelfth man to take Miller's place in the state side. He made 68 against Victoria in Melbourne out of a 138-run stand with Jimmy Burke and 93 against South Australia in Sydney, but had few chances with the ball, taking only five wickets in the season for 270 runs. Most of the leg-breaks dispensed by New South Wales bowlers at that time came from the Randwick club's Fred Johnston, who in 36 matches for the state took 125 wickets at 30.59, with five hauls of five wickets or more in an innings.

Recognising that Johnston was a very useful leg-spinner, Richie bided his time. He missed New South Wales' first two Shield matches in 1950–51 but appeared in his first international match against Freddie Brown's visiting England team in the state's third match. In the first England innings Richie had 1 for 75 from 16.5 overs. He did not get a bowl in the second innings, with Johnston taking 6 for 100. He kept making a useful contribution with the bat but wickets eluded him and after three seasons of Shield cricket he had dismissed only 15 batsmen for 576 runs and scored 416 runs, figures which raised doubts among cricket fans north of Sydney Harbour about the sanity of the state selectors.

This bewilderment over the selectors' policies increased when they picked Benaud for the fifth Test against John Goddard's West Indian team in Sydney, after a run of indifferent displays in the 1951–52 season. Benaud made 3 and 19 but had the satisfaction of taking his first Test wicket when he bowled Alf Valentine to end the match.

When Jack Cheetham's South African team toured Australia in 1952–53 those who thought the selectors could not possibly persevere any longer with Benaud were disappointed. He played in four of the five Tests, scoring 124 runs in seven innings and taking 10 wickets for 306 runs. His Sheffield Shield form disappointed, too, and all he had going for him was his brilliant fielding and his pluck in taking nasty knocks—John Waite shattered his upper denture into dozens of pieces in the third Test and kept him out of the match for two days.

His luck held, however, and he went off to England with Hassett's 1953 side and in three Tests scored 15 runs and took two wickets at 87 runs apiece. His tour appeared an absolute disaster when he went out to bat in the final match at Scarborough. Traditionally, this match was always a carefree affair in which batsmen entertained with big hitting, but early on Benaud batted cautiously. Then Len Hutton made some snide comment about playing for a good average. The remark stung Benaud and he proceeded to give Roy Tattersall and Johnny Wardle a fearful hiding. He made 135 of the 209 runs added while he was at the crease, hit 11 sixes and altogether collected 102 of his runs in boundaries.

The 1953–54 Australian season began with a marvellous performance from the former Sydney leg-spinner Bryan Flynn, who had been developed by the Paddington club before moving to Brisbane to further his big cricket chances. Flynn, one of the spinners passed over by selectors who preferred Benaud, took 8 for 148 and 3 for 92 but never again approached this 11-wicket effort. Benaud was completely eclipsed, taking 1 for 102 and 1 for 76. Flynn was killed some years later in a tragic boating accident in Darwin Harbour. Benaud improved to finish that season with three centuries and 30 wickets at 27.73 each.

His lacklustre form continued in 1954–55 when he played nine innings for 148 runs at an average of 16.44 and took 10 wickets at 37.70 each against Len Hutton's touring England team. By now the critics of his continued inclusion in the Australian team had multiplied but he went off to the West Indies in the side led by Ian Johnson for Australia's first-ever Caribbean tour.

Surrounded by brilliant players, he lifted his performance and now for the first time showed Test quality. He dismissed Everton Weekes four times, Clyde Walcott three times, Collie Smith twice, and Worrell once, to head the bowling averages with 18 wickets at 27 runs each, and average 41 runs with the bat in Tests. At Kingston, Jamaica, when Australia made 758, he was one of five Australian century-makers with 121, reaching the 100 in 78 minutes after scoring 50 in 38 minutes, and overall he played a big part in Australia's 3–0 series win.

He returned to Australia an established Test player. In a New South Wales side that dominated the Sheffield Shield competition under Keith Miller's leadership he took 25 wickets at 26.80 in the 1955–56 southern summer, but in England in 1956 under Ian Johnson he was a major disappointment. His tour was rescued by an innings of 97 in the Lord's Test but in his book, *Way of Cricket*, Benaud confessed that he was out before he scored when he edged a Trueman leg-cutter. The umpire gave him not out, and Benaud won praise for helping Australia to her first win in England since 1948.

Benaud had progressed out of the business department of the old *Sydney Sun* to learn journalism under some tough reporters in police rounds. Some of his reporting was impressive and his growing reputation as a cricketer encouraged management to try him out covering big crime stories and the Billy Graham religious rallies. Ian Craig beat him to the captaincy of the Australian team that toured South Africa in 1957–58.

Craig helped restore Australian prestige on that tour following the retirement of Miller, Johnson, Hassett, Morris, Johnston and other stars, but he could not have done it without Benaud's skilful leg-breaks and classy batting. Australia were unbeaten in five Tests, with Benaud's 30 wickets costing 21.93 apiece. He created a record with 106 wickets in all matches at 19.40. Overnight Benaud found himself a match-winner with 100 wickets and 1,000 runs in Tests to his credit.

Wisden said: 'Benaud was the outstanding personality of the tour, enjoying unbroken success in batting and bowling. Adding the googly to his leg-break and topspinner he once more revealed the South Africans' dislike of flighted spin out of the back of the hand ... only in the first Test did he fail to cause chaos but he made 122 in this match and added another century in the fourth Test. His all-round skill was a major factor in Australia's success.'

Australia's long search for a quality left-arm spinner appeared to have been answered with the displays of blond Victorian googly exponent Lindsay Kline, who in the Cape Town Test on that tour became the first Australian in 45 years to take a hat-trick. From a run-up culminating in a high kangaroo hop, Kline spun out three tailenders.

Back in Australia Benaud had further good fortune when Australia had to suddenly find a captain to replace Craig, who had fallen ill in the winter with hepatitis. Neil Harvey, Craig's deputy in South Africa and the senior Test player, appeared the logical choice, particularly as Australian selectors had traditionally shunned bowlers as captains. Benaud's aggressive image won him the appointment against all the odds and he led Australia in all five Tests against Peter May's English team.

From the start he showed a facility for extracting important performances from key players. His bowling perplexed May, and Cowdrey and Graveney appeared reluctant to go for their shots against him. All the Englishmen showed concern at the pace of Meckiff and the swing of Davidson, but it was the Benaud wrist-spin that swung the rubber. His 31 wickets at 18.87 more than doubled his pickings in his previous 13 Tests against England (20 wickets at 40 runs each), his hard-hitting with the bat and his brilliant catching in the gully delighted even his former critics but the big surprise was his resourceful leadership.

Even with his place as Australia's captain assured, Benaud continued to spend long periods in the practice nets, and on the arduous tour of Pakistan and India in 1959–60 he was rewarded with 47 wickets at 20.19 in the

One of the greatest feats of wicket-taking in Test history, with Benaud hitting Peter May's stumps at Manchester in 1961. Benaud pitched into rough created by Fred Trueman's follow-through to bowl May round his legs and set up an Ashes-deciding triumph.

eight Tests, bowling Australia to victory at Dacca (8 for 111), Delhi (8 for 76) and Madras (8 for 86).

His crowning achievement came in the 1960–61 series in Australia against the West Indies. He now bowled the googly with confidence and splendid judgment to fully test gifted strokemakers Kanhai, Sobers, Nurse, Smith, Hunte and Worrell and used the topspinner with control. On good batting wickets the West Indians made him pay 33.86 runs each for his 23 Test wickets but Australia won an enthralling rubber.

The sight of Benaud bowling to such an array of batting talent helped attract 90,800 spectators to the Melbourne Cricket Ground for the second day of the decisive fifth Test. His nerve held even when Kanhai played his famous falling-down sweep shot into the crowd off the first ball of the morning in one Test.

Under Benaud, the Australians were fashioned into a confident, versatile team that could cope with mishaps, with each member encouraged to give his ideas on tactics at team dinners before each big match. Overnight Ken ('Slasher') Mackay had been developed into a handy, wicket-taking seam bowler who could close up one end or fill in for an injured strike bowler. Davidson's batting skills had blossomed to give the side all-round value from a superb left-arm medium-pacer. With keeper Wally Grout geeing them up behind the stumps, they became a memorable fielding side, with O'Neill and Lawry joining Harvey to give the eleven outstanding throwing arms.

They went off to England in 1961 with team spirit high but in the first match at Worcester Benaud developed fibrositis in his shoulder that forced him to leave the side to get treatment in London. With Benaud under treatment, there was a strange reluctance to use Lindsay Kline's left-arm wrist-spin, though he took 57 wickets on the tour, and without spin Australia struggled to gain the upper hand. Lawry's brave batting in the 'Battle of The Ridge' at Lord's gave them victory and a one-up lead in the second Test, but England levelled by winning the third Test, thanks to Fred Trueman, who had a spell of 5 for 0 in Australia's second innings. The struggle was decided at Manchester in one of the most remarkable Tests ever played, which Australians argue was decided by skill, Englishmen by Benaud's amazing luck.

Benaud was fit to bowl with freedom for the first time on the tour but in the first innings it was part-time leg-spinner Bob Simpson who took the honours, bundling out England's last four batsmen for 12 runs in 26 balls. Australia has a fascinating history of producing batsmen like Simpson who occasionally bowl valuable leg-breaks, including Arthur Chipperfield (65 first-class wickets), Don Bradman (36), Sid Barnes (57) and, more recently, Ian Chappell (176 wickets). Of these men picked primarily for their batting, Simpson's 349 dismissals is unsurpassed.

On the last morning Davidson and McKenzie, Australian heroes in the Lord's win with 13 wickets between them, came together after the ninth Australian second innings wicket had fallen at 334, leaving Australia with a lead of only 157. They put on 98 in a thrilling stand, Davidson taking 20 off one over from David Allen on his way to 77 not out. Left to score 256 to win, England were 1 for 150 when Benaud began his historic onslaught.

Realising that Australia could not force a draw, he set about bowling England out, dismissing Subba Row for 49 and then having the rampaging Dexter caught behind for 76. Pitching his leg-breaks into rough created by Freddie Trueman's follow-through, he bowled May around his legs, had Close caught in the deep by O'Neill and then had Murray and Allen superbly caught by Simpson in the slips. His spell of 5 for 12 from 25 deliveries gave Australia the Ashes and an astonishing win by 54 runs. The Australians applauded Benaud from the field, his 6 for 70 in 32 overs having swung a match England appeared certain to win.

Back in Australia after taking 61 wickets on the English tour despite his injury, Benaud found critics praising him for rekindling interest in big cricket through his fighting approach. The post-mortems dwelt on the need to develop spinners who could support Benaud, with critics stressing the role would be best filled by a left-arm wrist-spinner. Ian Quick and his Victorian team-mate Lindsay Kline had disappointed in England so the best prospects appeared to be Johnny Martin and David Sincock. Martin narrowly missed selection in the 1961 team to England and spent that northern summer playing for Colne in the Lancashire League, defying those who claimed he would not take wickets in England by dismissing 70 batsmen. Sincock played in the same South Australian team as Martin in 1958–59 when Martin moved to Adelaide to further his Test hopes. Both were highly praised by the West Indian tourists in 1960–61, but both lacked the control required in left-arm googly bowlers.

Martin, a postman from Burrell Creek, near Taree, N.S.W., showed his enthusiasm by travelling overnight in the train to Sydney to appear every Saturday for Petersham–Marrickville in the Sydney club competition. He was a joy to spectators because of his habit of hoisting big sixes into the stands. He became one of the biggest hitters in first-class cricket when he made his debut for New South Wales in 1956–57 and despite limited opportunities took wickets consistently. His 45 wickets in the 1959–60 Sheffield Shield competition was the best haul for 10 years and attracted an offer to transfer to South Australia.

However, he was back in the New South Wales side in 1959–60 and in 1960–61 made his Test debut against the West Indies at Melbourne when he made 55 in 70 minutes in a 97-run partnership with Slasher Mackay. His first wickets in Tests—Kanhai, Sobers and Worrell—were sent back in four balls. His bowling proved too erratic for him to enjoy a long Test career but he toured England (1964), Pakistan and India (1964–65), South Africa (1966–67) and had two trips to New Zealand (1956–57 and 1959–60) with Australian teams. His eight Tests brought only 17 wickets

at 48.94, but in all first-class matches he had 445 wickets at 31.17.

Martin's popularity stemmed from a cheery nature. He cared little for statistics and never knew how many wickets he took but he could describe his six-hits at length. He made his only visit to England in 1964 in Bob Simpson's Australian team but was not used in Tests as the 35 wickets he took on tour were regarded as a little expensive at 32.62 apiece. He had better luck in South Africa in 1966–67 when he forced his way into the fifth Test with some outstanding hauls in minor matches, including 7 for 30 against Griqualand West. In this and in Tests against India and Pakistan he could never recapture the magic of his first three wickets in his Test debut. He died in 1992 at 61, after a long history of heart complaints which caused former team-mates to open a fund to help him pay his medical bills.

Sincock, born in North Adelaide in February 1942, began playing cricket in the backyard of his parents' house in the suburb of Plympton. His father, Harold Sincock, had played a few matches for South Australia in the 1930s and coached David, a natural games player who won prizes in baseball and had an outstanding scholastic career at Glenelg Sacred Heart College. Team-mates nicknamed him 'Stumps' when he began studies in dentistry at Adelaide University. Four Sincocks played for South Australia and his father's cousin Russell played for Victoria.

When David was invited to bowl to the touring West Indians in the Adelaide Oval nets in 1961, he stunned Frank Worrell's men by clean bowling four of their best batsmen, Kanhai, Hunte, Sobers and Worrell. 'He's the best left-hand googly bowler in Australia,' said Worrell. 'We just can't pick him. We can't understand why he is not playing for South Australia. If he's not playing for Australia within a couple of years, then I'm a bad judge.' Kanhai told reporters he was amazed by the amount of spin Sincock imparted to the ball. 'I get them in the middle, but they just slide off,' he said.

Sincock was picked for South Australia a week after this highly praised net display against the West Indies at the age of 19. Within a year noted critic Ray Robinson advocated his inclusion in the Australian team against Ted Dexter's touring England team. Robinson made this suggestion after watching the Englishmen flounder against Richie Benaud's spin in the first Test at The Gabba in 1962–63. Robinson said:

'The addition of Sincock's spin would increase England's worries left by Richie Benaud bowling for New South Wales and Australia. Though erratic and liable to punishment, Sincock has proved his ability to take the wickets of top batsmen. We would see some strange strokes as the Englishmen try to cope with his exceptional spin. Every time Sincock's left hand lands the ball on a good length it is a potential wicket-taker, and can be answered only by top quality footwork which the Englishmen are not trained to produce. None of the Englishmen have seen him and his selection would have big surprise-packet value.'

Sincock had played 10 first-class matches at that time and taken 50 wickets, most of them top-order batsmen— an entry into first-class cricket that recalled the early inroads made by Fleetwood-Smith, Bill O'Reilly and Jack Iverson. Robinson's proposal, made after he had seen all the English batting stars flounder against Johnny Martin and Richie Benaud on the Sydney Cricket Ground, where Benaud had his best-ever first-class bowling analysis of 7 for 18, was not followed by selectors, despite the English batsmen's astonishment at the ability of Benaud and Martin to turn the ball from six to 12 inches. Denys Rowbotham writing in *The Guardian* said England's batting, long weak against leg-breaks and googlies, had been timidly footbound and frail in its judgment against Benaud and Martin.

Australia's selectors ignored Sincock for the Tests against England, apparently because of his youth, but he made his international debut in March 1962, for South Australia against the visiting New Zealanders on Adelaide Oval. Ian Chappell, an 18-year-old leg-spinner unknown outside Adelaide, made his debut in the same match at the suggestion of West Indian Garfield Sobers. Chappell did not get a bowl but Sincock confirmed his promise by taking 6 for 54, bundling the New Zealanders out for 129 with some prodigious breaks.

Sincock, an ambidextrous fellow who wrote his university essays right-handed, loaded more spin on the

Ian Chappell, an aspiring wrist-spinner when he first came into big cricket, shows his style in a practice session.

ball with a wriggle of his body and a twist of his left wrist than any bowler Australians had seen since George Tribe, just after World War II. Vic Jackson, Arthur Mailey and others thought he imparted as much spin as the freakish left-hander Fleetwood-Smith. Spinning the ball developed huge calluses inside the knuckle of his third finger and alongside the forefinger nail, which he treated after lengthy bowling spells with a chemical mixture passed on by Richie Benaud.

Benaud's habit of providing exciting Test cricket ended in the dull 1962–63 series against Ted Dexter's England team, neither captain showing any desire to prevent three tame draws. The following summer he led Australia for the last time in the first Test against Trevor Goddard's South Africans. He handed over to Bob Simpson after scoring his two-thousandth Test run and taking his two-hundredth Test wicket in the Test in which umpire Col Egar no-balled Ian Meckiff four times for throwing. Benaud played the last three Tests of the rubber under Simpson and then retired.

Right to the end of his 63-Test career, Benaud drove himself hard in the nets and he deserved every one of his 945 first-class wickets. He was never a great spinner of the ball, and only as he approached his fiftieth Test and acquired the flipper did he become a match-winning bowler in the class of Mailey, Grimmett and O'Reilly, but he lifted a demoralised Australian team from decline and in the process restored all international cricket as a public entertainment. His 248 Test wickets at 27.03 each was an Australian record until Dennis Lillee took it to 355 (at 23.92), but it was Benaud's imaginative captaincy that benefitted cricket most. He took 10 wickets in a Test once, and 16 times had five wickets or more in an innings, best effort 7 for 42. He made 23 first-class centuries, three of them in Tests, and many of his 254 catches (65 in Tests) will long be remembered.

At 36, Benaud married Daphne Surfleet, a former secretary to the guru of English cricket writers, E.W. Swanton, and together they built a prosperous public relations company, culminating in their contract with Packer's World Series Cricket rebels. Despite a flat, humourless style and a limited vocabulary, he has become a household name, bobbing up as regularly as tax returns.

Benaud's success in 1961 encouraged selectors to continue the Australian tradition of sending successful leg-spinners to England, and in 1964 they included Reginald Hugh Durning ('Rex') Sellers in Bob Simpson's team. Sellers, born in 1940 at Bulsar, a tiny siding on the Bombay coast of India while his father worked there with the railways, migrated to Australia with his parents after the partition of India in 1947. Sellers boarded at King's College (now Pembroke College) in the Adelaide suburb of Kensington and when he finished school joined the Kensington club.

He made his debut for South Australia in 1959 but his results were disappointing until the 1963–64 season when he took 48 wickets in Sheffield Shield matches, three times

Wrist-spinners need to field well off their own bowling. Here Richie Benaud covers metres to his left to catch England's Peter Richardson in Brisbane off his own bowling in 1958–59.

taking five wickets in an innings. This clinched a spot in the team for England but before he left Prime Minister Bob Menzies had to virtually arrange Australian citizenship for him overnight, to avoid any doubts in England over his eligibility to play for Australia.

The tour proved a disaster because of a cyst on the tendon of his spinning finger—the third finger of his right hand—but even after this was removed he could not properly grip the ball in the cold English climate. Only when conditions warmed up did he settle to regular bowling and in the final weeks of the tour he took 30

wickets at 37.66. On the way home to Australia, he played in his sole Test in Calcutta, but bowled only five overs. The operation to his hand had not been fully successful and he retired after he arrived home.

Rex Sellers had a long spell as a South Australian selector and with his brother, Basil, remains an enthusiastic supporter of the Australian Test team. In the 1990s they sponsored a special clinic for fast bowlers, which Dennis Lillee conducted with Australian Cricket Academy chief Rod Marsh in a bid to solve the problem of Australia's lack of genuine pace bowlers.

12

Nervous John

Just as Benaud's flipper lifted him above orthodox leg-spinners like Victorians Jack Hill and John Wildsmith, Queenslander John Mackay, South Australian Jack Wilson, and the Sydney spinners Bob Roxby and Russell Waugh, David Sincock's googly put him in a class above other left-arm spinners. He was a bowler with the potential to win a Test in two overs or, at worst, to lose it in three. Only superlative fielding kept Sincock's outlay down to four runs an over in his Test debut against Pakistan, but his four wickets included Hanif Mohammad, whose 499 for Karachi against Bahawalpur in 1958–59 was the world's record first-class score until Brian Lara lifted it to 501 not out in 1994.

Sincock's freakish spin surprised batsmen but it also made field placements to his big googlies essential to his success. Experts found it very refreshing when the national selectors gambled by including him in the Australian team that toured the West Indies in 1965, but with orthodox right-arm leg-spinner Peter Philpott in the side and his own leg-breaks to fall back on, captain Bob Simpson did not call up Sincock until the fifth Test. Sincock took 4 for 143, after a dramatic start when he clean bowled his admirer and former South Australian team-mate Gary Sobers.

Sincock moved to Sydney to join the Randwick club in 1966–67 after appearing in his third and last Test in January 1966, against England, when his 20 overs cost 98 runs without bringing a wicket. By then it was clear that the gamble on him maturing into a consistent match-winner had failed, although the width of his spin continued to surprise batsmen. He retired in 1973. His brother Peter joined the South Australian team briefly in 1974–75, eager to uphold the family reputation for bowling quality wrist-spin but had to quit because of business commitments. This left the task of supplying leg-breaks for South Australia to Ian Chappell and Terry Jenner.

Ian Chappell was first selected to play for Australia as an all-rounder. He dismissed 176 batsmen in first-class cricket with a mixture of leg-breaks and topspinners, but at an average cost of 37.57 his wickets were expensive and he only once took five wickets in an innings. The demands of batting and captaincy gradually took up his time and allowed him to spend less time rolling his arm over at the bowling crease.

Chappell was Australia's captain when the Newcastle truck driver John Russell Watkins joined the side for the 1972–73 Australian tour of the West Indies, on the slim credentials of 10 wickets in five first-class matches. Watkins' selection was comparable with a 100-to-1 longshot winning the English Derby or Melbourne Cup, with most critics expecting the more accomplished Kerry O'Keeffe to be more suited to the spinning chores vacated by Ashley Mallett.

Watkins took time off from his job of delivering vegetables to take 6 for 38 at Newcastle, his birthplace, against the touring Pakistan side in December 1972. On this performance for Northern New South Wales he was picked for the third Test against Pakistan at Sydney a month later. He gave a warning of what was to come a week before the Test when he gave an erratic display for New South Wales in a Sheffield Shield match, bowling full tosses and wides that kept wicket-keeper Brian Taber on the hop.

Medium-pacer David Colley asked Taber if the pitch was taking spin. 'Don't know about the one we're playing on, but Watkins should be right for the Test,' said Taber, pointing to the adjoining pitch. 'He's getting turn out of *that* wicket.'

Watkins was so nervous in the Test it was difficult to assess if he could spin the ball. He bowled several wides in his six overs without taking a wicket, but with the bat made 36 not out in an 83-run ninth-wicket stand with Bob Massie, which contributed to Australia's 52-run win. The selectors stuck with him when they chose the team for the West Indies, but even with fellow leg-spinner Ian Chappell as his sympathetic captain he could not conquer his nerves long enough to settle down to bowling accurately. He played in only four matches on the tour, taking 10 wickets at 33.60, and disappeared from first-class cricket on his return home.

Watkins' abject failure left Jenner and O'Keeffe to provide all the spin in Tests in the West Indies, where Peter Philpott had been successful with leg-breaks on the

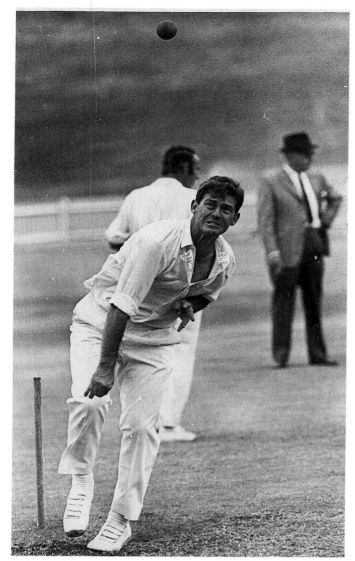

John Watkins, whose nervousness never left him out on the field in big matches. He won a West Indian tour with one outstanding performance which he was never able to repeat.

Kerry O'Keeffe bowled for Somerset and Australia with this distinctive action, thrusting his left arm across the body, right arm tucked into the midriff. He seldom turned his leg-break or googly much and some critics rated his off-spinner his best ball.

previous Australian tour in 1965, on pitches where Bedi, Prasanna and Venkat had set up victory for India two years earlier. O'Keeffe bowled with his wrist cocked well before he released the ball but usually turned his off-breaks more than his leg-spinners. Jenner was a seasoned right-arm leg-break bowler, with a splendid googly, who had earned his tour place with a series of impressive coups for South Australia.

Jenner began in club cricket for Mount Lawley, his birthplace, in the same team as Ashley Mallett. He found it hard to get a bowl when he broke into the Western Australian team in 1963–64, largely because of the presence of the leading English spinner Tony Lock. He made centuries with the bat but Lock did not give him the long spells Jenner felt were needed to develop his bowling and when Tony Mann began to take wickets regularly for Western Australia with leg-spin, Jenner

decided to move to South Australia. He and Mallett made the switch together in 1967–68.

Both won places in the South Australian team in their initial season in Adelaide. Prolonged spells did wonders for their bowling. Jenner's control and turn improved and his googly began to become a valuable weapon. On the Australian B team's New Zealand tour in 1969–70, Jenner was the most successful bowler with 32 wickets at 19.53. He made his Test debut in 1970–71 against England at Brisbane and in two Tests that summer took six wickets at 29.33 apiece. He was the tail-ender whom John Snow flattened with a bouncer in the Sydney Test. This incident caused Ray Illingworth to lead England from the field in protest at a demonstration that saw beer cans and fruit bounce around Snow.

Jenner took 13 Test wickets at 26.69 in the West Indies, including 5 for 90 in the fifth Test at Port-of-Spain, and 36 wickets at 28.50 on the entire tour. This was far superior to O'Keeffe's effort of 6 Test wickets at 50.50 and a tour bag of 20 wickets at 37.15.

Back in Australia, critics who had written off Jenner and O'Keeffe as potential match-winners started to admire the young left-arm wrist-spinner from Sydney's Waverley club, David Hourn. England's lanky Test all-rounder Tony Greig joined Hourn's fans when he returned from England for a season with Waverley, predicting that Hourn would become a famous Test bowler. Like Sincock, Hourn bowled occasional deliveries that made Test batsmen look inept. The ball hummed through the air on its way towards batsmen who had difficulty predicting the direction in which it would turn, but he had Sincock's problem of losing control of his action. In one Sydney grade match, Hourn bowled 26 no-balls, an absurd count for a slow bowler.

Hourn first appeared for New South Wales in 1970–71 and over the next 10 seasons took 161 wickets for the state without securing a Test berth. Part of his problem was over-stepping, which sapped his confidence, and periodically cost him his state spot. He still managed to take five wickets in an innings 11 times for New South Wales and twice took 10 wickets in a match. His best analysis was in Sydney against Victoria in 1978–79 when he took 9 for 77 and narrowly missed taking all 10, finishing with 11 for 172 from the match. He also had 12 for 113 against South Australia in 1977–78.

Crippled by a touch-football injury, he became almost immobile on the field, hobbling about on knees that did not respond to surgery. He was a complete duffer with the bat, averaging 6.32 in 52 first-class innings and holding only 12 catches in his 41 matches.

Hourn was more successful with the bat, however, than the long-serving Victorian right-arm wrist-spinner Jim Higgs, who managed to get through an entire English tour without scoring a run. Higgs bowled from an economical run, favouring the angled approach used by most spinners. He bowled the googly and leg-break and had a most unusual flipper, a delivery which skidded from the pitch and brought many mis-hits from batsmen attempting to pull what appeared to be short deliveries.

Higgs, born at Kyabram, Victoria, in July 1950, forced his way into the Victorian team in 1970–71 from the University club and soon learnt that on unresponsive pitches he usually had to wait to the last day to get a long bowl. He was an automatic selection for Victoria for the next 12 seasons. In that time he had some richly satisfying last-day hauls. When Victoria won their twenty-fourth Sheffield Shield in 1979–80, for example, it was Higgs' leg-spin that brought success on the last day against South Australia. With Ian Chappell in a threatening mood at lunch, South Australia appeared the likely winners, but Higgs dismissed Chappell quickly and finished with 6 for 57 off 20 overs to wrap up the Shield.

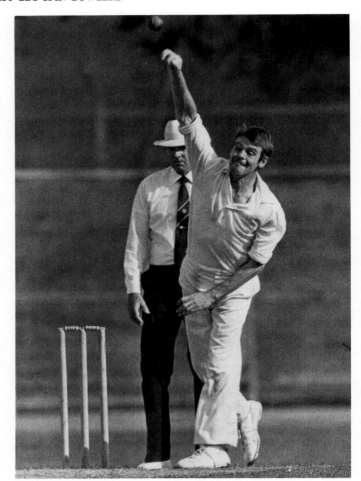

Long-serving Victorian leg-spinner Jim Higgs despatches another delivery. Higgs once toured England in an Australian team without scoring a run but delivered plenty of interest with the ball.

Higgs made three overseas tours with Australian teams. He clinched the first to England in 1975 under Ian Chappell's captaincy when he took 11 for 118 for Victoria against Western Australia just before the side was announced. Chappell only required him for eight first-class matches on this tour with Lillee, Thomson and Bob Massie dominating Australia's attack. He went to the West Indies in 1978 in the team led by Bob Simpson, when the Australians who signed to play for Kerry Packer's World Series Cricket were unavailable, and found himself forming the spin attack with Western Australia's Bruce Yardley. Higgs played in four of the five Tests and took 15 wickets at 25.60.

Higgs and off-spinner Yardley again exposed the West Indians' vulnerability against spin in minor matches but this was probably due to the absence of Packer's West Indian stars after the second Test. Bowling in tandem against Jamaica, Higgs and Yardley took 15 wickets between them to set up Australia's two-wicket win. At Port-of-Spain they had 12 wickets between them in Australia's six-wicket victory.

On his final overseas tour, to India in 1979, when Australia went without a win in 11 matches under Kim Hughes' captaincy, Higgs began splendidly with 7 for 143 in the first Test at Madras, suffering only from Kapil Dev's hitting late in the innings. Thereafter all India's leading batsmen mastered him, but in heat and monsoonal weather his 29 wickets from the tour at 32.86 was a satisfactory result.

The Packer revolt gave Higgs the chance to make 22 Test appearances during which he took 66 wickets at 31.17. He was much more at home playing for Victoria, for whom he took the majority of his 399 first-class wickets at 29.66, 19 times taking five wickets in an innings, best figures 8 for 66. He held only 43 catches in 122 first-class matches and his 399 wickets was 15 more than his run total. Since his retirement at the end of the 1982–83 season after 83 matches for Victoria Higgs has been a national selector.

One of the cricketers favoured by Higgs and his colleagues was the Queenslander Trevor Hohns, a smart left-handed batsman and right-arm leg-break bowler. Hohns was a long time attracting their eye, however, for he made his first-class debut in 1972–73 and did not win Test selection until 1988–89 when he appeared in the last two Tests against Clive Lloyd's West Indian tourists. In the 15 seasons of big cricket before his Test selection Hohns steadily improved both his bowling and batting but he was not rated one of Australian cricket's valuable assets when he toured South Africa with Kim Hughes' rebels in 1985–86 and 1986–87. The two rebel seasons accelerated his improvement, however, and on the second tour he took 33 wickets in his nine matches at 24.81, against some of the hardest hitting batsmen in world cricket.

By the time Hohns was picked for Australia's 1989 tour of England with Allan Border's team he was a fine player and his all-round skills made him a valuable player in five of the six Tests. He held vital catches, contributed very handy runs in the middle order, but most importantly, bowled his leg-breaks and googlies with great accuracy, breaking up threatening partnerships and preventing all chance of England regaining supremacy after Australia's strike bowlers tired. He did not attact the praise received by Mark Taylor, Dean Jones, Steve Waugh, Terry Alderman, Geoff Lawson and others in Australia's 4–0 win but his performances certainly merited it.

Hohns was persuaded to postpone his retirement for one season to captain Queensland's Sheffield Shield team in 1989–90. He quit with a career total of 5,210 runs at 27.13, which included 32 innings of 50 or more and 288 wickets at 35.90 which included 11 five-wicket hauls.

Hohns' dramatic improvement in the twilight of his career snuffed out a promising return to Test cricket by South Australia's talented right-hand batsman and leg-spinner, Peter Sleep. He made his first-class debut in 1976–77 from the Kensington club in Adelaide, where he received handy tips from Rex Sellers. He was 19 and an exciting spin bowling prospect because of the turn he imparted on hard pitches.

Sleep, born at Penola in May 1957, appeared in his first Test at Melbourne in March 1979, 18 months after his entry into big cricket, but he was discarded after one appearance in which his two wickets cost 78 runs. A solid performance in Shield matches—38 wickets at 22.26 and 495 runs at 35.35—won him selection later that year in the Australian team which toured India. He failed to take a wicket in his two Tests but selectors stuck with him for Australia's 1982–83 tour of Pakistan. Australia did not win a match on this tour, losing all three Tests. Sleep's one wicket in his only Test cost 159 runs and he dropped out of contention for Test teams for the next four years.

To his credit, he bounced back in 1986–87 when a sequence of strong displays for South Australia earned him selection for the fifth Test against England in Sydney. Amid intense excitement he clean bowled John Emburey to finish with 5 for 72 in England's second innings and give Australia her first Test win in more than a year. England had already won the series but this win enabled Australia to save face, with Peter Taylor twice dismissing

Trevor Hohns, who took valuable wickets on his 1989 English tour. Hohns' all-round skills gave Border's side valuable balance.

Botham cheaply with his bounding off-spinners and Dean Jones scoring a memorable 184 not out.

In 1987–88, with his Test place apparently assured, Sleep's bowling disappointed although he made 211 runs at 52.75 in three Tests against New Zealand, including his best Test score of 90, and he lost his spinning berth in the Australian team to Trevor Hohns. This setback persuaded him to an overdue move, dropping down the order to concentrate on his bowling. He appeared at Hobart in the 1989–90 Test against Sri Lanka, taking 3 for 26 and 2 for 75, and in one Test in Melbourne against Pakistan, taking 1 for 6 and 1 for 66.

Poor form saw him lose his place in the South Australian team but by concentrating on his bowling he returned for a final first-class season in 1992–93. Just before retiring to play in England he took seven wickets against Western Australia to complete his first-class career with 363 wickets at 39.36 apiece. With the bat he made 8,122 runs at 34.56. Disappointing results for a cricketer whose career had promised so much more.

Sleep was not alone in his leg-spin woes, of course. Around the Australian states there were similar tales of wrist-spinners who promised to win matches but failed to do so. Tasmanian Stuart Saunders, Queenslanders Malcolm Francke and Bob Paulsen, South Australian Malcolm Dolman, Victorians Leigh Baker, Edwin Carter, Geoffrey Cormack, Neil Crompton, Louis Germaine, Keith Kirby, Jack Potter and Keith Stackpole, New South Welshmen Geoff Davies, Gamini Gooneseena, Reg Pearce and Jack Treanor, and Western Australians Wally Edwards, Terry MacGill and John Rutherford have all bowled wrist-spin for their states at various times since World War I without influencing match results. Very few have won headlines because of their leg-breaks or googlies.

The strangest tale of all, however, is the failure of the Sydney all-rounder Bob Cristofani, on his return to Australia after a brilliant showing in England with Lindsay Hassett's Services XI just after World War II.

Desmond Robert Cristofani, born in the Sydney suburb of Waverley in November 1920, played three times for New South Wales in 1941–42 because of impressive bowling for the St George club, where he was coached by Bill O'Reilly. He bowled leg-breaks at a brisk medium-pace just as O'Reilly did and imparted turn that made him a nasty proposition for even top-class batsmen. A big future appeared assured for him when he went off to England with the RAAF in World War II.

He played a lot of cricket in England with Keith Miller, both for the Dominions XI and the Australian Services Team. At Old Trafford in the fifth Victory Test against England he turned in a dazzling performance, bowling his leg-breaks to a good length at a pace that made handling his sharp turn very difficult, restricting England to a total of 243 by taking 5 for 55 from 22 overs. His victims included famous Test batsmen Wally Hammond and Cyril Washbrook.

The Services, trailing by 70 runs on the first innings, were in desperate trouble when Cristofani went to the crease with the score at 8 for 105 in their second innings. Fearlessly hitting the bowling of Test stars Eric Hollies, Doug Wright and Bill Edrich, Cristofani aroused spectators to fever pitch with a succession of boundaries, and when he reached his century with a huge six off Doug Wright spectators stood and cheered for several minutes.

Cristofani and Graham Williams added 95 in 95 minutes for the ninth wicket, with Williams scoring only 12 of them before he was out to Lancashire medium-pacer William Phillipson. The applause was repeated when the Australian Services innings ended with Cristofani on 110 not out. English critics immediately acclaimed Cristofani as a certainty for Australia's immediate postwar Test teams, and recalled that in the earlier Victory Test at Lord's he had taken 5 for 49.

Cristofani returned home through India with the Services XI, but somewhere along the way lost all his bowling skill. He took only eight wickets in India at an expensive 38 runs each and his captain Lindsay Hassett was forced to rely on the spin bowling of Reg Ellis and Cec Pepper. When he rejoined the St George club in the Sydney grade competition, with restoration to the New South Wales side virtually assured if he performed reasonably well, he could not turn the ball at all. The magic critics had raved about in England had gone.

On hard Australian pitches his leg-breaks went straight through. O'Reilly, Arthur Morris and other St George team-mates suggested he slow down his pace until he began to deviate the ball again, but none of his experiments worked. Unable to regain his place in the New South Wales side, he returned to England, where he bobbed up with Accrington in the Lancashire League.

The thrilling all-round form he had shown in the Old Trafford Victory Test continued to elude him but he became a highly successful businessman and a director of one of the world's richest hotel chains. He was one of the few players to score more than 2,000 runs and take 200 wickets for St George first grade, the team in which he appeared with his brother Vic.

More fortunate than Cristofani was the sunny-natured Western Australian Tony Mann, born in the very month that Cristofani produced his pyrotechnics at Old Trafford in 1945. Mann's right-arm leg-spinners behaved impeccably when he needed them most and when Kerry Packer badly weakened Australia's Test attack with his signings, Mann went into the Australian team for four Tests at the age of 32. Selectors who plucked him from obscurity were elated to find him a colourful personality with a pugnacious but thoughtful approach to both his bowling and his batting.

Mann was the son of a noted vigneron from the Swan Valley near Perth and learnt his cricket on the verandah of the family home in the heart of the Houghton vineyards. Tony bowled for hours to his brother Dorham, the family batsman, while another brother, Bill, did all the fielding. They were encouraged by their father Jack

Mann, a lifelong supporter of the Middle Swan Cricket Club. The verandah permitted only a short approach so Tony bowled leg-spinners, sending the ball along the high side of the verandah and dropping it down at Dorham's feet.

Tony played first grade at 14 for Perth's Midland-Guildford club, and at 15 got a game for the Combined High Schools XI against the Governor's XI, which included visiting Test heroes Richie Benaud and Neil Harvey. John Inverarity captained the school's team and Rodney Marsh kept wicket. Tony took 7 for 45 and had Harvey stumped down the leg side by Marsh. At 19, he won selection in the state team but did not take a wicket in 15 overs and went in last. Selectors did not pick him again for two years.

When Mann returned to the state team he found he had a tough rival in Terry Jenner and an even tougher captain in Tony Lock. Jenner saw that he could not expect long spells with Lock doing most of the bowling, even if he beat Mann for the support role, so he went off to South Australia with Ashley Mallett. In 1969–70 Mann took five wickets in an innings against Victoria, New South Wales and Queensland, finishing the season with 25 wickets at 26.88. He hoped this would be enough to earn him a place in the Australian B team to tour New Zealand but selectors preferred Jenner and Kerry O'Keeffe.

Mann's all-round value became apparent when he hit a century in 1970–71 against Ray Illingworth's touring England team in Perth, but his state captains kept putting him late in the order, treating him solely as a bowler. He improved his control by spending three successive winters in England, first with Bacup in the Lancashire League and then in minor counties cricket with Shropshire. His feats won him an invitation to join the Cavaliers and play alongside Fred Trueman and Graeme Pollock. At Exmouth he hit a century in 44 minutes for the Cavaliers, who were glad to treat him as an all-rounder.

His big chance came when 12 of the players who had toured England with the Australian team in 1977 defected to Packer. He bowled Vishwanath with his seventh ball in Test cricket and took 3 for 12 in India's first innings. At Perth Bob Simpson sent him in as a night watchman in the second Test, after Australia lost 2 for 33. Mann did the job perfectly, remaining not out at stumps and carrying on next morning to 105, which turned out to be vital in a match Australia won by two wickets.

This enabled Mann to retain his place until the fourth Test, when selectors judged he presented little threat to batsmen of the calibre of Gavaskar, Amarnath, Chauhan and Vengsarkar, all of them brought up on spin, and preferred Bruce Yardley's off-spinners for the fifth Test. Although he never won an overseas trip with an Australian team, Mann continued to be an automatic choice for Western Australia until he retired in 1984, aged 38. He took 196 wickets at 33.63 for his state, including five wickets in an innings five times, and scored 2,355 runs at 24.27, which was very similar to his Test batting average. His four Test wickets cost a whopping 79.00 runs each.

Tony Mann, like his father's wine, took time to mature, but not as long as Robert George Holland, who did not get into Test cricket until he was beyond the age at which Mann quit. There is powerful evidence that Holland, known to cricket fans throughout the world as 'Dutchy', bowled better at 40 than he ever did at 20. He was a grey-haired grandfather when he returned leg-break bowling to the high place in Australian cricket it had not enjoyed since Richie Benaud's retirement 20 years earlier.

13

The Best Ball Club

Between 1978–79 and 1987–88 Robert George ('Dutchy') Holland restored the Australian public's interest in leg-breaks. Bowling mostly in partnership with orthodox left-arm spinner Murray Bennett, he took 316 first-class wickets, helped New South Wales win three Sheffield Shield championships, appeared in 11 Tests, and with Bennett ended the West Indies' run of 27 Tests without defeat. And he did it all at an age when most cricketers have retired.

Holland's popularity in his 10 seasons of big cricket grew with every match he played. Spectators became accustomed to the cocked wrist, the scheming grey head, the light-footed approach and the full swing of the right arm that kept batsmen in a spin. Helped by groundsmen who made Sydney Cricket Ground a spinner's nirvana, he achieved matinee idol status among the ground's regulars. There was something vastly appealing to this mellowed father of three hoodwinking world-class batsmen with deliveries many regarded as old-fashioned.

Dutchy may have come into big cricket late but he was a virtuoso with the art of leg-spin and googly bowling. His long apprenticeship had taught him never to underestimate the difficulty of landing each spinning ball on precisely the right spot, yet he could never resist the challenge from the moment coach Peter Philpott explained the basics of the art at a Sydney clinic.

Holland was born in the Sydney suburb of Camperdown on 19 October 1946 and began playing for the Southern Lakes Cricket Club at the age of 10 when his family moved to the western shores of Lake Macquarie, near Newcastle. He was in first grade before his fourteenth birthday, fascinated by the manner in which bowlers could impart bias to a cricket ball from the time he first donned whites. He took 48 wickets that first summer in the senior grade, 1960–61, which started an association with Southern Lakes that is still going strong in the 1990s.

In 1965–66, at the age of 21, he won selection in the Northern New South Wales XI beaten by Mike Smith's touring England team in Newcastle. His six overs were costly, yielding 68 runs without bringing a wicket. His job as an engineer took him to Grafton in northern New South Wales in 1967, but from there he again won a place in the Northern New South Wales XI, this time as an opening batsman against New Zealand. Further valuable experience came in 1968–69 when he was picked as a specialist spinner for the Country XI against the West Indies.

Holland accepted an appointment to the Bankstown Council in Sydney in 1970–71 and for two years played for the Bankstown club in the Sydney club competition. 'We did not have a bad side, but we had only four bowlers,' he said. 'We had two 19-year-old tearaways to open the bowling, one named Jeffrey Thomson and the other a fiery character called Len Durtanovich (later Pascoe). We used to let Thommo and Lennie loose for a session, and then Barry Thebridge and I would bowl out the rest of the day. Barry and I finished top wicket-takers with about 35 wickets each.

'Thommo and Lennie terrorised the whole of the Sydney competition. They were very fast but they were all over the place and never stopped arguing with umpires. It was quite lively cricket when they were on.'

Holland went back to Southern Lakes after two seasons in Sydney, disillusioned with his council job and with the high cost of city living. He probably was very grateful for his friendship with Thommo later on when Thommo played for Queensland against New South Wales. In 1973–74 Holland helped Southern Lakes to their initial Newcastle premiership, and he appeared set for a career as a country cricketer when an invitation came from the New South Wales Cricket Association that led to his career in international cricket.

'The NSW Cricket Association rang to ask if I would attend a wrist-spinner's school they were staging in Sydney with Peter Philpott as the head coach,' Holland said. 'I thought, "What's the point, I'm 30", and suggested they try to find some younger prospects. But they persevered and finally I agreed to go, mainly because I thought I might get in some good practice.

'But I learnt so much it wasn't funny. I'd taught myself to bowl leg-breaks, but up to that point I'd never thought about the theory or mechanics. Peter went right back to basics and over those few hours gave me a whole new perspective on the art and what was required to succeed.

Bob Holland, developed in Newcastle like Watkins, proved a far steadier, more reliable wrist-spinner although he got into big cricket late. Holland, a crowd favourite, won a Lord's Test for Australia on his only English tour.

For the first time I saw it as a challenge. Not long after that I got picked to play my first state game and things happened pretty quickly from there.'

Holland made his debut for New South Wales at the Sydney Cricket Ground at the end of the 1978–79 season and from the start looked at home there bowling against Queensland. But Wayne Broad and Don Regeling made centuries and Holland was probably fortunate to finish with 1 for 113 from his 20 overs. The selectors preferred Graeme Beard and David Hourn to supply the spin for the remaining matches that summer but the following season gave Holland an extended trial. He took 25 wickets in six matches and helped start a New South Wales revival after years in the doldrums.

Encouraged, Holland took 30 wickets in 1980–81, 27 in 1981–82 and 16 in 1982–83, and in 1984–85 had his career-best analysis of 9 for 83 against South Australia, which lifted his haul for the season to 59 wickets at 25.79. This performance played a major part in New South Wales winning the Sheffield Shield for the second time in three years.

He was rewarded with his first Test when he took seven wickets for New South Wales which contributed to the shock defeat of the West Indies in Sydney. His long-time partner Murray Bennett took eight wickets in this match but missed Test selection. Holland's Test career began in Brisbane in November 1984, in the second Test of that series. He did not immediately take wickets but made several West Indians look decidedly uneasy when he risked his googly.

At Sydney in the fifth Test came the coup every wrist-spinner dreams about. Bowling in good spells with Murray Bennett, he took 6 for 54 and 4 for 90. Bennett had 2 for 45 and 4 for 94. Their 16 wickets did the trick and Australia won by an innings and 55 runs, a stunning defeat for the side hailed as the world's best, but a wonderful reminder for all cricket lovers on the potential of leg-spin. Some angry clashes during the Test between players from both sides and West Indian protests about the umpiring had the crowd further enthralled.

The 14 wickets he took in the four Tests, culminating with that memorable haul, were particularly satisfying for Holland, the third-oldest Australian Test player on debut at the age of 38 years and 35 days. Only Bert Ironmonger, 46 years 237 days, and Don Blackie, 46 years 253 days, were older. No wonder Holland brought all his family, wife Carolyn, sons Craig, 22, Rohan, 29, and daughter Naomi, 18, to watch him humble the West Indies.

A wonderful season ended when he went to the crease at the SCG with New South Wales requiring 45 runs to beat Queensland and win the Sheffield Shield with two wickets left. Holland and Clifford made 34 runs before Holland departed. Dave Gilbert came in to replace him and Clifford greeted him with: 'I've been waiting all season for this so don't stuff it up for me now'. Gilbert hit a four and a three to leave Clifford to hammer away the winning runs.

The West Indian fragility against wrist spin, clearly shown in the defeats by New South Wales and Australia in 1984–85 and in later displays against Abdul Qadir, was understandable given their lack of forebearance with the style. Some of them show an irritation faced with sharply turning leg-breaks that suggests they do not think it is fair. Their obsession with fast bowling leaves them ill-prepared for wrist-spin of quality and few of the breed have come from the Caribbean.

A talented leg-spinner named Inshan Ali impressed in Australia in 1975–76 but played in only one Test on the tour. His career bag of 34 wickets at 46.67 was a sad testimony to his obvious gifts. Similarly Arthur Barrett had his potential submerged by pace bowling in his three Test series, at home against India in 1970–71, England in 1973–74 and on tour against India and Pakistan in 1974–75, and finished with only 13 wickets at 46.38 from six Tests. David Holford did a lot better in the late 1960s on tours of England, Australia and New Zealand, finishing with 51 wickets at 39.39 from his efforts with leg-breaks in 24 Tests. Bernard Julien allowed his skill with the bat to overshadow his left-arm Chinamen and googlies in the late 1960s, taking only 50 wickets at 37.36 in 24 Tests when his exceptional ability should have had a far higher career bag.

Sonny Ramadhin could hardly be classed a wrist-spinner although he did roll occasional leg-breaks down to confuse batsmen facing his unorthodox off-spinners. Garfield Sobers certainly rolled his wrist but he did so many other things effectively it is difficult to typecast him. Indeed West Indian wrist-spinners are so hard to find it is necessary to go back half a century to Wilf Ferguson, who took 34 wickets at 34.26 with leg-breaks in eight Tests. He was followed by Ivan Madray, a gifted leg-spinner who took 16 wickets in two Tests in the 1950s.

Back in the 1930s Tommy Scott had 22 wickets at 42.04, but bowled some marathon spells. Eleven of his Test victims came in Australia in 1930–31, four of them in nine deliveries in the Adelaide Test. The honour board of West Indian leg-break and googly bowlers is in fact a dismal record for a region of such flair and with such an ideal climate for spinners.

Shortly after Bob Holland had his two-match success against them he was named in the Australian team to tour England in 1985. Although he was then in his thirty-ninth year, he spun Australia to victory in the second Test at Lord's by taking 5 for 68. At this point his admirers watching telecasts in Australia predicted he would have a major influence on the entire rubber, but to their dismay Holland refused to bowl his googly for the rest of the tour, converting himself into a stock bowler of leg-breaks and topspinners.

The googly bowler's ace card has always been to let batsmen know he can bowl it. This casts doubt in their minds which, from its first exhibition, has the batsman concerned over when it will come along. He keeps looking for the ball that breaks the opposite way to the leg-break and this often forces errors in his strokeplay. As the ball's inventor B.J.T. Bosanquet demonstrated early this century, it's better to bowl googlies that bounce two or three times than not to bowl them at all.

Holland finished third among Australia's wicket-takers on that tour with 29 wickets at 34.06, bowling round the wicket for long spells and aiming at containment rather than dismissals. The decision to use him in such a fashion was perhaps the main reason Australia won only four of her 20 matches.

The Holland magic emerged on his return home when he took 8 for 33 for New South Wales v. New Zealand, bowling Martin Crowe with a ball masquerading as a lollipop that tempted Crowe to sweep and nipped round his legs into the stumps. In the very next match he took 6 for 106 and 4 for 68, a 10-wicket haul that gave Australia the second Test over New Zealand. Again the over-pitched ball inviting the sweep did the damage.

Holland remained a regular member of the New South Wales team until August 1987, after which he went to New Zealand to play a season with Wellington, taking 31 wickets in 1987–88. His 60 matches for the state had yielded 193 wickets at 32.38, his 11 Tests 34 wickets at 39.76, and in all matches he captured 316 wickets at 31.25. He was seldom a big scorer, as his career total of 706 runs at 9.67 showed, but he held some outstanding catches at all levels of cricket. He turned out every week for Southern Lakes, became president and head coach of the club, and in 1993 dropped himself from the first to third grade to make way for a younger player. By then he had scored 4,000 runs and taken 750 wickets in club cricket.

He did not remain in a lower grade long, however, and in March 1994, at 47, he returned to Southern Lakes' first-grade team to take 7 for 11 from 13.5 overs against Newcastle City. In his thirty-seventh year with Southern Lakes he tried in vain to win a major premiership for the club, one of the big gaps in a career of achievement.

Holland's success was carefully observed by administrators all round Australia. They were impressed by his figures, but most of them were more excited by the uneasiness he created among the West Indian batting heroes. Bill O'Reilly stressed that the lesson would take a long time for some officials to learn, but batsmen who face medium-pace and fast bowling with equanimity could be upset by well-controlled wrist-spin.

Selectors in all states now appreciate that the balance of their representative teams is complete only if they include a wrist-spinner. Captains, too, have become more conscious of the wrist-spinners' value and the need to plan field placements for them well ahead.

The 1994 crop in Australia featured some outstanding talent. The lively Sydney leg-spinner Adrian Edward Tucker, developed by the Balmain club, has steadily improved his control since his debut in the New South Wales team in 1989–90 against South Australia in Sydney. Some critics predict that Tucker, 24, will become a candidate for national honours within the next few seasons. He has already taken 44 first-class wickets, with 5 for 38 for New South Wales against Western Australia in 1990–91 his best analysis so far.

The 27-year-old South Australian Peter McIntyre, who toured Zimbabwe with an Australian B team that included Shane Warne in 1991–92, has 81 first-class wickets to his credit after six seasons in representative cricket and has tightened his control. McIntyre has taken five wickets in an innings three times.

The youngest of the group is Craig Howard, who has 35 wickets to his credit after only two seasons, with 5 for 42 against South Africa at Melbourne in 1993–94 his best figures so far. Howard is 21. Eleven years Howard's senior is Western Australia's part-time leg-spinner Tim Zoehrer, who has 38 first-class wickets. Zoehrer made his debut in Test cricket as a wicket-keeper against New Zealand at Wellington in 1985–86.

Between seasons he has played for Excelsior Twenty in Rotterdam as captain-coach, a venture that has allowed him to take off the gloves and develop his leg-break and googly. He plays cricket in contact lenses. Zoehrer showed on Australia's 1993 England tour that his googly is an attacking weapon, not easily detected by even the best players.

Apart from Zoehrer, who can be a very useful bowler for Western Australia, national selection could come to any of the crop if anything happened to Shane Warne. They deserve to be persevered with by selectors aware that wrist-spinners take a lot of experience to mature. The English selectors have shown they appreciate this in their

Alan Border celebrating Australia's win over the West Indies in Sydney in 1985. He later masterminded the plot that made Shane Warne an Ashes match-winner.

Ian Salisbury, the Sussex leg-spinner, in action against Pakistan at Hove in 1992, has the fingers of his bowling hand firmly wrapped around the ball. He did well for England in the West Indies in 1994.

handling of Ian Salisbury, the 24-year-old Sussex right-arm wrist-spinner. Salisbury has been heavily punished occasionally since his debut in 1992, but was included in the England team to the West Indies in 1994.

Aspiring young left-arm leg-break and Chinamen bowlers are fewer in number than budding right-armers, but in David Freedman New South Wales have an outstanding prospect. In Queensland, the left-armer Shaun Flegler has had some impressive results since he switched from finger-spinners to rolling them out of the back of the hand.

All of these players have at some time attended the Australian Cricket Academy or one of the Academy's camps for intensive coaching in the skills of wrist-spin bowling. Apart from Academy tuition, slow bowling clinics have been conducted over the past few years by Peter Philpott under an Australian Cricket Board program called Spinners Are Winners, which is sponsored by a container shipping line.

At all of these schools, lecturers repeatedly remind the young men of their responsibility to behave in a sportsmanlike manner and not allow their frustrations with opponents or umpires to result in nasty displays of temperament or sledging. Despite the warnings, however, there have been a lot of hot-tempered outbursts, which player-inspired Codes of Conduct, fines and even suspensions have failed to prevent.

Australian cricket leads the world in its enterprising coaching schemes and junior development programs, but some players' behaviour does not reach the same standard. A big challenge our young wrist-spinners face is the exposure to television close-ups undreamed of in the days of Arthur Mailey, Clarrie Grimmett, Bill O'Reilly and Bruce Dooland. O'Reilly in fact confessed that he would not have been allowed more than three matches had his behaviour been submitted to the pressures today's young players endure.

Big Bill retreating to his bowling mark with expletives pouring from him, gesticulations fiercely evident, particularly if he had just suffered the personal outrage of being no-balled, would have put Channel 9 off the air. But he was never more exciting to watch than when he was angry, and produced some of the greatest balls in cricket history when he was livid with rage.

The problems faced in South Africa in 1994 by the champion wrist-spinner Shane Warne have been building to a climax ever since Kerry Packer introduced the Pyjama Game and started planning how to get better coverage of the joshing and barbed comments that have always been part of cricket. The distinguished *London Times* cricket writer John Woodcock wrote in *Wisden* after watching Packer-style cricket in Australia that the cricket bore little resemblance to the sophisticated and skilful encounters of traditional cricket.

'Fired by chauvinism and the exaggerated gestures of some of the Australian players, as well as the frantic nature of some of the cricket, the atmosphere at times seemed more like that of the Colosseum than a cricket ground,' Woodcock wrote. 'These were days when gimmickry reigned supreme, a development which not only the most conservative of watchers viewed with some anxiety.'

There can be no denying the detrimental influence players' tantrums have on small boys learning the game and eager to find role models, but shows of temper are not new. Walter Robins, one of the pillars of amateurism, chairman of England's selectors, and captain of Middlesex on both sides of World War II, was famous for his reaction to an umpire's rejection of one of his appeals. The umpire offered Robbie his sweater and Robbie told him to 'stick it', and then, spotting the Middlesex badges on the sweater, added: 'Seaxes and all'. (Seaxes, emblem of the Middlesex club, are ancient swords or scimitars.)

Some cricket historians believe Robins was responsible for giving the left-arm wrist-spinner's googly with topspin—the flipper for right-arm wrist-spinners—its name of Chinaman. He had just been dismissed by such a delivery from the West Indian spinner Ellis Achong. 'Fancy getting out to a Chinaman!' Robins commented to Learie Constantine. 'Do you mean the bowler or the ball?' said Constantine.

Border rejoices in his own spin-bowling success when he took 7 for 42 against the West Indies in Sydney in 1989.

Ellis Edgar Achong, known to fellow cricketers as 'Puss', said he only bowled the ball as an experiment because he knew Robins' experience with ordinary leg-breaks and googlies meant he could detect normal deliveries. 'It pitched perfectly and turned back at pace and when Robins saw it coming back at him, he opened his legs and the ball went through and he was stumped.'

Achong, a slow left-armer, reported to be the first person of Chinese origin to play Test cricket, was born at Belmont, Port-of-Spain on 16 February 1904. He made his Test debut against England in 1930 at Port-of-Spain after bowling Trinidad to victory over England. He found the promotion to Test level difficult to handle, although he dismissed Patsy Hendren in his initial Test. A nasty injury sustained in that match put him out of cricket but when he returned in 1933 another splendid display for Trinidad earned him selection for the West Indies tour of England. He appeared in all three Tests on that trip with moderate success. He was also tried in two Tests against England at home in 1934–35, but disappointed.

Puss Achong's eight wickets at 47.25 runs each in his six Tests give no hint to his valuable contribution to West Indian cricket at a time when it was striving for acceptance in big cricket. At regional level and in the Lancashire League he represented his race with honour, taking more than 1,000 wickets. He took 10 for 147 for Trinidad against British Guiana in the final of the 1932 inter-colonial tournament and took 10 wickets in an innings for Burnley against Todmorden in 1945 at the age of 41. On his return to the Caribbean he became a Test umpire and was a prominent coach of island spinners.

There is no doubt that Puss Achong's famous Chinaman delivery would have attracted close scrutiny from television cameras had he played in the Packer era. He may not have been the bowling sensation Shane Warne has been, but he would have bowled the occasional delivery that produced membership of the 'best ball' club which Warne started in England in 1993.

14

Acts of Magic

Australia surprised the large contingent of sportswriters covering the 1993 tour of England by announcing that Shane Warne would play in the first match at Worcester, on the ground where Don Bradman thrashed the county bowlers on four successive tours. Warne was known to be one of Australia's major Ashes hopes and captain Allan Border was expected to carefully protect him from the possibility of a mauling before the Tests began. With big-hitting Graeme Hick in the Worcestershire XI, this appeared an ideal chance for the Zimbabwean-born batsman to avenge the county for what Bradman had done.

Border acknowledged the risk in playing Warne but added: 'If he doesn't put them on the right spot and a batting talent like Hick gets a pile of runs against us, it will give him a taste of what will happen when he gets it wrong.'

Hick was in such commanding form as one of the few English Test batsmen to succeed on a horror tour of India, this appeared a callous, avoidable selection. Hick faced 78 balls from Warne and hit him for 96 runs with the media wincing at every boundary. Border commiserated with Warne and spectators saw him giving the youngster advice that it happens to all leg-spinners occasionally. In fact, what Border was saying was to stick with the plot hatched with Bob Simpson and the team's tacticians. Nobody wanted Hick or the England batsmen watching on television to see Warne's googly, topspinners, the flipper he turned back at pace or the leg-break that drifted wide of the leg stump and then spun viciously towards the off bail.

Later the Fleet Street contingent realised they had been fooled, and recalled the winks and rib-jabbing among the Australians who knew what Warne could really do. Shane's parents had not been sympathising with him, as journalists had thought, merely offering encouragement. The contrived ration of what one critic called 'lollipopping leg-breaks' ended, however, when the first Test began at Old Trafford.

Years before, Bill O'Reilly had lamented the lack of leg-spinners who could exploit the poor footwork of the glamorous Test batsmen he watched for the *Sydney Morning Herald*. 'One day, Jack, a good young leggie will come along and the mayhem he will create throughout the cricket world will be a sight to see,' said O'Reilly. 'I only hope I am here to see it.' Sadly, he died not long before Allan Border threw Warne the ball and Warne marked out his short run to bowl to Mike Gatting; the time for kidding now over.

The ball that has gone into cricket history beat Gatting in the air as it drifted towards the on side. Adjusting for it, Gatting edged his bat towards the leg, leaving a gap through which the ball sped as it pitched on the edge of the pitch and darted sharply across the batsman into the off stump. Wicket-keeper Ian Healy saw the bails fly and threw his gloved mitts elatedly in the air. Warne jumped a few centimetres in the air in triumph. Gatting hesitated and then, as the truth of what had happened came to him, went off shaking his head.

Bob Holland said it was a ball all good leg-spinners bowl sometimes in the nets but not often in a match. The media called it the greatest delivery ever bowled, the ball of the century, but to Warne it was simply a model leg-break that came out right, first up. Spectators' amazement continued whenever Warne took the ball. His juggling seemed endless as he paraded his complete range of tricks.

Hick, who had dealt so brutally with his doddling leg-breaks at Worcester, appeared mesmerised as Warne served up his googly, a selection of topspinners which skidded like pebbles on the water, and leg-breaks that bounced far higher than at Worcester. Merv Hughes finished him off before Hick unravelled the puzzle. His Test career was in jeopardy but he was quickly joined by team-mates who looked just as inept against Warne.

'Test cricket is not a picnic,' said Border. 'It's tough out there.'

The havoc Warne created with his very first ball in a Test match in England continued throughout the series, with a succession of English batsmen returning to the pavilion bewildered by Warne's mix of googlies, fizzing topspinners and his remarkable flipper. The cricket world buzzed with discussion about how best to play him, but despite regular changes in their batting line-up the England selectors could not find men to resist Warne.

Shane Warne clean bowls Mike Gatting with his first ball in Test cricket in England. The ball spun back from outside Gatting's legs to remove the off bail. Some critics called it the 'ball of the century'.

Midway through the rubber the English chairman of selectors added to the confusion by resigning. Poor Ted Dexter. He felt he should take the blame for England's failures but Warne and the Australian brains trust produced a line of attack virtually unknown to Test cricket. It was a completely new problem for even the most seasoned batsmen to encounter and nobody Dexter's panel could have selected could claim to have experience against it.

Warne brilliantly upheld the tradition of Australian wrist-spinners in England by dismissing 34 batsmen in six Tests. Clarrie Grimmett took 29 and 25 in the 1930 and 1934 series, Bill O'Reilly 28 and 22 in the 1934 and 1938 series, and Richie Benaud 15 wickets in three Tests in 1961. Warne's aggregate was twice as many as any English bowler. Border commented: 'We picked Warne as a surprise packet but never thought he would turn out so surprising.'

Australia were badly weakened when Craig McDermott broke down and had to return home, but Warne and his off-spinning team-mate Tim May bamboozled England's best batsmen and completely outbowled English spinners on pitches that should have suited England more than Australia. Favoured by colleagues whose aggressive batting gave them plenty of runs to play with, Warne and May had a picnic.

Not the least surprising reaction to Warne's magic was the warmth of the praise he received from English critics. Normally they are inclined to grizzle over major defeats, but their admiration for Warne's role in restoring leg-spin to its rightful place in the game was unrestrained. After watching boring all-pace efforts for many years they unanimously applauded Australia's varied attack.

Coach Bob Simpson said the benefit of Warne's performance will be reaped for decades to come, and added that if Warne gave up tomorrow his deeds in 1993 will be talked about and written about as long as the game is played. 'The work we have done with Shane has been mostly on the tactical side of his craft,' said Simpson. 'We have worked long sessions on different lines of delivery, the varieties of his attack. Every other leggie goes for a basic off-stump line. All the old-timers did. By daring to bowl on the leg stump or outside it, Shane has changed the whole conception of leg-break bowling.

'In theory you would think the leg-stump line was the easiest and most natural for a leg-spinner because it provides more shoulder turn and leverage, hence a more comfortable rotation of the wrist in conjunction with the arm and the elbow. But hitherto the leg-stump line has frightened off leggies because the margin of error dramatically increases and you only have to be a couple of inches off beam to become meat on the sideboard for any decent bat.

'But if you are bold enough and strong enough in mind and hand and wrist for turn and bounce and are competitively determined to get it right, then the leg-stump line crucially assaults that batsman's territory we old hands call "the blind spot", but which now they call "the corridor of uncertainty". From the first, we planned that would be the line Shane would seek out. We knew English batsmen had never confronted anything like it.'

Warne's confidence that he could bowl to the leg-stump line was dramatically shown when he bowled Graham Gooch, who had been playing Test cricket since 1975,

Warne in magician's garb, which an Australian magazine considered appropriate after his dismissal of Gatting.

around his legs. Warne took bets with team-mates that he could get round Gooch's legs when Gooch repeatedly padded legside deliveries away.

Shane Keith Warne was born on 13 September 1969 in the Melbourne district of Black Rock and was educated at Hampton High. He cannot recall why he took up leg-break bowling, only that he was a 12-year-old playing junior cricket with East Sandringham and was intrigued by the bowling of the club's First XI leggie, Ron Cantlon. He went to Mentone High on a sporting scholarship, became captain of the combined Associated Grammar Schools XI, and University's Bowling Shield (Under 16) team, for whom he broke a long-standing run-scoring record. His father Keith, an insurance financial consultant, mother Brigitte, and younger brother Jason are among his keenest supporters.

He joined St Kilda, and under the direction of Shaun Graf moved quickly from the thirds to the first grade. After three matches for St Kilda firsts he won selection in the state squad and was given a scholarship to the Australian Cricket Academy in Adelaide. Test leg-spinner Jim Higgs introduced him to the flipper at a Melbourne training session before he left. 'The first few went over the back of the net,' said Warne. 'They were everywhere . . . I had no idea.'

At the academy, Warne developed quickly. He had immediate rapport with the founding head of the academy, Jack Potter, who arranged instruction on the basics of wrist-spin bowling. He was blessed with a naturally strong hand, the leg-spinner's major asset, as the stronger the hand the stronger the flick of delivery from wrist and fingers. Other leg-spinners carried squash balls to strengthen their fingers with constant handling but Warne did not need this.

He had played only 20 club matches and never taken five wickets in an innings when he was chosen for a West Indian tour by an Australian Youth XI, but was left out of a youth trip that followed to Sri Lanka for disciplinary reasons. Former Test leg-spinner Terry Jenner began to work with him at the academy and taught Warne the topspinner, the delivery which he often squeezes under good batsmen's bats.

Jenner said: 'The first time I saw Shane I recognised his great talent. He has fabulous hand strength but the curious thing is that he doesn't get a mark on his spinning fingers. He never has any calluses because of his strong wrist. He has problems with the googly simply because his wrist is so powerful, but he gets variations in the width of his leg-breaks through variations in his wrist direction.'

Jenner showed Warne how the overspinning topspinner and the smaller leg-breaks dropped quickly and bounced higher from hard wickets, particularly against a stiff breeze. The bigger leg-breaks spinning squarer on with less overspin floated on, but frequently drifted in towards right-hand batsmen before turning.

Rod Marsh took charge of the academy for the last few months of Warne's stay there in Adelaide. He was highly impressed with Warne's willingness to work hard. 'He set an example for all the others with his eagerness to practise,' said Marsh. 'With that fabulous hand strength, I was always confident he would make it big.'

Warne returned to Melbourne because he believed he could get more valuable practice there than at the academy and within a fortnight of his arrival played for Victoria. A year later he played for Australia. He had been the most successful bowler for the Youth XI in the West Indies, but Peter McIntyre and Paul Jackson appeared to have better qualifications for the Victorian spinner's job. Jackson had taken nine wickets in nine matches for the state at 41 runs apiece. McIntyre had emerged from three hard months at the Adelaide Cricket Academy with glowing reports of his skills.

Lack of a quality wrist-spinner had been a major weakness in the Australian team for several reasons, with Peter Taylor filling the role with assistance from Border. Border's left-arm tweakers had had some surprisingly good results but it was obvious that neither he nor Taylor were of Test match calibre.

Realising that they had to gamble on a young spinner, the selectors brought Warne into the Australian team for the Sydney Test against India. He made an inauspicious start with Ravi Shastri carting him all over the ground and finished with 1 for 150. Shastri became his first Test wicket but only after he had made a double century.

Warne looked overweight in his Test debut, a wide-bottomed blonde-haired lad with a double chin and bulging waistline, a fact that did not escape Bob Simpson and his other advisors. During the winter Warne worked very hard to lose weight and at the start of the new season bowled 400 to 500 overs in net sessions to improve his control. Despite his flimsy record he was picked for Australia's tour of Sri Lanka and this became the watershed of his career.

He was hammered in the first innings of the first Test, which ended with his career figures at 1 for 335. At this stage he wondered why he had laboured so hard all winter. Border sensed his frustration and told him: 'Mate, I'm a believer in guys who keep contributing, guys who keep trying. If you keep hanging in there, one day it will all click for you.'

For Warne, the turning point came when he made 35 in Australia's second innings of the third Test, sharing a 40-run last wicket partnership with that great battler Michael Whitney, which extended Australia's lead from 140 to 180. He then bowled Australia to an unlikely triumph by taking 3 for 0 in 11 balls, but it still left his statistics after four Tests at an unimpressive 4 for 386.

Back in Melbourne he spun Australia to a dramatic win over the all-conquering West Indies on the MCG by taking 7 for 52 in the final innings. None of the West Indians appeared to read him well. He held his place for the rest of that series, which the West Indies won by taking the fifth Test in Perth, and then went to New Zealand for three further Tests. He took another man-of-the-match

The exceptional strength in Shane Warne's hands is clearly shown in this shot of him soon after releasing the ball during his fine tour of England in 1993. Note the concentration, too.

award by taking 7 for 86 in the first Test at Christchurch and finished the three-Test rubber with 17 wickets.

Warne went to England for the 1993 tour an established match-winner. Martin Crowe, Richie Richardson, Gordon Greenidge, Ken Rutherford and Desmond Haynes, all batsmen noted for their skill against spin, acknowledged that he presented a whole new range of problems. By then he had taken 35 wickets in his eight Tests that season at 20 runs each. His repertoire consisted of at least seven varieties—leg-break, googly, topspinner, flipper, a back-spinner which he said was virtually a throw, with a variety of side-spin and over-spin for required effects, and an ability to slow or accelerate the pace of all of them. The English Test players may have heard about all of these deliveries, but cricketers generally remain sceptical about claims of dangerous deliveries, preferring to wait for first-hand proof of their threat. The Australian management did not want to enlighten them until the Tests began, and in Allan Border they had a canny, hard-nosed cricketer with old scores to settle—just the captain to trick the English into thinking Warne was no threat.

Border's five visits to England dated back to 1981, when Australia were savaged by Ian Botham's brilliance. Four years later as captain he had seen Australia's hopes again frustrated. The experience hardened Border and he returned in 1989 and 1993 a much changed leader, friendly but determined to limit socialising and ruthlessly chase victory. His team had been through so many downs he understood the hard-edged sledging they handed out to English players who thought Border was their buddy.

Unhappily, Bill O'Reilly did not live to enjoy the mayhem Warne created in Australia's 4–1 triumph. He died on 6 October 1992, seven months before Warne's fabulous first ball in an England Test. O'Reilly had had a leg removed because of a blood clot behind his knee and endured two years in a wheelchair before his death at 87. He defended the high place of leg-breaks in the game in 40 years of cricket writing. In one of his last articles he praised Shane Warne, without realising what a match-winner he was about to become.

Warne had taken time to adjust to the demands of Test cricket, but the talk Border had with him in Sri Lanka completed his baptism. 'I feel part of it now,' he said. 'I feel that if I bowl well I can take wickets at this level. I've never really thought about how I was attracted to leg-spinning. I am just glad I stuck with it.'

He showed he could bowl economically in the opening match of the English tour against Lavinia, the Duchess of Norfolk's XI at Arundel Castle, conceding only 26 runs in 10 overs against some talented strokemakers. At Worcester in his lusty innings of 187, Graeme Hick hit Warne for four sixes in 10 balls without getting a look at Warne's full range of tricks. The Australians kept the subterfuge going in the matches that followed against Somerset, where Warne's final innings 4 for 77 helped clinch victory, and Surrey, where Warne's seven wickets also brought a win, and did not use him in the one-day games.

In the last match before the first Test at Leicester, Warne finally went for the throat and on the last afternoon bowled three Leicestershire batsmen around their legs, and tossed up his entire mix of googlies, flippers and topspinners. There was only a small crowd in attendance and the dazed return to the pavilion of three batsmen who thought the ball that bowled them pitched on the uncut grass outside leg stump was not relayed to the England dressing-room. The trap was set and when the plot became public two days later the results were devastating for England.

Warne took 4 for 51 and 4 for 86 in the first Test, 4 for 57 and 4 for 102 in the second Test, 3 for 74 and 3 for 108 in the third Test, 1 for 43 and 0 for 63 in the fourth Test, 1 for 61 and 5 for 82 in the fifth Test, 2 for 70 and 3 for 78 in the sixth Test, and in between kept on taking wickets against the counties to take his total number of dismissals from 16 matches to 75 at 22.64. Tim May, his spin bowling partner, was the next best Australian bowler with 53 wickets at 26.96.

England captain Graham Gooch, an old friend of Border's from his days with Essex, resigned with grace, saying: 'We have been beaten by an outstanding side which first planned its campaign to perfection and then carried it out to the letter'. Border felt that the English media were so obsessed with the resignations of Gooch and Dexter and discussions about how to stop Warne's destruction of England's batting that they failed to give his team credit for its superb displays. Australian selectors had taken a big gamble sending so many young players to England and Border believed youngsters like Warne, Slater, Reiffel, Julian and Hayden deserved high praise for the effort they put in.

Overnight Warne had become a superstar and hundreds of small boys across the world were reported to be trying his over-the-wrist technique. Simpson said all the credit belonged to Warne for agreeing to the suggested line of attack and then putting in the effort to make it work. Like Jenner, Marsh and Border, Simpson was certain Warne's immense turn came from his strong hands. 'Shane bowled a flipper that simply took my breath away,' said Simpson. 'It came down like a fast-medium bowler's fastest. It was quite an extraordinary delivery to confront a batsman with, for the flipper is very tough work at the best of times. To get that sort of fizzing speed from it is simply unique.

'The flipper is spun out from under the wrist, the back of the hand facing the sky; it's like clicking your fingers to attract a waiter's attention—and heavens, it's hard enough to bowl with disguise and accuracy. To get real pace out of it as well is just sheer genius. It's been truly fantastic for an old cricketer like me to be involved with Shane and to revel in the reception he has received and the wonderment he has created in every corner of England.'

Richie Benaud was just as enthusiastic about Warne in an article he wrote for *Inside Edge* magazine. 'I think he is terrific,' said Benaud. 'He is the best young leg-

The ball almost disappears as Warne cocks his wrist prior to release in this 1993 shot from The Oval of the sixth England–Australia Test.

Clearly the required result has been achieved. Warne's victory dance later became a little more involved than this on the South African tour in 1994, attracting official fines.

spinner I have seen and the incredible thing about him is that he has so few technical problems at this early stage of his career. Bowling over-the-wrist spin is a very difficult business. It's hard on the fingers, tendons and shoulder, and the brain as well. There are plenty of tough days coming up, as well as a few good ones. Shane will be well aware now that batsmen are after him. It's his job to attack the batsmen, and at the same time, give them nothing.'

Benaud's forecast proved valid immediately Warne returned to the Test arena in 1993–94. First the New Zealand batsmen had a crack at ending his marvellous run, but after the departure through injury of Martin Crowe they lacked the class to combat him regularly. He ended the calendar year 1993 with 71 wickets, the only spin bowler in history to exceed 60 wickets in a year. In the last of the three Tests against New Zealand he was named man-of-the-match, despite a sprained finger on

his spinning hand, his eight wickets also earning him the man-of-the-series award.

At that stage Warne's first 20 Tests had produced 83 wickets at 25.74 and he had managed a wicket every 69 deliveries. This put him ahead of great leg-spinner Richie Benaud (45 wickets in his first 20 Tests at 27.03, with a wicket every 77 balls) but behind Bill O'Reilly (101 wickets in 20 Tests at 22.59, with a wicket every 59 balls), Arthur Mailey (90 wickets in 20 Tests at 33.91, with a wicket every 62 balls) and Clarrie Grimmett (112 wickets in 20 Tests at 24.21, with a wicket every 67 balls). Warne's strike rate is still good enough for Sir Richard Hadlee to suggest he might be the first bowler to take 500 Test wickets. At 24 he appeared certain to rewrite the bowling record books.

Initially the South Africans had just as many problems with Warne as the other Test batsmen he had faced. He took 1 for 63 in the first Test against them in Melbourne in 1993–94, 7 for 56 and 5 for 72 in a brilliant second Test performance at Sydney, and 1 for 85 and 4 for 31 in the third Test at Adelaide. This took him to 101 wickets in only 23 Tests at an average cost of 24.19 runs per wicket. This prompted Bill Brown, former Australian opening batsman, to comment: 'As regards spinning the ball, Warne spins it more than any right-arm spinner I have ever seen, more so than Grimmett or O'Reilly.'

This is a view one of the Victorian Sheffield Shield team batsmen would agree with, for Warne converted him to tears in a 20-minute net session. He could barely make contact with the ball, and his embarrassment and the unkind guffaws of team-mates left him wiping the tears away.

Largely because of his cricket commitments Warne and his fiancee Simone Callahan, a striking pair at Allan Border's celebration dinner, had to postpone their wedding until after he completed the second part of his clash with the South Africans on their home pitches. Here the sledging and gesticulating that had become an irksome part of his bowling in big matches got him into trouble. He and Merv Hughes were each fined 1,000 Rand, the Australian equivalent of $450, for abusing South African batsmen they had dismissed. The Australian Cricket Board did not consider these fines heavy enough for verbal abuse that had caused the umpires to report them to match referee David Carr, and imposed an additional fine of A$4,000 each for what the Board said was a flagrant breach of the players' Code of Conduct.

Shane Warne's path to a unique place in cricket history seems likely to be troubled but he still remains the greatest wrist-spinner any of us have ever seen. Mailey, O'Reilly, Benaud and Grimmett may have been more subtle but they could not match Warne's remarkable range of spinning deliveries. He comes out as No. 1 in the whole history of leg-break bowling, matched against Freeman, Wright, Qadir, Kumble and other overseas exponents of the style, but it is illogical to compare him directly with O'Reilly, who was really a medium-pacer.

Shane Warne goes down on one knee to appeal for a lbw decision during the second Test against South Africa at Cape Town in 1994.

Shane Warne jumps high with elation after taking a wicket for Australia against South Africa at Sydney Cricket Ground in 1994.

Appendix

Ross Dundas

LEADING WICKET-TAKERS

Bowler	Country	Tests	Wickets	Average	Stk/Rt
R. Benaud	Australia	63	248	27.03	77.05
B.S. Chandrasekhar	India	58	242	29.74	65.96
Abdul Qadir	Pakistan	67	236	32.81	72.56
G.S. Sobers	West Indies	93	235	34.04	91.91
C.V. Grimmett	Australia	37	216	24.22	67.19
M.H. Mankad	India	44	162	32.32	90.65
S. Ramadhin	West Indies	43	158	28.98	88.22
S.P. Gupte	India	36	149	29.55	75.73
W.J. O'Reilly	Australia	27	144	22.60	69.61
H. Verity	England	40	144	24.37	77.59
Intikhab Alam	Pakistan	47	125	35.92	83.79
J. Briggs	England	33	118	17.74	45.18
S.K. Warne	Australia	26	116	23.97	68.84
D.V.P. Wright	England	34	108	39.11	75.32
J.H. Wardle	England	28	102	20.39	64.67

LEADING BOWLING AVERAGES

Bowler	Country	Tests	Wickets	Average
C.S. Marriott	England	1	11	8.72
J.B. Iverson	Australia	5	21	15.24
T.K. Kendall	Australia	2	14	15.36
J. Briggs	England	33	118	17.74
H. Ironmonger	Australia	14	74	17.97
B.F. Butcher	West Indies	44	5	18.00
H.L.E. Promnitz	South Africa	2	8	20.12
J.H. Wardle	England	28	102	20.39
W.J. O'Reilly	Australia	27	144	22.60
A.E.E. Vogler	South Africa	15	64	22.73
J.V. Saunders	Australia	14	79	22.73
L.F. Kline	Australia	13	34	22.82

BEST STRIKE RATE
(Balls per wickets)

Bowler	Country	Tests	Balls	Wickets	Stk/Rt
C.S. Marriott	England	1	247	11	22.45
B.J.T. Bosanquet	England	7	970	25	38.80
T.K. Kendall	Australia	2	563	14	40.21
B.F. Butcher	West Indies	44	256	5	42.66
J.V. Saunders	Australia	14	3,565	79	45.13
J. Briggs	England	33	5,332	118	45.18
A.E.E. Vogler	South Africa	15	2,764	64	45.31
H.V. Hordern	Australia	7	2,148	46	46.70
R.O. Schwartz	South Africa	20	2,939	55	47.98

MOST WICKETS IN A TEST SERIES

Bowler	Series	Tests	Wickets	Average
C.V. Grimmett	1935–36 Aus v SAf in SAf	5	44	14.59
A.E.E. Vogler	1909–10 SAf v Eng in SAf	5	36	21.75
A.A. Mailey	1920–21 Aus v Eng in Aus	5	36	26.27
B.S. Chandrasekhar	1972–73 Ind v Eng in Ind	5	35	18.91
M.H. Mankad	1951–52 Ind v Eng in Ind	5	34	16.79
S.P. Gupte	1955–56 Ind v N.Z. in Ind	5	34	19.67
S.K. Warne	1993 Aus v Eng in Eng	6	34	25.79
C.V. Grimmett	1930–31 Aus v W.I. in Aus	5	33	17.96
C.V. Grimmett	1931–32 Aus v SAf in Aus	5	33	16.87
H.V. Hordern	1911–12 Aus v Eng in Aus	5	32	24.37
J.V. Saunders	1907–08 Aus v Eng in Aus	5	31	23.09
H. Ironmonger	1931–32 Aus v SAf in Aus	4	31	9.54
R. Benaud	1958–59 Aus v Eng in Aus	5	31	18.83
R. Benaud	1957–58 Aus v SAf in SAf	5	30	21.93
Abdul Qadir	1987–88 Pak v Eng in Pak	3	30	14.56
G.A. Faulkner	1909–10 SAf v Eng in SAf	5	29	21.89
C.V. Grimmett	1930 Aus v Eng in Eng	5	29	31.89
R. Benaud	1959–60 Aus v Ind in Ind	5	29	19.58
W.J. O'Reilly	1934 Aus v Eng in Eng	5	28	24.92
B.S. Chandrasekhar	1977–78 Ind v Aus in Aus	5	28	25.14
W.J. O'Reilly	1932–33 Aus v Eng in Aus	5	27	26.81
W.J. O'Reilly	1935–36 Aus v SAf in SAf	5	27	17.03
S.P. Gupte	1952–53 Ind v W.I. in W.I.	5	27	29.22
S. Ramadhin	1950 W.I. v Eng in Eng	4	26	23.23
J.H. Wardle	1956–57 Eng v SAf in SAf	4	26	13.80
J.W. Gleeson	1968–69 Aus v W.I. in Aus	5	26	32.46
R.O. Schwarz	1910–11 SAf v Aus in Aus	5	25	26.04
C.V. Grimmett	1934 Aus v Eng in Eng	5	25	26.72
W.J. O'Reilly	1936–37 Aus v Eng in Aus	5	25	22.20
M.H. Mankad	1952–53 Ind v Pak in Ind	4	25	20.56

MOST WICKETS IN A TEST

Bowler	Series	Venue	
N.D. Hirwani	1987–88 Ind v W.I.	Madras	16/136
J. Briggs	1888–89 Eng v SAf	Cape Town	15/28
H. Verity	1934 Eng v Aus	Lord's	15/104
C.V. Grimmett	1931–32 Aus v SAf	Adelaide	14/199
Abdul Qadir	1987–88 Pak v Eng	Labore	13/101
M.H. Mankad	1952–53 Ind v Pak	Delhi	13/131
C.V. Grimmett	1935–36 Aus v SAf	Durban	13/173
A.A. Mailey	1920–21 Aus v Eng	Melbourne	13/236
J.H. Wardle	1956–57 Eng v SAf	Cape Town	12/89
B.S. Chandrasekhar	1977–78 Ind v Aus	Melbourne	12/104
M.H. Mankad	1951–52 Ind v Eng	Madras	12/108
S.K. Warne	1993–94 Aus v SAf	Sydney	12/128
J. Briggs	1891–92 Eng v Aus	Adelaide	12/136
A.P. Freeman	1929 Eng v SAf	Manchester	12/171
H.V. Hordern	1911–12 Aus v Eng	Sydney	12/175
A.E.E. Vogler	1909–10 SAf v Eng	Johannesburg	12/181
L. Sivaramakrishnan	1984–85 Ind v Eng	Bombay	12/181
H. Ironmonger	1931–32 Aus v SAf	Melbourne	11/24
J. Briggs	1886 Eng v Aus	Lord's	11/74
H. Ironmonger	1930–31 Aus v W.I.	Melbourne	11/79
C.V. Grimmett	1924–25 Aus v Eng	Sydney	11/82
C.S. Marriott	1933 Eng v W.I.	The Oval	11/96
R. Benaud	1956–57 Aus v Ind	Calcutta	11/105
W.J. O'Reilly	1934 Aus v Eng	Nottingham	11/129
Intikhab Alam	1972–73 Pak v N.Z.	Dunedin	11/130
S. Ramadhin	1950 W.I. v Eng	Lord's	11/152
H. Verity	1933–34 Eng v Ind	Madras	11/153
C.V. Grimmett	1930–31 Aus v W.I.	Adelaide	11/183
Abdul Qadir	1982–83 Pak v Aus	Faisalabad	11/218
W. Ferguson	1947–48 W.I. v Eng	Port-of-Spain	11/229
B.S. Chandrasekhar	1966–67 Ind v W.I.	Bombay	11/235
C.V. Grimmett	1935–36 Aus v SAf	Cape Town	10/88
A.P. Freeman	1928 Eng v W.I.	Manchester	10/93
C.V. Grimmett	1935–36 Aus v SAf	Johannesburg	10/110
W.J. O'Reilly	1938 Aus v Eng	Leeds	10/122
W.J. O'Reilly	1932–33 Aus v Eng	Melbourne	10/129
R.G. Holland	1984–85 Aus v W.I.	Sydney	10/144
J. Briggs	1893 Eng v Aus	The Oval	10/148
H.V. Hordern	1911–12 Aus v Eng	Sydney	10/161
R.G. Holland	1985–86 Aus v N.Z.	Sydney	10/174
D.V.P. Wright	1947 Eng v SAf	Lord's	10/175
Intikhab Alam	1969–70 Pak v N.Z.	Dacca	10/182
Abdul Qadir	1987–88 Pak v Eng	Karachi	10/186
Abdul Qadir	1983–84 Pak v Eng	Lahore	10/194
G.T.S. Stevens	1929–30 Eng v W.I.	Bridgetown	10/195
C.V. Grimmett	1930 Aus v Eng	Nottingham	10/201
A.P. Freeman	1929 Eng v SAf	Leeds	10/207
Abdul Qadir	1987 Pak v Eng	The Oval	10/211
S.P. Gupte	1958–59 Ind v W.I.	Kanpur	10/223
L.O. Fleetwood-Smith	1936–37 Aus v Eng	Adelaide	10/239
A.A. Mailey	1920–21 Aus v Eng	Adelaide	10/302

CONCEDING LEAST RUNS PER OVER

Bowler	Country	Tests	Balls	Runs	BPO
H. Ironmonger	Australia	14	4,695	1,330	1.70
J.B. Iverson	Australia	5	1,108	320	1.73
A.J. Richardson	Australia	9	1,812	521	1.73
H.L.E. Promnitz	South Africa	2	528	161	1.82
R. Kilner	England	9	2,368	734	1.85
H. Verity	England	40	11,173	3,510	1.88
J.H. Wardle	England	28	6,597	2,080	1.89
W.J. O'Reilly	Australia	27	10,024	3,254	1.95
L.F. Kline	Australia	13	2,373	776	1.96
S. Ramadhin	West Indies	43	13,939	4,579	1.97

FASTEST TO 50 WICKETS

Bowler	Country	Tests
A.A. Mailey	Australia	9
J.V. Saunders	Australia	10
A.P. Freeman	England	10
C.V. Grimmett	Australia	10
H. Ironmonger	Australia	10
W.J. O'Reilly	Australia	10
A.R. Kumble	India	10
A.E.E. Vogler	South Africa	11
S. Ramadhin	West Indies	11
N.D. Hirwani	India	11
G.A. Faulkner	South Africa	12
R.W.V. Robins	England	12
S.P. Gupte	India	12
Pervez Sajjad	Pakistan	12
B.S. Chandrasekhar	India	12

FASTEST TO 100 WICKETS

Bowler	Country	Tests
C.V. Grimmett	Australia	17
W.J. O'Reilly	Australia	20
S.P. Gupte	India	22
B.S. Chandrasekhar	India	22
M.H. Mankad	India	23
S.K. Warne	Australia	23
J. Briggs	England	25
S. Ramadhin	West Indies	25
H. Verity	England	26
J.H. Wardle	England	27
Abdul Qadir	Pakistan	28
D.V.P. Wright	England	32
R. Benaud	Australia	32
Intikhab Alam	Pakistan	41
G.S. Sobers	West Indies	48

BEST BOWLING ON DEBUT

Bowler	Series	Venue	
N.D. Hirwani	1987–88 Ind v W.I.	Madras (1)	8/61
N.D. Hirwani	1987–88 Ind v W.I.	Madras (2)	8/75
T.K. Kendall	1876–77 Aus v Eng	Melbourne	7/55
C.V. Grimmett	1924–25 Aus v Eng	Sydney	6/37
G.H.T. Simpson-Hayward	1909–10 Eng v SAf	Johannesburg	6/43
C.S. Marriott	1933 Eng v W.I.	The Oval	6/59
F.A. Ward	1936–37 Aus v Eng	Brisbane	6/102
W.H. Cooper	1881–82 Aus v Eng	Melbourne	6/120
A.M. Moir	1950–51 N.Z. v Eng	Christchurch	6/155

BEST MATCH BOWLING ON DEBUT

Bowler	Series	Venue	
N.D. Hirwani	1987–88 Ind v W.I.	Madras	16/136
C.V. Grimmett	1924–25 Aus v Eng	Melbourne	11/82
C.S. Marriott	1933 Eng v W.I.	The Oval	11/96

HAT-TRICKS

Bowler	Series	Venue
J. Briggs	1891–92 Eng v Aus	Sydney
T.J. Matthews	1912 Aus v SAf	Manchester (1st inns)
T.J. Matthews	1912 Aus v SAf	Manchester (2nd inns)
L.F. Kline	1957–58 Aus v SAf	Cape Town

THREE WICKETS IN FOUR BALLS

Bowler	Series	Venue
J. Briggs	1888–89 Eng v SAf	Cape Town
W.J. O'Reilly	1934 Aus v Eng	Manchester
R. Benaud	1954–55 Aus v W.I.	Georgetown
J.W. Martin	1960–61 Aus v W.I.	Melbourne

WICKET IN FIRST OVER IN TEST CRICKET

Ball	Bowler	Series		Venue
1st	Intikhab Alam	1959–60	Pak v Aus	Karachi
2nd	J.H. Cameron	1939	W.I. v Eng	Lord's
2nd	C.L. McCool	1945–46	Aus v N.Z.	Wellington
2nd	P.I. Philpott	1964–65	Aus v W.I.	Kingston
2nd	B.A.G. Murray	1967–68	N.Z. v Ind	Wellington
3rd	R.O. Jenkins	1948–49	Eng v SAf	Durban
4th	D.V.P. Wright	1938	Eng v Aus	Nottingham
4th	D.A.J. Holford	1966	W.I. v Eng	Manchester
5th	G.H.T. Simpson-Hayward	1909–10	Eng v SAf	Johannesburg
6th	E.W. Clark	1929	Eng v SAf	The Oval
6th	V.V. Kumar	1960–61	Ind v Pak	Delhi
7th	A.L. Mann	1977–78	Aus v Ind	Brisbane
–	M. Leyland	1928	Eng v W.I.	The Oval

MOST WICKETS IN AN INNINGS

Bowler	Series	Venue	
Abdul Qadir	1987–88 Pak v Eng	Lahore	9/56
S.P. Gupte	1958–59 Ind v W.I.	Kanpur	9/102
A.A. Mailey	1920–21 Aus v Eng	Melbourne	9/121
J. Briggs	1888–89 Eng v SAf	Cape Town	8/11
H. Verity	1934 Eng v Aus	Lord's	8/43
M.H. Mankad	1952–53 Ind v Pak	Delhi	8/52
M.H. Mankad	1951–52 Ind v Eng	Madras	8/55
N.D. Hirwani	1987–88 Ind v W.I.	Madras (1)	8/61
N.D. Hirwani	1987–88 Ind v W.I.	Madras (2)	8/75
B.S. Chandrasekhar	1972–73 Ind v Eng	Delhi	8/79
L.C. Braund	1903–04 Eng v Aus	Melbourne	8/81
B.J.T. Bosanquet	1905 Eng v Aus	Nottingham	8/107

Leg-Spin Test Records

LEG-SPINNERS TEST CAREER AVERAGES
(Minimum 5 wickets)

Bowler	Debut	Age	M	Balls	Runs	Wkts	Avrge	5 wi	10 wm	Best	Stk/Rt	RPO	Tests per Wickets							
													5	10	25	50	75	100	150	200
AUSTRALIA																				
W.M. Armstrong	1901-02	22	50	8,022	2,923	87	33.60	3	-	6/35	92.21	2.19	13	17	21	30	42	-	-	-
R. Benaud	1951-52	21	63	19,108	6,704	248	27.03	16	1	7/72	77.05	2.11	3	4	14	24	29	32	40	49
D.D. Blackie	1928-29	46	3	1,260	444	14	31.71	1	-	6/94	90.00	2.11	2	2	-	-	-	-	-	-
I.M. Chappell	1964-65	21	76	2,873	1,316	20	65.80	-	-	2/21	143.65	2.75	5	18	-	-	-	-	-	-
A.G Chipperfield	1934	28	14	924	437	5	87.40	-	-	3/91	184.80	2.84	4	-	-	-	-	-	-	-
W.H. Cooper	1881-82	32	2	466	226	9	25.11	1	-	6/120	51.78	2.91	1	-	-	-	-	-	-	-
B. Dooland	1946-47	23	3	880	419	9	46.56	-	-	4/69	97.78	2.86	1	-	-	-	-	-	-	-
S.H. Emery	1912	26	4	462	249	5	49.80	-	-	2/46	92.40	3.23	4	-	-	-	-	-	-	-
L.O. Fleetwood-Smith	1935-36	25	10	3,093	1,570	42	37.38	2	1	6/110	73.64	3.05	1	4	6	-	-	-	-	-
J.W. Gleeson	1967-68	29	30	8,857	3,367	93	36.20	3	-	5/61	95.24	2.28	3	5	10	15	21	-	-	-
C.V. Grimmett	1924-25	33	37	14,513	5,231	216	24.22	21	7	7/40	67.19	2.16	1	1	5	10	14	17	28	36
J.D. Higgs	1977-78	27	22	4,752	2,057	66	31.17	2	2	7/143	72.00	2.60	2	3	7	16	-	-	-	-
J.C. Hill	1953	29	3	606	273	8	34.13	-	-	3/35	75.75	2.70	2	-	-	-	-	-	-	-
T.V. Hohns	1988-89	35	7	1,528	580	17	34.12	-	-	3/59	89.88	2.28	2	5	-	-	-	-	-	-
R.G. Holland	1984-85	38	11	2,889	1,352	34	39.76	3	2	6/54	84.97	2.81	3	3	9	-	-	-	-	-
H.V. Hordern	1910-11	28	7	2,148	1,075	46	23.37	5	2	7/90	46.70	3.00	1	2	3	-	-	-	-	-
P.M. Hornibrook	1928-29	29	6	1,579	664	17	39.06	1	-	7/92	92.88	2.52	2	5	-	-	-	-	-	-
H. Ironmonger	1928-29	46	14	4,695	1,330	74	17.97	4	2	7/23	63.45	1.70	2	3	6	10	-	-	-	-
J.B. Iverson	1950-51	35	5	1,108	320	21	15.24	1	-	6/27	52.76	1.73	2	2	-	-	-	-	-	-
T.J. Jenner	1970-71	26	9	1,881	749	24	31.21	1	-	5/90	78.38	2.39	2	4	-	-	-	-	-	-
T.K. Kendall	1876-77	25	2	563	215	14	15.36	1	-	7/55	40.21	2.29	1	2	-	-	-	-	-	-
L.F. Kline	1957-58	23	13	2,373	776	34	22.82	1	-	7/75	69.79	1.96	2	4	-	-	-	-	-	-
C.G. Macartney	1907-08	21	35	3,561	1,240	45	27.56	2	1	7/58	79.13	2.09	4	5	9	-	-	-	-	-
A.A. Mailey	1920-21	34	21	6,119	3,358	99	33.92	6	2	9/121	61.81	3.29	1	3	4	9	13	-	-	-
J.W. Martin	1960-61	29	8	1,846	832	17	48.94	-	-	3/56	108.59	2.70	3	5	-	-	-	-	-	-
T.J. Matthews	1911-12	27	8	1,081	419	16	26.19	-	-	4/29	67.56	2.33	3	5	-	-	-	-	-	-
C.L. McCool	1945-46	30	14	2,504	958	36	26.61	3	-	5/41	69.56	2.30	3	4	11	-	-	-	-	-
K.J. O'Keeffe	1970-71	21	24	5,384	2,018	53	38.08	1	-	5/101	101.58	2.25	2	7	12	21	-	-	-	-
N.C. O'Neill	1958-59	21	42	1,392	667	17	39.24	-	-	4/41	81.88	2.88	29	40	-	-	-	-	-	-
W.J. O'Reilly	1931-32	26	27	10,024	3,254	144	22.60	11	3	7/54	69.61	1.95	2	3	5	10	14	20	-	-
P.I. Philpott	1964-65	30	8	2,262	1,000	26	38.46	1	-	5/90	87.00	2.65	1	3	8	-	-	-	-	-
A.J. Richardson	1924-25	36	9	1,812	521	12	43.42	2	-	2/20	151.00	1.73	3	7	-	-	-	-	-	-
D.T. Ring	1947-48	29	13	3,024	1,305	35	37.29	2	-	6/72	86.40	2.59	1	3	8	-	-	-	-	-
J.V. Saunders	1901-02	26	14	3,565	1,796	79	22.73	6	-	7/43	45.13	3.02	1	3	5	10	14	-	-	-
R.B. Simpson	1957-58	21	62	6,881	3,001	71	42.27	2	-	5/57	96.92	2.62	11	15	31	51	-	-	-	-
D.J. Sincock	1964-65	22	3	724	410	8	51.25	-	-	3/67	90.50	3.40	2	-	-	-	-	-	-	-

Bowler	Debut	Age	M	Balls	Runs	Wkts	Avrge	5 wi	10 wm	Best	Stk/Rt	RPO	Tests per Wickets							
													5	10	25	50	75	100	150	200
AUSTRALIA																				
P.R. Sleep	1978–79	21	14	2,982	1,397	31	45.06	1	—	5/72	96.19	2.81	5	7	13	—	—	—	—	—
K.R. Stackpole	1965–66	25	44	2,321	1,001	15	66.73	—	—	2/33	154.73	2.59	10	15	—	—	—	—	—	—
G.H.S. Trott	1888	21	24	1,891	1,019	29	35.14	—	—	4/71	65.21	3.23	7	15	23	—	—	—	—	—
F.A. Ward	1936–37	27	4	1,268	574	11	58.18	1	—	6/102	115.27	2.72	1	2	—	—	—	—	—	—
S.K. Warne	1991–92	22	26	7,985	2,780	116	23.97	5	1	7/52	68.84	2.09	5	5	10	14	19	23	—	—
ENGLAND																				
R.W. Barber	1960	24	28	3,426	1,806	42	43.00	—	—	4/132	81.57	3.16	2	7	16	—	—	—	—	—
K.K. Barrington	1955	24	82	2,715	1,300	29	44.82	—	—	3/4	93.62	2.87	6	12	75	—	—	—	—	—
B.J.T. Bosanquet	1903–04	26	7	970	604	25	24.16	2	—	8/107	38.80	3.74	2	2	7	—	—	—	—	—
L.C. Braund	1901–02	26	23	3,803	1,810	47	38.51	3	—	8/81	80.91	2.85	1	3	10	—	—	—	—	—
J. Briggs	1884–85	22	33	5,332	2,094	118	17.74	9	4	8/11	45.18	2.35	7	7	12	16	20	25	—	—
F.R. Brown	1931	20	22	3,260	1,398	45	31.06	1	—	5/49	72.44	2.57	3	6	12	—	—	—	—	—
D.W. Carr	1909	37	1	414	282	7	40.29	1	—	5/146	59.14	4.09	1	—	—	—	—	—	—	—
E.W. Clark	1929	27	8	1,931	899	32	28.09	1	—	5/98	60.34	2.79	2	3	7	—	—	—	—	—
A.P. Freeman	1924–25	36	12	3,732	1,707	66	25.86	5	3	7/71	56.54	2.74	1	3	7	10	—	—	—	—
J.W. Hearne	1911–12	20	24	2,926	1,462	30	48.73	1	—	5/49	97.53	2.99	2	3	9	—	—	—	—	—
W.E. Hollies	1934–35	22	13	3,554	1,332	44	30.27	5	—	7/50	80.77	2.24	2	3	6	—	—	—	—	—
R.O. Jenkins	1948–49	30	9	2,118	1,098	32	34.31	1	—	5/116	66.18	3.11	3	3	7	—	—	—	—	—
R. Kilner	1924	33	9	2,368	734	24	30.58	—	—	4/51	98.66	1.85	3	4	—	—	—	—	—	—
M. Leyland	1928	28	41	1,103	585	6	97.50	—	—	3/91	183.83	3.18	28	—	—	—	—	—	—	—
C.S. Marriott	1933	37	1	247	96	11	8.72	2	1	6/59	22.45	6.00	1	1	—	—	—	—	—	—
T.S. Mitchell	1932–33	30	5	894	498	8	62.25	—	—	2/49	111.75	3.34	3	—	—	—	—	—	—	—
C.H. Parkin	1920–21	34	10	2,095	1,128	32	35.25	2	—	5/38	65.46	3.23	2	3	8	—	—	—	—	—
I.A.R. Peebles	1927–28	19	13	2,882	1,391	45	30.91	3	—	6/63	64.04	2.89	3	6	9	—	—	—	—	—
R.W.V. Robins	1929	23	19	3,318	1,758	64	27.46	1	—	6/32	51.84	3.17	1	5	6	12	—	—	—	—
I.D.K. Salisbury	1992	22	6	1,141	812	15	54.13	—	—	4/163	76.07	4.27	1	5	—	—	—	—	—	—
G.H.T. Simpson-Hayward	1909–10	34	5	898	420	23	18.26	2	—	6/43	39.04	2.80	2	4	—	—	—	—	—	—
J.M. Sims	1935	32	4	887	480	11	43.63	—	—	5/73	80.63	2.84	2	4	—	—	—	—	—	—
G.T.S. Stevens	1922–23	21	10	1,186	648	20	32.40	2	1	5/90	59.30	3.27	3	9	—	—	—	—	—	—
R.K. Tyldesley	1924	27	7	1,615	619	19	32.57	—	—	3/50	85.00	2.29	1	3	—	—	—	—	—	—
H. Verity	1931	26	40	11,173	3,510	144	24.37	5	2	8/43	77.59	1.88	4	6	10	14	19	26	—	—
J.H. Wardle	1947–48	25	28	6,597	2,080	102	20.39	5	1	7/36	64.67	1.89	4	6	10	17	22	27	—	—
L.L. Wilkinson	1938–39	22	3	573	271	7	38.71	—	—	2/12	81.85	2.83	2	—	—	—	—	—	—	—
D.V.P. Wright	1938	23	34	8,135	4,224	108	39.11	6	1	7/105	75.32	3.11	1	3	7	16	22	32	—	—
INDIA																				
C.G. Borde	1958–59	24	55	5,695	2,417	52	46.48	1	—	5/88	109.51	2.54	7	11	20	33	—	—	—	—
B.S. Chandrasekhar	1963–64	18	58	15,963	7,199	242	29.74	16	2	8/79	65.96	2.70	1	4	8	12	19	22	37	48
S.P. Gupte	1951–52	22	36	11,284	4,403	149	29.55	12	1	9/102	75.73	2.34	2	4	7	12	17	22	—	—
N.D. Hirwani	1987–88	19	14	3,878	1,799	58	31.02	3	1	8/61	66.86	2.78	1	1	3	11	—	—	—	—
V.V. Kumar	1960–61	25	2	605	202	7	28.85	1	—	5/64	86.42	2.00	1	—	—	—	—	—	—	—
A.R. Kumble	1990	19	17	5,692	2,103	86	24.45	5	1	7/59	66.19	2.22	2	4	7	10	14	—	—	—
M.H. Mankad	1946	29	44	14,686	5,236	162	32.32	8	2	8/52	90.65	2.17	2	3	9	15	19	23	40	—
S.G. Shinde	1946	22	7	1,515	717	12	59.75	1	—	6/91	126.25	2.83	3	4	—	—	—	—	—	—
L. Sivaramakrishnan	1982–83	17	9	2,313	1,145	26	44.04	3	1	6/64	88.96	2.97	2	2	8	—	—	—	—	—

Bowler	Debut	Age	M	Balls	Runs	Wkts	Avrge	5 wi	10 wm	Best	Stk/Rt	RPO	Tests per Wickets							
													5	10	25	50	75	100	150	200
NEW ZEALAND																				
J.C. Alabaster	1955–56	25	21	3,992	1,863	49	38.02	–	–	4/46	81.46	2.80	7	11	14	–	–	–	–	–
R.C. Blunt	1929–30	29	9	936	472	12	39.33	–	–	3/17	78.00	3.02	1	5	–	–	–	–	–	–
W.E. Merritt	1929–30	21	6	936	617	12	51.41	–	–	4/104	78.00	3.95	3	5	–	–	–	–	–	–
A.M. Moir	1950–51	31	17	2,650	1,418	28	50.64	2	–	6/155	94.64	3.21	1	3	16	–	–	–	–	–
M.J.F. Shrimpton	1962–63	22	10	257	158	5	31.60	–	–	3/35	51.40	3.68	9	–	–	–	–	–	–	–
PAKISTAN																				
Abdul Qadir	1977–78	22	67	17,125	7,742	236	32.81	15	5	9/56	72.56	2.71	2	3	9	13	23	28	44	53
Intikhab Alam	1959–60	17	47	10,474	4,494	125	35.92	5	2	7/52	83.79	2.57	2	5	17	27	35	41	–	–
Mushtaq Ahmed	1989–90	19	13	2,410	1,074	29	37.03	3	–	3/32	83.10	2.67	4	5	11	–	–	–	–	–
Mushtaq Mohammad	1958–59	15	57	5,260	2,309	79	29.22	3	–	5/28	66.58	2.63	16	18	29	46	53	–	–	–
Pervez Sajjad	1964–65	22	19	4,145	1,410	59	23.89	3	–	7/74	70.25	2.04	3	3	8	12	–	–	–	–
Wasim Raja	1972–73	20	57	4,092	1,826	51	35.80	–	–	4/50	80.24	2.68	4	13	24	54	–	–	–	–
SOUTH AFRICA																				
X.C. Balaskas	1930–31	20	9	1,572	806	22	36.63	1	–	5/49	71.45	3.07	5	5	–	–	–	–	–	–
G.A. Faulkner	1905–06	24	25	4,227	2,180	82	26.58	4	–	7/84	51.54	3.09	1	3	8	12	–	–	–	–
Q. McMillan	1929	25	13	2,021	1,243	36	34.52	2	–	5/66	56.13	3.69	4	6	12	–	–	–	–	–
S.J. Pegler	1909–10	21	16	2,989	1,572	47	33.44	2	–	7/65	63.59	3.15	3	6	8	–	–	–	–	–
H.L.E. Promnitz	1927–28	23	2	528	161	8	20.12	1	–	5/58	66.00	1.82	1	–	–	–	–	–	–	–
R.O. Schwartz	1905–06	30	20	2,639	1,417	55	25.76	2	–	6/47	47.98	3.22	2	3	8	17	–	–	–	–
V.I. Smith	1947	22	9	1,655	769	12	64.08	1	–	4/143	137.91	2.78	1	8	–	–	–	–	–	–
A.E.E. Vogler	1905–06	29	15	2,764	1,455	64	22.73	5	1	7/94	45.31	3.15	2	6	9	11	–	–	–	–
G.C. White	1905–06	23	17	498	301	9	33.44	–	–	4/47	55.33	3.62	7	–	–	–	–	–	–	–
WEST INDIES																				
A.G. Barrett	1970–71	28	6	1,612	603	13	46.38	–	–	3/43	124.00	2.24	3	3	–	–	–	–	–	–
B.F. Butcher	1958–59	25	44	256	90	5	18.00	1	–	5/34	42.66	2.11	32	–	–	–	–	–	–	–
C.B. Clarke	1939	21	3	456	261	6	43.50	1	–	3/59	76.00	3.43	3	–	–	–	–	–	–	–
W. Ferguson	1947–48	30	8	2,568	1,165	34	34.26	3	1	6/92	75.52	2.72	2	2	5	–	–	–	–	–
D.A.J. Holford	1966	26	24	4,816	2,009	51	39.39	1	–	5/23	94.43	2.50	5	6	15	24	–	–	–	–
B.D. Julien	1973	23	24	4,542	1,868	50	37.36	1	–	5/57	90.84	2.46	3	6	14	–	–	–	–	–
S. Ramadhin	1950	21	43	13,939	4,579	158	28.98	10	1	7/49	88.22	1.97	2	2	4	11	17	25	40	–
O.C. Scott	1928	34	8	1,405	925	22	42.04	1	–	5/266	63.86	3.95	3	3	–	–	–	–	–	–
G.S. Sobers	1953–54	17	93	21,599	7,999	235	34.04	6	–	6/73	91.91	2.22	3	5	22	36	42	48	63	80

Index